THE KEYS OF TRANSFORMATION

BOOK ONE

Also by David Ashworth

Dancing with the Devil as You Channel in the Light

Ocean of Emotion

VISION

The Yellow Kite

Revealing Truth
DVD of full day workshop on evolution of consciousness

The Vision Journey – www.thevisionjourney.com
On-line Journey including Spiritual Lessons

THE KEYS

OF

TRANSFORMATION

BOOK ONE

Birth of a New Light

———

DAVID ASHWORTH

Crucible Publishers

MMIX

Crucible Publishers,
4 Monmouth Paddock, Norton St. Philip, Bath, BA2 7LA, UK
e-mail: sales@cruciblepublishers.com

David Ashworth 2009
First published, July 2009

ISBN 978-1-902733-12-8

1

The Golden Section
The published version of this book, as opposed to the Print on Demand version, is produced to the
dimensions of Sacred Geometry, the Golden Section. All imagery for the cover was given through
insight and is presented to uplift and empower the individual seeker of truth.

Book Cover: Cover Illustration by the late Nick Clarke

Death Becomes Her
The background to the Front Cover is from a Space Photograph of Cassiopeia, entitled *Death
Becomes Her,* from the online library of Nasa's JPL Laboratory. Located 10,000 light-years away,
Cassiopeia A is the remnant of a once massive star that died in a violent supernova explosion,
possibly observed by John Flamsteed on 16th August 1680, according to astronomy historian
William Ashworth, (no relation to the author) in 1980. It consists of a dead star, called a neutron star,
and a surrounding shell of material that was blasted off as the star died.

   A section of the photo was used as a base to provide Universal Energy in one of its most
amazing transformational processes, the energy of supernova death creating the matter for rebirth.
Elements of the photo were then airbrushed to create a base for the guided imagery to be used.
To read more about this image, see:

   http://photojournal.jpl.nasa.gov/catalog/?IDNumber=PIA03519

After Nick's untimely death the line work for the Golden Section was added by Chris Peach to
complete Nick's final work for me in this life. Thanks for everything, Nick.

Illustrations: Line Illustrations by Chris Peach

Set in 11 on 13pt Monotype Bembo
Typeset by Christian Brett

Printed in Great Britain by Henry Ling Limited, Dorchester

For Denise

Who has been my constant companion on the path.

For the Chosen Ones

Who are awakening.
Who are ready to discover who they are and why they are here.

Jesus said,

> I will choose you, one out of ten thousand,
> and two out of ten thousand,
> and they shall stand boldly being a single One.

Jesus said,

> 'Happy are the Chosen for you shall find the Kingdom
> Because you are from the heart of it,
> You shall return there again.'

The Gospel of Thomas

Contents

Introduction

As we begin this adventure together, we are going to bring ourselves forward through the last century in an attempt to see and understand the birthing of the incoming illuminating light of the Age of Aquarius. We will observe the actions of the Aquarian Light as it shows itself through the unfolding patterns of the evolution of consciousness of humanity throughout recent history. By keying ourselves into this timeline and understanding how we have become a part of this conscious opening, we will be better able to understand our choices. We can observe, feel and become a part of this evolution of human consciousness, or we can choose to step out and deny it. Either way, at least you will be informed in a way that will help you to see with clarity the changes that are upon us through practical, down-to-earth, everyday observation.

I have used some sayings of the *Gospel of Thomas* throughout the book, which seemed appropriate at this time. As I have worked on myself over the years I have constantly searched for messages and deep meaning, instruction and guidance for life and evolution. I have searched for illumination on my path. One of the things I have tried to do is get as close as I can to the original words of the spiritual teacher Jesus, as his words have always had great resonance to me personally, as have those written by Richard Bach in *Jonathan Livingstone Seagull*, which I quoted extensively in my previous book, *Dancing with the Devil as You Channel in the Light*. There have been many great enlightened teachers who have all resonated at some level with those who are awakening. I have read many ancient texts and continue to do so, although, I seek them out less these days, as I have come to rely on the fact that when something is needed for one's evolution it is always provided, no matter from which source. However, it was my discovery of the Gospel of Thomas that really lit that fire of understanding within me. Working with the sayings, or logia, of Jesus confirmed so much of what I had experienced personally. It seemed as if I had been prepared for the confirmations that this source would bring me. Those who have walked the spiritual path will know that confirmation of your insights is very necessary and is always sent forth at the right moment.

Before you think that the Gospel of Thomas and the words of Jesus might be some sort of religious guidance, I would point out most clearly that Jesus was not a Christian, as we understand the term through the religious institutions of Christianity, and he had nothing to do with the church. The established church came many years after his passing and was not really enshrined in statute until the Council of Nicea in 325 CE, at which time many of the early teachings were taken out of what was to become the accepted Bible, the Gospel of Thomas being one of them. These early Gospels or recordings of the words of a teacher were merely the news of the day. There are many great sources of light and wisdom in the writings of the teachers and sages throughout the ages, but the teachings of Jesus seem to light my lamp, as it were. However, I am fully appreciative and revere all spiritual and mystical teachings in the way they speak to different people in different ways leading us, as they ultimately will, towards a common goal. Those of us who are seekers after truth will find what we are looking for in the words of those who came before and recorded them for us. Anyone who is seeking or perusing spiritual texts is bound to find what he is looking for under Universal Law. Seek and you shall find. Knock and it shall be opened unto you.

The Gospel of Thomas was discovered in the desert near Nag Hammadi in Egypt in 1945. As formulated and reworked by Hugh McGregor Ross in his wonderful work *Jesus untouched by the Church*, I have found this to be the most powerful and effective form of presentation of this Gospel. It feels just right and constantly teaches me many things, as my vibration rises to a point where I can perceive and understand the hidden meanings within Jesus' teachings of how to address yourself in order to transcend the mundane world. Like all spiritual works of great truth, the light and power shines through every word and the more you read it, the more the light within those words opens the light at the core of your own being.

Jesus said,
    'He who drinks from my mouth will become as me.'

A Journey Through Time

Although, my awakening began in the late 80s, *The Keys of Transformation* describes part of my evolutionary pathway between 1998 and January 2005. It is my journey of revelation and illumination and I refer to periods within this timeline to help you understand the processes I went through and how they fit with the unfolding of this new age, leading me to a point where I could begin to adopt the mantle of teacher. In fact, I did not so much adopt it as have it forced upon me, with little choice. Well, we might think there is always a choice, but the choice comes at a cost which is too high when you begin to realise that you have been chosen to bring something of great import to the world of man. The only choice is to step up and follow the guidance.

The key period, between May 2002 and May 2004, is when the most phenomenal transformation took place as my consciousness was expanded, for want of a better description. The book illustrates how this period fits into a larger picture of who or what I was becoming. Therefore, you will find dates appearing in order to present an understandable chronology.

The Guides Speak

In this book, we are going to tell you things which you won't believe. Mark our words now. You will find yourself saying, 'I don't believe that'. You will think that what you are reading is ego talking. Or you will think it is imagination gone mad. Or, you will think it is some kind of flight of fancy. And, in all probability, you may even put the book down and not return to it, ever. Let us say that its assertions might even offend you on some level.

We can see it coming and we can see how it will work within you. Let us say this. When the light within this book touches you, it will challenge you. It will challenge many aspects of what you are prepared to believe and that is when you will be offended. You will find that the energy of challenge causes you to feel angry. That is when you will put the book down, for anger will be your self-defence mechanism for something that you do not wish to look at, something that you do not wish to attempt to open yourself to. However, if you don't pick up the book again, then that will be your loss. For what will be happening to you is that the light of evolution which radiates from these words will challenge you at a level of truth to which you cannot stretch or accept, and that will be the point of your limitation.

If you do not go beyond that limitation, by facing the challenge and opening your mind to the possibility of what you read, then that will be your marker in time, the point at which your evolution of consciousness stalled. It will be the place on your path beyond which you will not pass. You will become limited by your acceptance of what you consider to be true and possible, and that will be your limitation.

Until you have the courage to face the things which challenge you, then you will not evolve. Until you have the courage to face the things which limit you, then you will not evolve. The journey of the path involves finding courage at every stage of the way. If you are not open-minded to things that go beyond your present level of reasoning, then you close your mind to the creation of your own future. You limit your potential for evolution of consciousness to zero. Quite simply, a closed mind or a life controlled by inner fear, especially that which uses anger as a defence to protect it from opening, reaches a point beyond which evolution of consciousness cannot proceed.

About The Guides and Guidance

During the writing of this book, and in no particular pattern, the guidance of higher consciousness opens up and blends with me as I write. I sometimes refer to this as The Guides and sometimes Higher Consciousness or Guidance. When this happens, the writing begins to flow through me rather than me creating it, as it were, and one of the signs that this is happening is when you see the terms 'we', or 'we might say,' being used. Often when I am writing, I may be in the middle of a piece when the higher consciousness comes through with guidance or a teaching for us. Even though I understand my work in an everyday sense, sometimes the Guidance takes this kind of opportunity to enlighten me as to how a subject works, in practical, everyday terminology.

When this higher conscious guidance or teaching came through, I used to try to separate what I was writing from what was being given to me, so that there was clarity as to who was speaking. However, I found that this was hard work, gave me more to do, tended to be a little jerky and lacked flow. Sometimes, The Guides will come through with just one sentence, or a few words, which will fit with something I am trying to express to you, and sometimes it can be pages of writing delivered over an hour or so. Eventually, I decided just to allow things to flow as they came. The book, therefore, becomes a mixture of sources all flowing onto the page whenever any particular aspect of consciousness decides to throw something in for our benefit. View it as if there are a group of people all contributing at the same time. I think you will very easily get the feel for when guidance and teaching are coming from a higher place. The guidance has a feel all its own, often very challenging as it tries to open your mind to higher realities and often extremely smooth as it tries to take you on a softer journey of illumination within yourself.

Finally, if you really don't like something, then ask yourself what it is reflecting in your own make up and personality. Then that will be another great opportunity for the evolution of your consciousness.

Dave Ashworth
Prestwich, June 2008

Getting the Terminology Right

His disciples said,
    'Show us the Place where you are,
    because it is necessary for us to seek after it.'

He said to them,
    'He who has ears let him hear:

        There is Light
        at the centre of a man of Light,
        and he illumines the whole world.
        If he does not shine,
        there is darkness.'

    The Gospel of Thomas

What is God?

We could say that the answer to this question is Who Knows?

Quite simply, when we are incarnated into a human body our consciousness is too limited for most of us to even contemplate the vastness of such a concept as God or God Consciousness, an all-pervading power of creative consciousness, which can be acknowledged within every atom of matter. Humans are just too small and too limited to form a comprehension of something this big.

Why Ask this Question?

When you begin to work with spiritual light, you will begin to experience expansion. Your consciousness will begin to expand and open to perceptions, which you will find at times amaze you, at other times turn you inside out and sometimes challenge you beyond your comprehension. Yet you have an inner knowing that they are true. In short, your consciousness will begin to evolve. At some point you will have to realise and accept that you have been chosen to work with something far more intelligent than you are, something which has unlimited power to bring about change to peoples' lives and to show you what you need to see in order to be active within the evolution of your own consciousness.

You will find that you need a word or phrase to describe this thing that is working with and through you. There are perhaps many terms which can be found to identify with this all-pervading consciousness of All That Is: The Universe; The Universal Mind; Oneness; The Great Spirit; The Creator; The Lord of all Creation; Unity; Universal Consciousness; The Creative Force, Divine Source, etc., and of course, not forgetting the word that many people avoid using because of the fear of being perceived either as a crackpot at one end of the scale or an evangelising religious freak at the other. That word is God.

In the present time though, many people in the west are beginning to overcome the fear of using the word God, as their consciousness opens and this force begins to align with them. They begin to realise that whatever it is that is working through them needs some description. It doesn't matter at all what term you use, because that almighty consciousness of unity will know your thoughts anyway. You can't hide from it, but you can still feel the fear of identifying with it in public. Most people, as they realise the need to use a term to describe the feeling they experience, eventually tiptoe towards that word God. How can such a small word create so much fear? Well, I am sure we will answer that somewhere on this journey.

It is not important right now to determine what God is, or what word is correct to use to describe God. Just nod your head in acknowledgement when you come across it in the text and mentally replace it with a word that feels right to you. That goes for your life journey too. At any point on that journey, just use the word that feels right, but at the same time, don't be afraid to abandon or change the use of that word as you unfold and change. Align with what feels right and that will bring you into the closest alignment with the power of the God force within you. Eventually, you will find that every time you don't use the word God you are actually in denial of that force, trying to lay it off for some term that has less power or less risk of offending.

From my own perspective, which has evolved through my own experiences, I mix the terminology up a bit, but more often than not, I do prefer to use the term God. It is a simple word and everyone knows what it means, although I might also use any of the other terms, depending on what comes when I am in the flow of writing or speaking. When in that flow, you cannot be distracted by what might or might not be politically, or otherwise, correct. One is focused on delivering the message of the moment, and that is how it should be, undiluted and full of the power that is creating it. In that way, that power of creation will touch you deeply in the right place with truth.

Limitations and Challenges

I do realise that the word God challenges and even offends some, and there are also those who think that God belongs only to their religion, as if they have some kind of monopoly or personal ownership of the term and all it encompasses. There are others who think that you shouldn't utter the name at all. That is not my issue, it is theirs. Some people are afraid of acknowledging there is a Universal Consciousness or a God at all. Many more are actually afraid of Him or It coming into their lives, and others write most vociferously that nothing of the sort exists. Mmm, that's some delusion that the rest of us are experiencing then!

No matter. Do not fall into judgment. Everyone is on their own path at the exact point in their evolution where they are. All I ask for now is that if you are not ready to use my terms for God in your own life, then humour me. It's not a big issue. From time to time I need to use such a term to help you to learn and I need to know that you understand what I mean when I use it. The name of the game is simplicity. So, let's keep things simple shall we? There is already too much complication in the world of men, especially where trying to find the path of understanding is concerned.

Man is man and God is God and this journey is about dissolving the separation between them. As quoted in the saying of the teacher Jesus at the head of this chapter, 'if he does not shine, there is darkness.' Indeed there is darkness within all of humanity and that is why we are here in this realm, in order to learn how to dissolve that darkness and shine more brightly. This work is dedicated to bringing you the knowledge and understanding of what that darkness is and how to transform it so that you can shine more brightly; so that you can begin to 'illumine the whole world'.

2

A Short and Simple Journey

Sit beneath the Great Oaks,
and Know.
They hold the Keys to forever.
The Keys of Time and Space.

And humans,
in their ignorance,
Reduce their wisdom to ashes.

David Ashworth
24th February 2007

This book is devoted to helping you understand something of energy, then healing and evolutionary light and how it works in stages to unlock you and illuminate your life. I mention healing and evolutionary light deliberately, as during my own journey I have come to appreciate the difference, a huge difference and one that has largely gone undiscovered or has been misunderstood as we have begun to shift quickly beyond the Age of Healing and into the Age of Evolution of Consciousness, the new Age of Aquarius. The reasons will become apparent as you move through the book.

As you learn how to work with light successfully, you will attain evolution of consciousness. Through this process you will gain self-empowerment, step by step. Although, my personal journey has covered many distinct areas of healing and lightwork, the Guidance that works with and through me has steered me progressively beyond healing and ever more towards empowering others through evolutionary processes. When you say to someone, 'I used to be a healer,' you can see their mind asking, 'Is there something beyond that, then?'

My own journey into light has opened me as the vehicle for some fascinating, powerful and unique streams of light, which have now been thoroughly anchored into our Earth plane and are available to help unlock the evolutionary potential of others. The journey of preparation for such a task has been a constant battle, like climbing a great mountain, ever wondering will the peak come into view. The battle, or struggle is an internal one, as the light reveals and illuminates the things that need to change within me, in order to hold the next level of light.

The journey leading to the explosion in my consciousness of these new evolutionary and unique streams of light has been a fascinating one of exploration and self-realisation through vibrational energy work. New and hitherto unknown information, which can help empower further those who are already well developed Light workers and practitioners, has been revealed.

As well as empowering the already powerful and knowledgeable amongst us, the information is also aimed at all levels of practitioner, from the newly awakening neophyte to the highly experienced intuitive healer and light-worker. There is something to empower everyone. It is also important to note that it is through sharing knowledge and information and selflessly uplifting others into their power, that we reap the whirlwind of further empowerment ourselves, as teachers and facilitators for the light. The nature of this process will be revealed in the Universal Laws later. The more we learn to use the power, which is available to us for the benefit of others, the more we are empowered from above. I will, therefore, be sharing with you as much as I can, or shall I say, as much as I am given to share, for indeed, I have been trying to share some things for a long time and the guidance which brings me the most amazing information and concepts regarding setting yourself free has often said, 'they are not ready for this yet.' But, the days are close when much more will be revealed through this series of books, *The Keys of Transformation.*

Simplicity

Whatever healing or evolutionary work you are doing with and for others, it should be easy, or at least 'easyish', if you are doing it right. If you are struggling then you are doing something 'wrong'. However, we can never really say that anything is wrong, but if you are struggling at some level, then you are still trying to learn something that the Universe is presenting to you. By Universal Law, if you are on the right track then it becomes easy. Learn to follow the intuition and the heart in order to make it simple and observe the Universal Laws.

After delivering this message of simplicity for many years through my teaching and workshops, I was pleased to discover an ancient poem, which gives us the same message from the Chinese Saint, Chuang Tzu.

> Easy is right,
> Begin right and you are easy,
> Continue easy and you are right,
> The right way to go easy,
> Is to forget the right way,
> And forget that the going is easy.

The essence of the message, of course is, 'just do it!'

Learning to be Unlimited

I always try to keep things simple. In some of my work these days I have been able to effect transformational situations for people with very little effort indeed. My Guidance often asks me what I want out of life, in terms of work. They tell me I can be very busy dealing with the most difficult cases and burning myself out in the process or I can sit in the garden all summer and bring more light onto the planet than I could possibly imagine, through the evolutionary light which passes through me. 'What do you want?' they say. 'You tell us what you want and we will bring it to you. Don't limit yourself in any way.'

What I want to share with you, amongst other things, is learning to be unlimited, to expect that you will be more powerful than you can imagine. Or, it might be more accurate to say that 'you can be as powerful as you *can* imagine, for imagination is one of the keys to unlocking the power within you. Unfortunately, when people begin to sense and feel this power emerging within them, they often then step away from it through the inner fears that the power brings to the surface in the cleansing process.

The evolution of human consciousness is the key to continually unfolding our potential and the key to our success as a species. The story goes way beyond success as a species, but using the various Keys of Transformation correctly and at the appropriate time begins to bring you in to the timeline of the Evolution of Universal Consciousness. Each of us is a singular aspect of that process. As we ascend ever higher on the ladder of eternal possibility we evolve our consciousness, not just for this lifetime, but in preparation for the next and those beyond that. Our mission is to learn how to see ourselves in a process that is unfolding to a point where we can once again rejoin that unity, which was the original thought that created everything there is. At this point in Earth history we have a better opportunity to evolve than ever before. If you are reading this book, you have done much work in previous lives, for this book is only speaking to those who are ready to move forward, ready to take the awakening to an undreamed of level, ready to learn how to surf the Wave of Time.

Although, I am still learning, as are we all, I have reached a point where everything just unfolds for me. It has always unfolded for me in one way or another since I was pushed into my own healing journey in the late 1980s. I might say that I have now learned how to see what is coming and act as it comes. As a result, The Guidance often shows me what is coming for a number of years in advance, so that I can work towards creating the vision of the future that the higher guidance is presenting as its desire. This future view helps me prepare myself to receive. I never know by which route the future vision will manifest, but I sure know it will and it always does. But just because it unfolds does not mean that its been easy. I am shown the vision on the one hand and on the other given the work to do in order to attain it.

The Journey

We are all on a journey, whether we understand it or not, 'the journey through life, the journey into our own evolution.' I could say that there is no destination, there is only the journey, but that would be untrue. The journey can be a long one, and so it is better to view it as unending, but what some of us find is that we do suddenly reach the destination when we least expect it. Perhaps the destination should remain a surprise, for now anyway.

Many of you who are reading this book will have journeyed with each other in many previous lives. The call of the Soul Grouping is sounding as it transmits its signal to the warriors of light, awakening them from their slumbers; awakening them for the next march towards Unity. You may have journeyed with me and I with you in previous times. It is possible that we are now coming back together to help each other move forward once again. Whether we actually speak or meet is of no matter, for it is the light, which uplifts, binds and bonds us together and carries us forward. It is the light, which raises us into our potential and it is the soul-grouping consciousness, which will have brought you to this book and into the energy once again, so that you can feed from the light as it bathes you from the words as you read.

Other soul groups will be gathering too, to continue their journey together. We are all drawn to different paths and different things. Sometimes, you may think that your friends are crazy for being drawn to a certain teacher, mode of healing or shamanic practices, which do not make sense to you. Quite simply it is they who are being called, not you. When you are called, you absolutely know it so deep within your being that you have no doubts. When you are called, then that is the path that you must follow at that particular time, and wild horses will not divert your attention until you have learned or experienced what the Universe is guiding you towards. Sometimes, that experience can merely involve being in the light or vibration of a single person for a half hour or so, often leaving you wondering why you were so drawn, and why now it seems like such a disappointment. It is never a disappointment if you know how it works and how to view it. In the Age of Aquarius, the Masters of Light will emerge. We are in the foothills and beginning to climb that mountain to a new world view; a new view for humanity to attain. As we attain the heights of the mountain, so each step of the way will bring greater understanding of what is being prepared for us.

Just by being in the light, which is embedded in the guided words of this book, you will be awakening to new levels. A 'knowing' will emerge within you that you are once again connecting. There are patterns within these words, which your soul will recognise. A remembrance of the calling to the meetings in the forests of old. A whisper of memories of the gatherings beneath the moon to witness the acceleration of one and all. A knowing of the shared unspoken truths in times past. Memories awaken you to the possibilities, which lie within the new journeys on the next wave of your evolution.

I haven't put the patterns in the words deliberately, but I know that they are there. My words are, more often than not, guided, and The Guides always know what they want to achieve with their message. I may be the person writing the book physically, but who is bringing you the message? Certainly, much of this work is the result of my own experiences, but how did I get those experiences? None of them were accidental or coincidental. I can tell you that for certain. It is all part of the great plan which is unfolding. We are living in exciting times. If you can see how to connect into that energetic expression of light, which is holding open the door for you, then you will transform your consciousness again in this lifetime, you will ride that train to glory as you have before, and you will continue to open your potential into the reality of a new paradigm shift, and The Age of Aquarius, which will bring ever more brightness into your life.

Going Boldly

Each working day for me is a new adventure. Like Captain Kirk and the crew of the Starship Enterprise, I will boldly go where no man has gone before, or very few, anyway, as my consciousness opens the doors into 5th dimension reality. However, my journeys are not into outer space, as they are for the Enterprise, but into the inner space of the consciousness of my fellow man, to unlock the secrets within that prevent their evolution in the moment. These inner journeys are no less exciting, though.

It is not just the consciousness of man that I journey into. Depending on the task in hand, it may be the consciousness of the Earth Mother, the Nature Spirits or Essences, or indeed the consciousness of anything, which is animated by the forces of God. However, there are many similarities to Kirk's journeys in the Enterprise, as many of the realms we can visit, with a little practice and development, are indeed Universes in their own right. Some are even Universes within Universes.

Evolution of Human Consciousness

This story though, is about those journeys into other people's minds and emotions, sub-conscious and deeper consciousness, past lives and karmic lessons, hopes and fears. My work is essentially that of uplifting and empowering others through revealing the truth within them. I am steered and focused by my Guidance as we course through the universe within you, unearthing the blockages, which prevent you from attaining your next level of perfection and flowing into your true potential. We bring light into your darkness and that light then begins a process of illumination and transformation.

From these journeys come profound offerings of mental patterns, emotional stresses, strains and blockages within the subtle energy system, sometimes created by the person themselves, sometimes the result of inharmonious interactions with other people, such as a partner or work colleagues. Sometimes amazingly complex patterns have been set up by the subconscious mind to sabotage you, patterns that are almost outside of your control. And, believe it or not, your own Higher Self sometimes throws a spanner in the works if it is trying to stop you going down the wrong path.

Seeing thoughts and emotions very clearly in another person, complete with the detail of how they have developed and manifested, ultimately sabotaging the person's life, can be fascinating. It is wonderful to be able to present the visions of the inner workings to someone as tools for them to work with, helping them understand what is happening deep within and why; helping them understand how they are held back from achieving their potential. Very often a potential that they are unaware of. Sometimes, the person can identify with the issues immediately, but have not been able to 'pin it down' or 'put it into words' before. Sometimes they have an inkling, but have been too afraid to look, or sometimes the journey is just too painful to contemplate. In other instances, when the issues are below the surface, a person can find initial difficulty in identifying with them as they may be in places within consciousness that are beyond awareness until some of the 'surface noise' has been cleared by powerful evolutionary processes. This can bring deep healing to reveal that deeper imagery.

Learning Through the Lessons of Others

This work has been a great teacher for me, too, as I can see an issue being played out in a client and I recognise it as one which is active within myself. It is often a revelation to see how it works within others, and to feel the same emotions in them as in me. When I see and feel an issue in another person at a deep level, it opens doors for me to explore my own limitations as a human and then helps me address these issues or lessons and overcome them, leading to a vibrational shift and further evolution. Of course, it is not as easy as I paint the picture here. If it were, we would all be perfect. Wouldn't we be a boring species then?

When seeing issues within the consciousness of others, my Guidance often gives me great insight and draws analogies that the person can relate to, in order to help them grasp the picture of what is taking place within them. In some instances whole chapters of philosophical guidance are given to illuminate their understanding and bring the clarity needed to work on the issues and move beyond them. At other times a simple reference to the action of a simple item of household equipment holds that clarity, such as a vacuum cleaner or some plumbing hoses. Guidance is always personal and makes the journey as simple as possible to interpret and understand from the student's or client's perspective.

Learning to Reach Out for Help

You all have the most amazing gifts and talents waiting to be unlocked, but you may find that you will need the help of others to unlock them. You all have the potential to be able to do what I or even others greater than I do. However, those of you who are drawn into the worlds of spiritual work and helping others are the lucky ones, because you are connecting to people in an area of humanity which is fast awakening and evolving. Those who work with energy and light are in the vanguard of the evolution of human consciousness. You know that anyway. There are many people in all walks of life who are not as privileged as you in having so much light to play with or opportunity for change surrounding you. You are very blessed.

One of the most important Universal Laws that you can understand is that mankind cannot make it alone. Those of you who work as healers, therapists and practitioners need to know this more than any other group in the world today. The most important thing to learn right at this very moment is that you can't do it by yourself. *You must learn how to reach out and ask for help.* By the time you get to the end of this book you will understand why. When you learn how to do that you might just find that your hidden gifts and talents begin to emerge very quickly. Mine certainly did.

The Clarion Call to the Old Soul Group
You won't have picked up this book without that old connection from previous lives calling to you, or the new light of Aquarius now entering, which is awakening the Seeker of Truth within you. It will be calling you to remember who you are, calling you to awaken again and take your rightful place on the continuing wave of progress towards perfection, towards Unity. As in previous times in the Earth Realm, we are once again journeying together and sharing the light and information, which will guide us on our path to completion. Drink and refresh yourself from this fountain of knowledge and wisdom, and continue your journey. It is my enormous privilege to be able to share the beauty of what I have been shown with you in the hope that you may make a further transformation towards holding the light of a new reality.

A short and simple journey with a good guide who knows the way is worth more than any price you can put upon it. Therefore, learn to reach out and ask the way.

I bid you Good Journeys.

PART ONE

All We Need is Truth

3

Perceiving the Dawn

When the Moon is in the Seventh House,
and Jupiter aligns with Mars,
Then peace shall guide the planets,
and love will steer the stars
This is the dawning of the Age of Aquarius ...

Harmony and understanding
Sympathy and trust abounding
No more forces of derision
Golden living dreams of visions
Mystic crystal revelations
And the mind's true liberation

5th Dimension

It is very important to recognise and understand the bigger unfolding picture of which you are part, as the dawn of the Age of Aquarius rises to illuminate our lives. In the following few chapters we are going to journey back and forth in time over the last century or so. We will touch into the periods of both light and darkness to get a 'feel' for the changes manifesting through the different consciousness patterns of recent history as they push and pull at each other. It is like the spinning of a yin/yang symbol in which each path of darkness or light contains a little bit of its opposite, by understanding this principle we can learn to feel the polarity of the forces of both light and dark within us. But to start, let's take a ride through recent time as we key you in to the timeline of the birthing of a new age.

Of Aeons and Ages

An aeon is an indeterminate period of time usually associated with an age, such as a geological age, or an astronomical age. For our purposes an aeon represents a time period of around 2,000 years, the present aeon being the Age of Pisces, or the Age of the Fish, or indeed, the Age of Jesus and his teachings, whose symbol is often given as the fish. When we progress from one aeon to the next there is a shift in vibration, which brings with it a corresponding awakening in human consciousness. You can clearly note this conscious movement towards greater enlightenment between the biblical writings of the time of The Old Testament and those which came later in The New Testament. You can see a clear progression in thinking from retribution in sayings such as, 'An eye for an eye' to, 'Do unto others as you would have done unto yourself'; a complete shift from revenge to turning the other cheek and encouragement to, 'love thy neighbour as thyself.'

The ages are displayed and understood in the firmament above through what is known as The Precession of the Equinoxes. This pathway is described in the heavens as the sun slowly moves backwards through the astrological signs. The sun entered the astrological sign of Pisces around the time of Jesus' birth and it is now approaching the astrological sign of Aquarius, which it will pass through over the coming 2,000 years or, before entering the next sign, which is Capricorn.

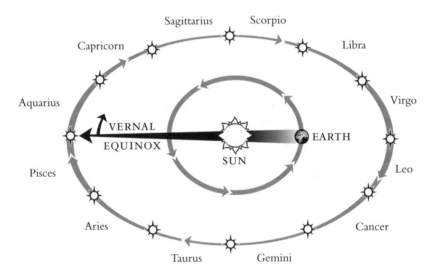

Precession of the Equinoxes

The Earth's axis is slightly off centre. Imagine a needle running through the earth from south pole to north pole and projecting outwards into space. Because the axis is slightly off centre, as the earth turns one complete revolution over a period of just under 28,000 years, it describes or draws a circle through the heavens with this needle-like point. This single cycle is called the Great Platonic Year, after Plato. An average astrological sign occupies about 30 degrees of the sky. There are 12 astrological signs. 12 multiplied by 30 gives us 360 degrees, or a full circle of the heavens, by observing the position of the sun at the spring equinox you can determine what sign you are in and what age you are in. The Standard Precessional Period is around 2,160 years as the sun traverses the sky from one sign to the next.

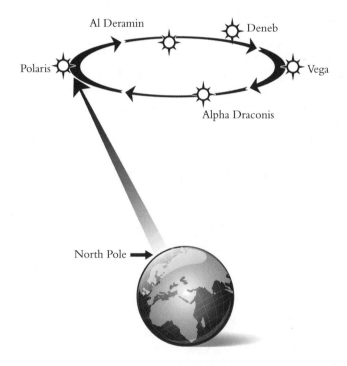

The Great Platonic Year

As the Earth turns, because its axis is slightly off-centre, it wobbles. Together, the Precession of the Equinoxes and the way the earth wobbles clearly shows how we go through warm and cool periods on earth and at present we are coming out of a cool period and things are warming up a bit. Because we wobble, we are constantly changing our position to the sun and this brings the changes of warm and cool periods.

When Does The Age of Aquarius Actually Begin?

It is not easy to say accurately when The Age of Aquarius begins, but with a little thought it is possible to get a good feel for the time period when its energies begin to influence the consciousness of people, and that is what is most important for us to understand. It doesn't start on one particular day, month or year, rather it begins to influence us as we move closer to it, just as we feel more warmth as we move closer to a fire.

Let us first look in chronological order at some notable dates as offered by spiritually aware people from our recent past. Then we will have a look at working it out for ourselves, based on some very simple principles. Here are some extracts from the website at www.greatdreams.com (for which I am very grateful.)

1898:   According to Hindu chronology, the Kali Yuga (Age of Iron) began in the year 3102BC. As the Yuga has a duration of 5000 years, its end occurred in 1898. Therefore, according to the Kali Yuga a new age or period began around 1898/1900.

1905:   Gerald Massey used the Standard Precessional Period of 2160 years for each zodiac sign of 30 degrees and assumed a starting point of 255BC, which meant that the beginning of the Age of Aquarius was in 1905. He used the correct precessional period, but his starting point seems only to be justified because it is significant to Massey, rather than for humanity as a whole, but maybe he knew something else that he forgot to share.

1911:   Madame Blavatsky predicted that the reality of a Universal Church would become possible towards the close of the 20th century. The Theosophical Society based their calculation for the dawning of the Age of Aquarius on the channelling of the Lord Maitreya by Krishnamurti in 1911. Indeed we have seen many movements and teachers who open their doors to all comers regardless of belief systems or religions in this time period. To any who are awakening, it is becoming ever more clear that the belief systems of religions are being exposed for their weaknesses regarding truth. As ever more awaken, they begin to see through the illusion that is often presented by belief systems.

1936:   Edgar Cayce stated that during 1936 the terrestrial axis had begun to shift, an unstoppable process, which would activate the transition between world ages. The change would accelerate rapidly, with cata-strophic consequences. A well-known American geologist, whose identity is not listed, apparently confirmed that this axis shift did indeed begin below the Earth's surface in 1936. (See Edgar Cayce's books for information.) Certainly, we have all noted that the planet is changing quickly at this time.

1945: Alice Bailey determined that the transition to the Age of Aquarius occurred in the 1930s, as described in *The Externalisation of the Hierarchy*. In 1945 the Master Djwahl Khul gave out *The Great Invocation,* which invoked the powers of Light, Love and Divine Purpose irrespective of all religions; and in 1946 Alice Bailey wrote, *'the day is dawning when all religions will be regarded as emanating from one great spiritual source.'* (See Alice Bailey's books).

1962: Peruvian spiritual messenger Willaru Huayta of the Quechua Nation, a part of the ancient Inca confederation, believes that the Age of Aquarius began in February, 1962.

1975: Dane Rudhyar, the father of Karmic Astrology designated 1975 as the time when the Avatar of the New Age would appear. Interestingly, he allowed the possibility that it might not be the second coming of Christ as anticipated by many, but that the Christ Light could be car-ried by a series of individuals who would be agents for this message.

Following on from what Dane Rudhyar said and before I had seen or read of this theory anywhere, I had a series of amazing, but sometimes frightening insights where I began to see the emerging Christ Light in others as I was doing my work. A little at a time, so as not to overwhelm me, I was taken ever deeper into the consciousness of clients and shown the process of the Christ Light in its active and awakening state. These insights clearly showed that the Christ Light would begin to awaken in many people simultaneously and indeed that this would be the definition of the second coming of Christ. Since I had those insights I have seen this Christ Light manifesting, as it begins to illuminate some people's deeper consciousness. It is both glorious and terrifying at the same time. The Guides refer to these people as The Chosen Ones, those chosen to carry the light of Christ, or the God-consciousness, into the world for the illumination of all those who are called and awakening. It will work by radiating outwards, from the centre of whomever has been chosen to carry it and as it radiates so it will illuminate and stimulate the awakening of others.

The above gives you a flavour of possibilities for the Dawn of the Age of Aquarius. Many other dates could also be considered. Because energy and light don't just switch on or off, but rather rise and set like the sun, all these dates and the methods by which they have come to us, whether calculation, channelling or Divine message, will have some merit. Personally, I feel the shift every single day as the Aquarian Light opens me more, liberates my mind and consciousness more. How I attained this ability is what I want to share with you so that you too can perhaps walk this same path, if you so desire. The first step is to help you to perceive that dawn yourself, by learning both to observe the patterns of its coming—which will give you understanding—and to feel the changes in consciousness as it touches you—which will give you Inner Knowing. We all need to be able to feel, perceive and Know it in the heart.

At What Period in Time can we Observe the Aquarian Light?

Rather than going by specific date, I think the way to view the beginning of the Age of Aquarius is through a transition period from one energy to the next. From the perspective of my work today in unlocking the evolutionary potential of seekers of truth, I feel and know that the doors most definitely are opening as we speak.

A better question to ask ourselves would be, 'At what period in time can we actually observe some kind of conscious shift in humanity, which may have been brought about by the incoming Aquarian Light?'

If we look at the question from an astronomical and mathematical point of view and use the Standard Precession Period of 2160 years between ages, and we then begin to count from the time of Jesus' death, we see the Dawn of the Age of Aquarius in the year 2160CE. However, if we work with the energies we understand and can, 'feel' as we live and work on the earth today, we may be able to get a better idea of the time we enter the Light of the Age of Aquarius. Firstly, think of the saying 'as above, so below' and about the dawning of each day. When the sky is clear of cloud you can often see it brightening an hour or so before sunrise, depending on where you are on the planet, of course. Equatorial regions react more quickly to approaching light and dark. The question you could ask yourself is, 'When does the day dawn?' Is it when you see the sky begin to brighten or is it when the sun actually appears over the horizon?

The point I am making is that dawn is the approaching light of the coming day before the sun actually rises. We can say exactly the same thing about the coming or rising of a new age, but rather than seeing the light, we, 'feel' it because it is dawning in our consciousness rather than at a visual level. It is illuminating our minds, our inner being and our perception, or bringing, 'The Mind's True Liberation' in the words of the song at the head of this chapter.

Look at this a different way. Each birth is associated with an astrological sign and those of us who are sensitive to energy can sometimes tell a person's sign from the energy they carry. When working with an air sign for example, you might be able to determine that the subject had more water than air in their astrological makeup merely from the way their energy feels. When a person is born on the cusp, they are born on the day, or in the period when the astrological sign changes. Because the energies don't change instantly from one sign to the next, but morph through the cycles from Fire to Earth or Air to Water, for example, the person can have characteristics of both signs, but often more of one than the other. In terms of energy and the sun's influence upon the individual there is a gradual changeover during a period of four to six days as the sun passes from one sign to the next — two to three days before the energies of the sign flip to the next energetic pattern and two to three days after they do.

So, if we say that three days either side of the cusp is the period of influence, as one sign truly changes to the next, we have a total energetic influence period of six days, or about one fifth of a monthly astrological cycle. Progressing this upwards to one fifth of an astrological age of 2160 years, we get a changeover period of around 432 years when we truly pass from one age to the next. If we divide 432 by 2 it gives us 216 years either side of the cusp of the age. So we could say that 216 years is the period of the dawn of an age, as we could also say that an hour or so is the average period for the dawning of a day. Easy, isn't it?

If the current year count began at the death of Jesus, and the period of an age is around 2160 years, then the cusp of the Age of Aquarius should be at 2160CE. If we were visually seeing the dawn of Aquarius we should be seeing the light begin to brighten the sky about 216 years before 2160CE. We can't see it with our eyes, so we must learn to feel it with our hearts, but at the same time we can, 'observe' it acting upon the consciousness of humanity. Using this very simple method of calculation we could say that we should have begun to feel or observe the light touching the consciousness of those who were ready to awaken, around the year 1944, give or take a few years.

As a matter of interest, a few days after I worked out this date of 1944 I discovered that, *The Great Invocation* was given out in April 1945. This Mantram is considered to be a vibration for the Age of Aquarius and in particular resonates to the frequencies of the Christ Consciousness. Some say that it is the replacement for the Lord's Prayer, which of course was given by Jesus for the Age of Pisces.

The Great Invocation
From the point of Light within the Mind of God
Let light stream forth into the minds of men.
Let Light descend on Earth.
From the point of Love within the Heart of God
Let love stream forth into the hearts of men.
May Christ return to Earth.
From the centre where the Will of God is known
Let purpose guide the little wills of men—
The purpose which the Masters know and serve.
From the centre which we call the race of men
Let the Plan of Love and Light work out
And may it seal the door where evil dwells.
Let Light and Love and Power restore the Plan on Earth.

Here is a quote from website: www.goodwill.f9.co.uk/aboutinv.htm and I might suggest that it is well worth reading this site if you want to connect with a powerful spiritual light.

> *'The Great Invocation is said to be the complete new utterance of the Christ, as well as a tool given to humanity to aid in the preparation for the reappearance of the Christ.'*

With the dawning of each new age, new rules or laws apply as we constantly ascend. We should learn to let go of the structures of the past and ascend into the new light of the new dawn. The Age of Aries and the Old Testament was the age of revenge, of continually giving back the energy that was given out. In the Age of Pisces Jesus taught us to, 'turn the other cheek,' not to give back the same energy as was given you, otherwise things would never change and you would never be free of the revenge cycle. Absorb what evil comes towards you and transform it into love, then give out the love. Be a transformer and transmitter.

As we move into the Age of Aquarius the mantra will be 'harmony and understanding, sympathy and love abounding'. What these words are really all about is the dawning in our consciousness of the realisation that what we do to others, we do to ourselves. It is an expression of The Law of Reflection. Whenever something is drawn to us that we don't like, it is because it is teaching us a lesson we need to learn. It is reflecting something of our own inner being that needs transforming. It is teaching us that whatever we are putting out is being returned to us, but the illumination of the new age will bring the possibility and opportunity to see that and then change our thoughts and behaviours around it, and thus we will be liberated through our learning.

4

Waves of Equal Force

Jesus said,
   'I will overturn this house,
   and no one will be able to build it again.'

The Gospel of Thomas

Observing the Shift
How can we judge the shift from one age to another? Well, if the gap is measured in hundreds of years we won't live long enough to make any meaningful measurements through personal observation. However, there are patterns, which can be felt by those who are sensitive and observed by those who are seeking to understand. The key you are looking for is an evolutionary shift in human consciousness, which brings a change in behaviour. The clearest way to observe the shift is to look at the work of the Sensitives in our midst, those people who are more awake in the heart than their contemporaries.

The Sensitives
I speak of the poets, musicians, writers, artists, clairvoyants, astrologers, healers and mystics of any particular time; those who are 'sensitive' to the more subtle vibrations of the different levels of reality around them and are also sensitive to and aware of a higher expression of Divine Light within themselves. They have true self-belief, can step out of the crowd and stand alone as an expression of individuality, rather than huddle with the herd for safety. They are sensitive to the driving force, which guides them to proceed in a single and focused direction of their own choosing, rather than following the crowd. These people are ultimately the liberators of our own spirit when we see, hear or read their work. And of course, they are often ahead of their time and so are not fully honoured or recognised until they have passed. The

collective consciousness of the day is simply not illuminated to a degree that can understand their perspective.

When the earth goes through a major shift in consciousness, such as when we shift from one age to the next, it is always a gradual process. Old ways of thought and action have to fall away for the new to emerge in their fullness, like a plant dying back in the autumn so that it can grow anew in the spring. It is a period of transition and re-birthing. The energies and light stream forth upon humanity, and as they do, new thought begins to emerge and the greater cultural picture slowly changes. However, it is important to under-stand that as light comes to change us, resistance to change *will* most definitely emerge within the consciousness of many people, who will strug-gle to let go of old patterns and structures. Large groups of people, tribes or nations, have their own overall patterns of collective consciousness, which take longer to change than individual consciousness because of the mass of energy associated with such a large grouping of people. There will be waves of resistance, a kind of undertow, pulling back against the forward momen-tum of change, which will be very strong. To bring change on such a scale is an interesting business. Firstly individuals are illuminated to a point where they begin to change their own lives, not necessarily challenging the old ways as that necessitates force and force is the old way. Passive change from within brings the most powerful results. Illumination gives birth to new ideas and perceptions and these then spread into small groups. Eventually, there is such a swell of inner cultural change that governments and nations begin to vibrate on a different, higher plane. But the undertow which pulls back is always there, held strongly in place by those who want to stick rigidly to what they know and trust. Fear of change is the controlling force from within the individual consciousness and this is amplified by the fundamental programme of the deeper collective consciousness of humanity as a whole. This is the 'if things don't change, then I'll be safe' pattern, which presents itself to the world through the mental body of the aura.

The Waves of Ebb and Flow

Energy always imitates water and can simulate the action of waves on the ocean as a new age begins to dawn. Imagine waves breaking on a shore. The incoming wave is moving forward, it breaks and rolls up the beach and then slides out again beneath the next incoming wave. The incoming wave flows over the ebbing wave, which is returning to the mass of the ocean. The ebbing wave creates the undertow, a pulling backwards, which takes some of the power and surge out of the incoming wave. We might even say that the ebbing wave calms the incoming wave a little. See the incoming wave as the new power, bringing light and glorious energy from its source, seeking to serve it with its breaking action upon the beach of humanity's consciousness. See the ebbing wave as having seen the beach and wanting to return to something it already knows, which it perceives as unchanging.

The incoming, surging wave of the Age of Aquarius brings new energies to bathe the planet and our lives in its glory. The ebbing wave is very much connected to the deeper experience of the age we are leaving behind. The two struggle together, the heavier wave beneath, taking some of the power out of the lighter, newer wave on the top, slowing it down a little and tempering its power. Those people with the lighter consciousness change more easily, adapting and flowing with the incoming wave. Those with a lighter consciousness float more easily to the surface, unattached to the place they are leaving behind. Those with a heavier, denser vibration struggle to adapt and change, remaining rigid and attached to the depths of the old. So, the undertow of the collective human consciousness is exemplified by people grouping together to stand against the change, which the light of the new age is bringing.

Domination and The Fear of Change

You can see this pattern acted out at every level of society, business and government. The expression of the new younger voices being drowned out by the heavier older voices. It is best observed at an individual level first, as played out in family environments. Then you can see how it works as you progress that pattern to larger organisms like groups of people, tribes or nations.

In households across the world you see one person trying to dominate the others. They are acting out of *Fear of Change*. An unchanging life is a safe life. Change is often very frightening. Usually fear of change, of experiencing a new situation 'or just something, which threatens the *status quo*' can be the trigger for a great revolt within an individual who is rigidly fixed in time, space and habits. Living our lives by daily habits, which are rigidly fixed is a safe place to be. A situation in which mother and father dominate their children leads in the next generation to husband dominating wife or *vice versa*, depending on how unsafe they feel, then again to parents dominating children. The patterning is merely passed on from generation to generation. Scale up this pattern and you see nations trying to dominate nations. It is just one simple subconscious pattern but expressed in a singular way through an individual, or in a mass way, within a national identity; through the collective unconscious and conscious.

In those who are truly terrified of change, you can observe a pathological desire to maintain the *status quo,* resisting at all costs having change served upon them. These people might, as individuals, commit extreme acts to protect themselves from their own fear. On a national level, they may even rise up and try to take over the human race, imposing their will so that everyone must conform to their ways or be damned or annihilated in the process. The national consciousness becomes an unwilling participant through being a part of that consciousness, which emanates throughout the masses as the energy of mind and thought washes through them by mere association with their neighbours.

The Opening of The Door

If you observe the patterns, you can see the energy of the Age of Aquarius beginning to open at the beginning of the 20th century. You can see sudden flushes of change throughout the world, with periods of darkness, followed by ever greater periods of light.

As we approach 1920 we are coming out of the period of the First World War, a period of horrendous darkness. Europe was the chief theatre for this war and there was great devastation and loss of life, but the new inventions of the age were beginning to spread. Electricity was introduced to homes, the radio transmitted information and music. There was a speeding-up of travel as the motor car and then the aeroplane were developed. Stop and think for a moment where we are today in terms of engineering and technology compared to a hundred years ago. The mode of transport then was foot, horse, canal barge or railway. So today's scenario is quite some progress in only a couple of generations, compared with the changes which took place in the five hundred years prior to 1900.

More Speed

A New Age is characterised by an increase in speed. A higher vibration is moving in to the planetary auric field and the Universe is radiating a higher frequency of light towards us. Everything begins to vibrate faster, or on a higher level. This begins the shift in consciousness. As conscious change comes upon us we develop new thought patterns, which result in new thoughts and abilities, which in turn produce new products. So, on the one hand minds are developing new things which are an expression of the surging wave of change which is incoming, but at another level, the undertow and weight of the Age we are still experiencing is trying to slow the change down, trying to pull things backwards. Nostalgia always says that it was better before, and for certain, some things were.

Think for a moment about the struggle a tiny bird has in order to break out of the egg. Life must move forward, but the chick has to break through a barrier first in order to experience it. However, it has come into this world with all the tools to enable it to succeed in breaking through the barrier. Also, think about the symbolism of man taking to the air. A higher vibration allows the consciousness to rise. As the energies of Aquarius spill upon the shores of Earth, they begin to illuminate minds which very soon solve the problem of heavier-than-air flight. At once we find ourselves overcoming the gravitational forces which have kept us Earth-bound since the dawn of our time as a species.

The Great Depression

The Great Depression affected more or less the whole world on some level, but more so, the young and still emerging American nation. Consider the parallel of a child suffering a measles outbreak. It will crash and go down with illness more quickly and easily than an adult, but often recover much more quickly too. See America as very much a child nation, emerging and growing alongside the energy of the older established nations of Europe. America is the new kid on the block with the bright ideas and symbolises that surging wave of new consciousness breaking with glee on the shores of the world. The roaring 20s saw money and spending grow dramatically in certain circles. This was the surge of the top wave creating an artificial picture of the reality of wealth. But beneath it, the undertow was preparing for the great depression of the thirties. Some were riding the wave whilst the majority were sinking beneath it.

The First World War had seen an attempt to dominate and control on a national level and ten years later, by 1924, we see the same pattern emerge within the new nation of America as the Ku Klux Klan reaches the height of its influence. By the end of the year the Klan will claim to have 9 million members, but will decline drastically in 1925 after financial and moral scandals rock its leadership. You can see that things are happening quickly and when they do there can be some destabilisation as old and new energies fight it out.

By 1929, the richest 1 per cent of Americans owned 40 percent of the nation's wealth. The bottom 93 percent had experienced a 4 percent drop in real disposable income in the six years between 1923 and 1929, but individual worker productivity rose an astonishing 43 percent from 1919 to 1929. However, the rewards are being funnelled to the top: the number of people reporting half-million dollar incomes grows from 156 to 1,489 between 1920 and 1929, a phenomenal rise compared to other decades.

By 1929, we see the surging wave turning into the ebbing wave and recession begins in August 1929, two months before the stock market crash.

The stock market crash begins on October 24th. Investors call October 29th 'Black Tuesday'. Losses for the month will total $16 billion, an astronomical sum in those days.

History shows that 1932 and 1933 are the worst years of the Great Depression. Since 1929, 10,000 banks have failed and about $2 billion in deposits have been lost. Over 13 million Americans have lost their jobs and the top tax rate is raised from 25 to 63 percent. When the people are down, the government kicks them.

A Military Coup in America

In retrospect, can you believe this? Alarmed by Roosevelt's plan to redistribute wealth from the rich to the poor, a group of millionaire businessmen, led by the Du Pont and the J P Morgan empires, plans to overthrow Roosevelt with a military coup and install a fascist government. The businessmen try to recruit General Smedley Butler, promising him an army of 500,000 men, unlimited financial backing and generous media spin control. The plot is foiled when Butler reports it to Congress.

By the following year, 1934, we are about to see the beginning of the next incoming, surging wave as Sweden becomes the first nation to recover fully from the Great Depression, following a policy of Keynesian deficit spending. Two years later, in 1936, Germany becomes the second nation to recover fully from the Great Depression, through heavy deficit spending in preparation for the next war. Two years later again, by 1938, Britain becomes the third nation to recover as it too begins deficit spending in preparation for war.

Finally by 1939, 10 years on from Black Tuesday, the United States will begin emerging from the Depression as it borrows and spends $1 billion to build its armed forces. The Depression is ending worldwide, a symbol of light returning again. The emerging light lifts up the power within people and there is high activity in every quarter as money moves about and work is more plentiful. We see the light uplifting the aspirations of individuals and driving things forward. In the midst of this process we are about to witness a most unusual phenomenon. Something you would never imagine light could do, until you understand it a little better.

Waves of Equal Force

We see the power of light illuminating the old pattern of Fear of Change, which, as always, is played out through the domination of others in an attempt to control outside forces and thereby avoid change. The incoming light is actually activating the old darker forces as nations prepare for the coming hostilities. World War II starts with Hitler's invasion of Poland on September 1st 1939, and energetically we observe a complete overlap of the incoming and outgoing ages. At this point in time we can say that the energies from the incoming Age and the outgoing Age are perfectly balanced and exactly equal in force. Neither one is more powerful than the other. Lots of people want peace and prosperity, but they are all caught up as the pawns in a war.

In his attempt to avoid change by attempting to dominate humanity, Hitler falls into the trap of the Aquarian Light. The Light opened his fears to the degree that he acted to close down all the freedoms of humanity and dominate it entirely. Eventually that great force of resistance within him was smashed by the very light which brought it to the surface. Although the fear of change of the Age was expressed through Hitler, it was representative of all the hidden fears of the collective consciousness of the Age of Pisces. The incoming wave of light used the wave of darkness to destroy itself. The light pushed the fear to breaking point where it was exposed for what it was as it was exposed through the actions of Hitler. The world suffered human loss, but the outcome was the rebirth of a world society in which more freedoms would be allowed and tolerated. Of course, immediately after the war, we can still see those old patterns displayed through countries like Russia and China, where the people are not yet enjoying freedom, but essentially, the close of this period of history was a turning point in the new wave of incoming consciousness versus the old wave of diminishing resistance to change.

The saying of Jesus at the head of this chapter speaks of breaking the patterns of consciousness. Once a certain pattern of resistance within the consciousness has been 'overturned', then it cannot be 'rebuilt', or, the vibration cannot function at the same level of intensity. When consciousness evolves, then it cannot regress. The old life or old world must be left behind through the evolution of consciousness. It is interesting to observe those people who stood against fighting, the conscientious objectors, as they were called. These were the people who stood in the face of collective consciousness and said that what the world was doing was evil. They were truly the carriers of the new light and that light helped them to summon the courage to stand their ground and swim against the tide in the face of almost certain death by firing squad, as the old consciousness demonstrated the lengths it would go to in order to purge itself of any form of thinking that rocked the boat of certainty. There was no room for those who would turn the other cheek, but they were the thin end of the wedge of the coming of the Aquarian Light. The conscientious objectors were labelled cowards, but in reality, they were the ones with the highest moral courage.

Although, the war is the largest tragedy in human history, the United States emerged as the world's only economic superpower. The new kid on the block is now a teenager with power and energy at his elbow and is ready to cut a swathe through the world. During the period 1945 to 1963 America will experience the greatest economic boom it has ever known, establishing its position on the world stage. Because America was a young nation with little in the way of restriction, it moved more easily energetically; it wasn't held back by convention or the entrenched energies of history. America was populated by people who had been prepared to take a journey to try to move their lives forward. It was almost as if that incoming, uplifting wave was working for America even when people were suffering throughout the depression. Patterns were being laid down. This was America's time to be able to take full advantage of the new energies awakening minds, which created huge growth unprecedented anywhere else in the world.

(Information on the Great Depression copyright Steve Kangas, *"The Great Depression: Its Causes and Cure," Liberalism Resurgent* (THE_GREAT_DE-PRESSION.htm, 1997 http://www.aliveness.com/kangaroo/)

Let us Step Backwards a Few Years

Out of the darkness of the First World War was born the surging wave of the Roaring Twenties in North America. This was the first sign of an uplift in consciousness, a first taste of new freedoms, of changes to come and a period, which has been described as one of the most colourful decades in history. It was a time for the confident emergence of the feminine as women began to step into a new role of work and entering society and public life. Remember, Aquarius is a feminine energy. To those who were ready it was a time of great excitement. In post war Britain too this energy was visible and the twenties are often referred to as the decade, which changed Britain.

Art was also developing rapidly during the 1920s. In America Art Deco was taking hold in a big way, expressing itself with such grace in examples like the Chrysler Building in New York City. In Europe the expressionists emerged, followed by surrealists such as Dali. However, as America was changing rapidly and becoming incredibly colourful and attractive, to the less fortunate in Europe, this taste of freedom began to awaken the fear of change lying in wait in the collective unconscious of the older nations of Europe. The collective unconscious mind then reacted on a major scale with economic collapse and a need to dominate in order to avoid change. The greatest expression of this need to dominate was from Adolph Hitler, and Hitler, of course, being an artist, was a Sensitive.

Hitler was born 20th April 1889, the first day of Taurus the Bull. One might conjecture that he was a late birth and should really have been an Aries, the first sign of the zodiac, but being on the cusp of both Aries and Taurus is probably just about perfect to describe this man. Aries, being the first sign, is often child-like, or like a child in its expression of life, and the imaginations of children know no bounds. Being the first sign can mean being like a baby, having tantrums to get what you want. Shout loudly and bang your spoon on the table and someone will take notice, no matter how old the baby is. Imagine then a baby who is full of the *Fear of Change*, driven by the fire of Aries with the determination, stubbornness and power of Taurus the bull and you have a cocktail, which spells out, 'I am going to get what I want and if you stand in my way I will drive my horns right through you.' In Hitler we have the sensitive artist with a fear of change and a determination to avoid it at any cost. He is an expression of one of the last great walls of resistance to the incoming Age of Aquarius. His work can be seen as one of the last great battles to hold back the evolution of human consciousness. Or was it?

Let's leave this era with a comment from Billy Price, which seems to echo well my descriptions as I allowed my consciousness to travel back into those energies. '*The revolution in art which began in the late 19th century shattered conventional forms and accepted standards, and seemed to many to herald a new, uncomfortable and confusing era. Hitler felt that the collapse of "eternal" values in aesthetics could only lead to decline. The fine arts were in danger of being divorced from the people: the new concepts of "beauty" were incomprehensible to those who were bound to an older world. Hitler's art clearly reflected his personal convictions, which were a reaction against both imagined and real threats of a changing world. As an artist, he adhered to those standards he considered "worthy," "comprehensible," and "eternal."*' (http://www.adolfhitler.ws/index.php)

The Turning of the Tide

As we step out of the 1940s and leave that great battle of subjugation and domination behind us, we enter a period of personal struggle for many in Europe, but also calm and recovery. This is a little like when you are ill. Sometimes, you get a little worse before you get better and although the pressures of war were over, things could be worse as people came to terms with helplessness, personal loss and emotional desolation. But, this period is also the respite, the still water, before the surge of the next wave of Aquarian light. Not only were we waiting for the next wave, but the end of the 1940s was also the turning of a major tide.

Tides come in and go out and waves are a constant movement upon the tide. The end of the Second World War was approaching the slack water before the next major incoming tide. Since 1900, there had been three major waves of darkness in the two World Wars and the Great Depression, interspersed with the growing glimmer of a new reality. After 1945, the world was poised between war and peace. It was poised in the slack water between the outgoing tide of domination and fear and waiting for the next incoming tide of new light and possibility. We see that the 40s were a time for reflection in those still waters. The tide was already turning. The darkness was being submerged by the incoming waves of light, then the tide gained momentum and Elvis Presley came on the scene. Suddenly, for a new generation, life suddenly got a whole lot better, but boy, did their parents kick up a fuss!

5

One for the Money

Well, its one for the money,
Two for the show,
Three to get ready,
Now go, cat, go.

Carl Perkins, *Blue Suede Shoes*

Waves of Sound

Let us slip back for a moment and revisit the 1920s, to see the emergence of another wave of light. Remember that a new age is characterised by an increase in speed. We see radio waves being used for the first time to transmit the energy of speech. In 1921 Westinghouse develop four major broadcasting radio stations — in Pittsburgh, Boston, New York and Chicago. By the end of the following year, there were over five hundred radio stations in America. In 1922, radio was also taking off in Britain and by 1927, the BBC was enshrined by Royal Charter as the national broadcasting authority. Although, not many people had radio receiving sets yet, this was going to be the first time in history that human beings had harnessed invisible vibrations in the form of radio waves in order to transmit vibrations of sound over great distances. And, of course, radio was developed on that incoming wave of the roaring twenties.

As we leave the dark outgoing tide of the late 40s, the waves of the next incoming tide are preparing to bring an influx of new Aquarian Light onto the surface of our planet. By now radio is well developed and is being used for both speech and, more importantly, music. Of all the different forms of art produced by the Sensitives, because of radio, music was going to become the biggest influence on the changing consciousness of the masses.

The first rock record, *Rocket 88* by Jackie Brenston emerged in 1951, but it took another three years for Bill Haley and the Comets to come up with

Rock Around the Clock as the acclaimed first rock record to enter the collective consciousness, or to put it another way, to become a hit. Radio was now a medium, which was reaching millions on both sides of the Atlantic and musicians were becoming the new messiahs, awakening souls by developing many new genres of vibrations, illuminating the desire in others to, 'feel' the beat.

Of all the people bursting onto the music scene, Elvis most represented the next shift in human consciousness. He was setting the young people alight with excitement and possibility. The words of his song at the head of this chapter could almost be an anthem for the Age of Aquarius ..., *Three to get ready, now go cat go*. In the Summer of 1953, Elvis goes to Sun Studios to record his first songs. By November 1955, Elvis signs with RCA for an unprecedented $40,000. By January the following year, he releases the famous, *Heartbreak Hotel*, which would be his first Gold Record, selling over a million copies. The symbolism of gold and hearts is apt, as in order to truly move into the age of Golden Light, one has to break the bonds of the heart. Things were moving fast. This was truly a wave to be surfed, and in Hawaii, that's exactly what was about to happen.

However, this stage was not the smoothest place to be for the burgeoning of this new sound, thought and rhythm. Elvis suffered the slings and arrows of outrageous fortune as a staid society rose up and tried to ban his concerts and keep its teenage children, especially daughters, away, which is to say; safe from those devilish gyrating hips. Music has always suffered as being the expression of the devil when it suits those still struggling with changes that are coming. Music is merely at the forefront of the expression of emerging light through human consciousness, and when that light is emerging through the likes of Elvis, from a source so powerful and pure as an Aquarian wave of energy, then it will illuminate thousands and, as history has proved, there is nothing, which can stop it.

Waves of Light

During this period, television was also developing quickly, so that vision as well as sound was now being transmitted and received by the public. Although, America had been very quick to develop radio and television and American artists were leading the way in the new music of the time, almost bizarrely and against great opposition from the old school, a young graduate named Jack Good managed to get a new music show for teenagers onto the BBC in Britain.

The *6.5 Special* was first broadcast at 6.05p.m. on a Saturday night, February 16th 1957. At that time, we really didn't have any rock and roll artists to speak of in Britain, and because of union problems and restrictions, the new show couldn't get any American artists to perform either, but on that first night, they did manage to air a film clip of Little Richard's, *Long Tall Sally* from *Don't Knock The Rock'*.

American band leader Ray Anthony appeared on The *6.05 Special* and when asked what he thought of it, he replied, "I think it's great. I've not seen any excitement like this for a long time." When asked did they have anything like this on American television, he replied. "No, I'm afraid they don't, and we want some more of it. Yes we do!" It wasn't long before Dick Clark's people were sent over to Britain to have a look at *The 6.05 Special* so that they could bring American Bandstand up to date. (Film clip info courtesy of www.spencerleigh.demon.co.uk/Feature_6.5Special.htm).

Billed as a kind of magazine programme because Jack wasn't allowed to do only music, *The 6.05 Special,* nevertheless, was a huge success, breaking lots of new ground. However, Jack left the show because of his ongoing battles with the hierarchy who continually looked down their noses at his product, probably considering that it was a bit of a disgrace on the BBC. Jack moved to the only commercial TV station in the UK at the time and on Saturday September 13th 1958 he launched *Oh Boy*, the first music programme completely dedicated to the popular music of the day.

Acceleration of Aquarian Light

You can clearly see that once the emerging consciousness of the day, as expressed through the new generation of Sensitives, the Rock and Rollers, begins to be transmitted over the airwaves in both sound and vision, it opens a huge new portal, which can spread the message and vibration of the times into the lives of millions. You could say that the late fifties were the period in which incoming Aquarian Light can be seen to be accelerating for the first time, rather than battling with the outgoing age, and when light wishes to emerge you can't stop it. As we see with Jack Good's work, the old school at the BBC tried to stop him bringing forth the new vibration, but the commercial stations were ready to run with it and the new message of the day was delivered.

The History of Delivering the Message

At this point, let's take a moment to look at the technology which has allowed the message to be delivered — not just the spiritual message, but any message. Prior to the 15th century, information was always brought by word of mouth or read from scrolls or parchments to an assembled crowd. Spiritual teachings though, were usually passed from teacher to student on an individual basis by word of mouth and the chosen students would be allowed to read and study the ancient texts in whatever form they had been recorded.

The earliest writings and indeed books were of mystical, spiritual or self-development-type subject matter, so the self-help book is not a new thing, as many seem to think it is. In those times it was called News, or if it was considered to be especially important, Good News or Gospel. Self-help has been around since information was first recorded. Hand written parchments developed into a series of parchments bound in animal skin and known as a codex. Some of the most important of these early books surviving today are known as the Nag Hammadi library. Dating from around the 3rd century CE, this collection of codices, was discovered buried in a jar in the Egyptian desert by peasants in 1945. The library consists of an amazing array of early Gospels, amongst them, The Gospel of Thomas, perhaps the most powerful expression of the teachings of Jesus known to us in the present time. This type of hand written and bound document was usually only for study by the mystical or spiritual student, though, and not something the public could easily obtain for themselves.

America was of course a long way from existing in the guise we know it today. Europe was in the Dark Ages from 400 to around 1000CE, when the only form of cultural expression and opportunity of advancement was through the beautiful Illuminated Manuscripts produced by scribes in the monasteries. Even today these are considered perhaps the most beautiful books ever produced. Again, these were not for public consumption.

Other than Illuminated Manuscripts, little changed from the time of the codices, shortly after Jesus, for over a thousand years. Then, sometime prior to 1450 Johannes Gutenberg of Germany developed a system of moveable type and a printing press. Between 1452 to 1455, he began to print the famous Gutenberg 42 Line Bible, the first commercially printed book and still one of the most famous of early printed books. 48 examples are known to have survived and are spread quite widely among major libraries of the world today.

With the development of printing with moveable type, the general public began to have access to information on an unprecedented scale.

Printing with moveable lead type continued into the 1970s, almost unchanged from Gutenberg's original invention. The craft was practised continuously for five hundred years. As a matter of interest, compositors — i.e. those who compose type — were the last artisans in Britain allowed to carry a sword in public, such was their standing in society. In the 1970s, on the back of those great breaking waves of the 1960s, typesetting began to move into the new era of photo-composition. I trained as a compositor on the very first photo-typesetting systems to come to Britain from Germany, where they were developed. They were the forerunner of desktop publishing and the personal computer age. When we were working with screens and keyboards in the 1970s, the personal computer as we know it today hadn't been invented, although computers did exist. We forget that the PC has only been with us a very short time, but in that short time its power has grown dramatically.

So, around 1450 the printed word began to accelerate. The next great shift in information transmission was in the 1920s, when Radio was born and then in the 1950s, television came along. By the 1980s, the personal computer was developing and by the 90s, the internet arrived. October 29th 1969, was the first time a device called a computer communicated with another computer via a router. Again, look at the timing. Right at the point where Hendrix was setting fire to his guitar on stage and his music was becoming the co-narcotic, with marijuana, of the soldiers in Vietnam as they tried to touch new perceptions with the mind. This is when it was all happening. However, the internet as we know and use it today really developed through the early-to-mid 1990s. Let us remember our focus. What we are interested in observing is 'speed', and the speed of the development of the computer in around three decades has been dramatic in comparison to five hundred years of moveable type and prior to that, two thousand years of hand written manuscript.

The internet, now running at broadband speeds, is already developing into super-broadband speeds. You can also use the internet as a great library for research, you can read books on it; you can hear radio and watch television programmes from all over the world on it and you can communicate with virtually anyone anywhere in the world who has a personal computer or can access an internet café. Even if they don't own one, most people at least have access to a computer. Mobile phone technology now also allows you to access the internet, so from a small device you can keep in a purse or a pocket you can communicate across the globe. Just look at the rate of development since the end of the 1960s, the speed is incredible and we have barely yet attained the Age of Aquarius.

The Opposing Forces of Light and Dark

Any device with the power to transmit a message, whether it be art, a book, radio, television or the internet, can transmit either Light or Dark energy. Power always attracts power and in the early days of radio and television that power attracted clean, clear and intelligent minds producing what we might describe as wholesome material for the listener and viewer. This was a great period for knowledge and culture to be spread via the new media by the people whose minds were being illuminated by the incoming light of the emerging consciousness of the new age. Subsequently, though, dark-force aspects began to infiltrate and degrade these media and the quality of programming began to fall during the late 1980s. In Britain during the nineties, we saw changing patterns in programming. We were entering the era of emotional stimulation and manipulation. Television in particular became like a dealer, persuading the viewer to try the latest drug of choice. A little at a time, the dealer began to feed the viewer ever more powerfully charged visions of bad language, violence and sex, which would stimulate emotional responses. Emotional responses are the cause of creating addictions. Unknowingly, you become addicted to certain feelings, which are produced by the stimulus. The result is that those of weak willpower become prisoners of their desires. This then leads to a greater inner weakness and they become easy to control, or pacify. If you scale this up to a collective conscious level, you find that whole nations can be controlled by the same programme at the same time on the same night of the week. Now, that is some force at work.

Darkness has crept in and the quality has gone down, as it has in movie-making to some degree. There is a power struggle in the media between the forces of light and dark. We saw this very clearly in the British newspaper market, as tabloid papers began to produce articles little better than school-boy humour and smut, pandering to a consciousness, which was happy where it was without the need to struggle to awaken itself. The result of this unchecked dark-force activity has led to journalists having little or no respect for their fellow human beings on any level, seeing the likes of you or I as nothing more than carrion to feed upon, in the name of bringing a photo, invented story or even plain lies to the pages of their publication; for the emotional gratification of the addicted vultures who consume such matter. The hounding of people in this way, whether a celebrity or not, is evil of the most pernicious kind in action and destroys lives. It is nothing less than stalking your prey, but the laws on stalking don't seem to apply to these people. Perhaps the ultimate expression of this was the way in which Princess Diana's car was pursued by photographers on motorcycles, like a pack of hyenas in some wildlife programme determined for a kill. They even stood around taking photos as the occupants of the car lay dying. This is a good example of choosing your path in life, choosing the actions of light or the actions of darkness. Judge for yourself what you make of such a situation, but if you had to state whether you think these actions to be good or evil, then what would you say?

The Future

The energies of the Age of Aquarius are an irresistible force for change and so change will come. Within that change you will see the battle between light and dark continue and one or the other will at times have the upper hand. Already, people are vying to control the internet and the Chinese government, for example, is forcing Google to limit access to certain websites. This is that old pattern of Fear of Change again, but expressed as Fear of Truth. But the internet has a great power to bring truth to those who are seeking it. In the past, books were burned, radio and television programmes were subject to court orders banning publication, but the internet is a different animal. Although you may have to trawl through spurious matter to find the truth, you will eventually find it, because the Age of Aquarius is the Age of revealing Truth to those who seek it and the internet is one of the keys to accessing that Truth.

As we have seen, wherever a medium of transmission exists the message can be from a source of light or a source of darkness. We have seen the degeneration in all the forms of media and the rise in pornographic magazines, garbage radio programmes, gambling on television and all three of these on the internet. However, the internet is the present state-of-the-art form of communication, allowing anyone and everyone to publish their thoughts and ideas. Light and dark are only different sides of the same coin. The only way you will ever change the consciousness from darkness is through a shift in vibration producing an evolutionary event. As consciousness evolves, people will learn to live and create from a higher expression of perception, from the deeper consciousness within themselves. An evolutionary shift accesses more of the pure aspect within, which is the seed of the God-consciousness. This resides within the deepest point in the heart of all humans.

Transmitting Spiritual Light

Spiritual knowledge and the spiritual message have always been available through the first of the three media we have discussed, the beauty of type and the printed word. However, the spiritual message through radio and television has been extremely limited because those who govern these airwaves are always concerned with revenue and viewing figures and more people will view a film with lots of sex and violence than will view a programme of spiritual teaching by the Dalai Lama, for example. With the internet, you have the choice of what you view, whereas with radio and television, you can only view what the 'controllers' wish to transmit. So, don't get too hung up about the darkness on the net, just avoid viewing it, then you don't give it any energy. You have the choice, so you have the power. Where do we begin?

The internet has the most amazing power to transmit not only a spiritual message, but Spiritual Light itself. Following my Guidance, I have already been using it for this purpose for a number of years, but more so since around 2003, though without fully realising what this was leading up to. In January 2007, my Guidance gave me the most amazing insight, which could trigger the start of an evolutionary process within the consciousness of millions of people merely by logging-on to a website. What that website might contain, we will discuss later. But, the important thing to note here is that the internet and mobile phone technology is the initial communication medium for the Aquarian Age and the Aquarian Light. The Age of Aquarius is all about the evolution of human consciousness and the most recent wave of incoming energy, which brought us these media is now bringing us the message and the light to transmit upon it. The only thing that can hold back what is unfolding is your own limiting beliefs in yourself or your ability.

So, it's ...

Three to get ready,

Now go, cat, go.

Communications Time Line of The Word

Recording of the Word

c5000 BCE – Glyph-like impressions on pottery, from Harappa, Pakistan

c3100 BCE – Sumerian and later Egyptian symbols appeared on clay tablets.

c3100 BCE – Papyrus used for scrolls.

    100 CE – The Dead Sea Scrolls, some on copper sheet and others on parchment.

    200 CE – Codex: Parchment or papyrus used in sewn sheets and bound in leather to form the first books, known as a codex.

    500 CE – Earliest Examples of Illuminated Manuscripts but the majority of surviving examples are from the Middle Ages to the 15th century.

    c1450 – Guttenberg develops moveable type and the printing press.

Electronic Transmission of the Word

1921 – Westinghouse develop 4 radio stations across America.

1922 – Over 500 radio stations in America.

1923 – The first demonstration of television.

1936 – The BBC began the world's first television broadcasts.

1939 – By 1939 there were 20,000 television sets.

1955 – Elvis signs with RCA.

1957 – The first TV programme to transmit Rock and Roll was the *6.05 Special* on the BBC in the UK.

1961 – Man goes into Space. Russian, Yuri Gagarin orbits the earth.

1973 – First Generation Mobile Phone—the size of a house brick!

1981 – IBM announced the first Personal Computer.

1984 – Apple Macintosh introduces Desktop Publishing.

1985 – The First Domain Name is registered.

1985 – Microsoft Windows is launched.

1987 – 25 million PCs sold in the USA.

1991 – World-wide Web (www.) is open for business.

1991 – The first SMS message was sent in the UK.

1996 – 45 million people are on-line

1999 – Google arrives and there are now 150 million people on-line.

c2000 – Broadband speeds begin to develop.

2002 – Over 500 million users on-line

2004 – Internet available on mobile phones

From the first decade of the new millennium, the mobile phone has become a pocket device that can transmit and receive all manner of calls, internet pages, tv and satellite information. In less than 20 years, the speed of communication has seen an unprecedented acceleration. Where will it go next?

6

Voodoo Child

'If I don't meet you no more in this world,
Then I'll see you on the next one,
And don't be late, DON'T BE LATE!'

Jimi Hendrix, *Voodoo Child*

The rhetoric of key movers and shakers of the 50s, Beat Generation such as Allen Ginsberg (*Howl* 1956), Jack Kerouac (*On the Road* 1957) and William S. Burroughs, (*Naked Lunch* 1959), was opening the minds of a new generation and preparing the ground for new thought. Music had become *the* medium for the message and Bob Dylan's, *The Times They Are a Changin'* could, on the one hand be seen as prophecy, and on the other, the reality of the moment.

As we entered the 1960s, the conscious change really began to gather momentum. The sound of popular culture suddenly took another shift as God gave a hand to four lads from Liverpool. The Beatles came on the scene and in no time at all there were pictures on television of screaming and fainting girls, demonstrating a mass desire to associate with the guys making this new music — something never before seen on such a scale. Something quite unusual was happening in dear old over-conservative Britain and of course, because America was already awakening, The Beatles became a huge success over there too.

The Divine Feminine
One of the most important aspects of stepping through the door into the Aquarian Age is that it heralds the emergence of the Divine Feminine. Generally speaking, the receptive feminine has been subjugated, crushed, denied, ignored and undervalued by the dominant masculine throughout most cultures of the world since time immemorial, but in this coming age, as

the feminine emerges, we will observe a complete change in the way the world works and at this point in the evolution of our species, we will not be able to imagine how that might happen. Our world presently functions through force being applied in a masculine way in order to meet the desires of those applying the force, or, in other words, those at the top of the food chain.

Of course, there have been many prominent heroines in history, such as Boudicea, who gave the Roman Army a thrashing, Joan of Arc, who gave the English Army a thrashing, Florence Nightingale, Amy Johnson. Mother Teresa, etc. There are also many lesser known, but equally important figures such as Marie Curie, the Polish scientist and double Nobel Prize winner, Rosa Parks, the black woman who refused to give up her seat on the bus to a white passenger, which culminated in the acceleration of the civil rights movement in America, Aung San Suu Kyi, the opposition leader under permanent house arrest in Myanmar. But these are perhaps exceptional examples rather than everyday women stepping forward.

What we have seen as women have become more prominent in business and politics throughout the latter part of the 20th century and the first part of the 21st, is that those women are often extremely masculine in the way they approached their work. What we might say here is that rather than bringing forward the Divine receptive Feminine, they competed and played the game exactly as the pushing competing masculine did. They enter the battlefield and play, by the existing masculine rules, rather then bringing forth the feminine light. This has largely been one of the problems with the Feminist Movement. This first show has been one of separation and conflict as the female has tried to emerge as if they were entering a battle of us against them. This is a perfect reflection of how the masculine functions through a national identity; where it views other nationalities as something to be dominated if they are not on board with the same message. However, the Feminists took it a stage further in that they didn't want the masculine on board with any message. This is what is meant by separation. In evolutionary terms, separation ultimately leads to a dead end and the process of evolution is all about coming together in unity and balance. So, what we can see are early expressions as the Divine Feminine tries to find its voice. As with the birth of all new things, balance and understanding needs to be found in order to succeed.

This will all change and to some degree we have already witnessed the emergence of the Divine Feminine in the way Hilary Clinton approached the most recent Presidential elections in the United States. She is a woman playing by her feminine rules from the heart, although, getting carried away with it sometimes when she's dodging bullets in the heat of the moment. It was time to move on from the Texas cowboy style of leadership and coming to the fore in the race were the white woman, Hilary Clinton and the black man, Barack Obama, both of them brilliant symbols of a changing world. The dominant masculine attitudes in the USA at the time still managed to push Hilary down, but as soon as Obama became President elect, he reached out and pulled her onto the podium with him. It almost didn't matter who won with these two though, as what was most important to the human psyche was the symbolism of huge change.

We began to see the emergence of the feminine through the actions of the Suffragettes in the early part of the 20th century. Throughout the Second World War, women turned to work in a big way, managing and farming the land for food, working in the factories making planes and munitions, and also flying the planes as they delivered them where they were needed by the Air Force. Women took on the roles of the men who had gone to war and this change allowed the work ethic to continue for women after the war. Women were becoming empowered and discovering value to their lives and their own self-worth. As we reach the liberating 60s, the Divine Feminine is finding her voice and power of expression through the protest singers such as Joan Baez, Joni Mitchell and others. The screaming girls at Beatles gigs were another expression of that voice emerging. By 1979, we saw the first female Prime Minister in the UK in Margaret Thatcher, the daughter of a grocer. In September 1981, a group of women chained themselves to the fencing outside an American Military base in the UK to protest against the decision of the Government to allow the US to site nuclear weapons in the British countryside. The female camp grew as ever more women joined the protest and the strength of this movement eventually succeeded when the missiles were removed ten years later in 1991. The women finally left 19 years to the day later.

In this New Age, the desire to be at the top will diminish and the people who will be chosen to lead will be those who truly have integrity, but also a lack of ego. Ego does nothing for the world and its problems, but allows those who use it to shout loudest, yet all ego is proclaiming is itself. We might think ego-driven leaders are our representatives, but they are not and that truth will be revealed more and more as the light of the Aquarian Age reveals the truth at a level where ever more people will see the illusion.

As the Divine Feminine emerges, ego will begin to dissolve in the light of truth from the heart, whether the feminine emerges through men or women, and it will emerge in both. For example, anyone in their right mind would not wish to battle to become the leader of a modern day America or Britain with all the attendant problems that have been created by the recent incumbents. If these countries were businesses, then they would have ceased to exist a long time ago, consigned to the financially and morally bankrupt scrapheap of things that don't work.

With the birth of the Age of Healing, women are very much in the vanguard of bringing energy and light to help those individuals who are ready to seek change. As each individual benefits from the change they facilitate, so it is that the world will change.

In many cultures, the feminine is still crushed to the degree that it doesn't even attempt to raise its head above the parapet, let alone think about bringing change for the better. Even in the west women still have to fight to gain equal rights. However, using force is the masculine way and that is not how the change will come. Think passive and receptive and watch how the world comes to you. It will be a silent revolution. As a simple example, let us give you this image to work with. Women have often been at the forefront of trying to prevent war and disharmony. The disharmony is always perpetrated by the masculine aspect. If women truly harnessed their power and refused to bend to the desires of the masculine, then they could wipe out war and disharmony in a couple of generations. If they withdrew from the masculine entirely, then this would prevent the birth of the next generation and that would prevent the continuation of the old programme of the collective unconscious. If you think about warring societies, the children are already programmed with the battle scenario at an early age. As they grow, they naturally continue the fight because that is what they know. If there is no new generation, then there is no continuation. The warmongers would die out and a new age would prevail. This is perhaps an extreme version of how to bring lasting change. Another way of attaining the same goal is to remove the children from the influences of the old programme and bring them up with new values. Such is the saying of Francis Xavier:

'Give me the child until he is seven, and I'll give you the man.'
Francis Xavier (co-founder of the Jesuit Order).

What this means is that the mind of a child is a blank canvas and you can paint upon that mind with light or dark, good or evil. You can select your own images and present any form of reality and the child will be a reflection of the reality you endow it with. Therefore, consider this. If you gave birth to a child in an Eastern culture and then sent it to a western culture for the first few years of its life, who would that child be? It would be the product of a different culture, regardless of who its parents and birth culture were. Therefore, even in a war torn province, if you shield the child from the war and anger, and endow it with good virtue, then what will you have? You will have lasting change, for the child will not easily be able to assimilate the warring posture. It will be outside of its mind-set and understanding. The Devine Feminine has such power at its elbow to change humanity, but will it ever see this opportunity? The power has always been there, but it takes courage and determination to bring that kind of change. First you must change yourself, then you will become the example for others to learn from.

'Be the change you want to see in the world.'
Mahatma Gandhi – revered for his doctrine of none violence.

Perhaps the most visible sign of the Divine Feminine at this time can be seen through the emergence of men and women choosing same sex partnerships. In only a few years gay men have found ever more courage to display their feminine side and enter society more openly. Like any period of change, this has met with great opposition in certain quarters, but their strength is growing and their visibility spreading. The gay women of these recent years are also very different to the sometimes strong and loud feminists who emerged through the 60s and 70s. To be feminine, you do not have to be anti-masculine, but there was a strong expression of this attitude in early feminism. The strange conundrum in this is that it is the masculine aspect, which attempts to create the wall of force between the male and female. Therefore, the feminine was trying to emerge through feminism, but using the forceful pushing energy of their own masculine side to create separation from men. That masculine force is not present in the later generations. The old voice is dying away as a greater confidence in the feminine self emerges, although, there is still a strong element of separation and mistrust at some levels. Both gay men and women are ever more able to take their natural place in society in greater peace through a greater acceptance of the truth of self. As the environment of the collective consciousness continues to be influenced by the emergence of the Divine Feminine, the gay community will become a greater part of the overall community. Separation will become a thing of history.

The Mind's True Liberation

The Aquarian Age is about the liberation of the mind and going beyond its known and understood limitations; self-imposed limitations, really, or shall we say imposed by society's programming of what is acceptable or possible and what is not. Aquarius will dissolve those self-limiting programs as people learn to find the courage to express their unlimited potential through individuality. The people of the 1960s were already entering and exploring the new age through experimenting with mind-altering herbs and chemicals such as Cannabis and LSD. Necessity being the mother of invention, if you don't try something, you don't find out. People were looking for answers and if you had money, then you could pursue those answers. By 1967, The Beatles and their music were well established on the world stage, but we could also see the members as individuals trying to find answers, as they veered towards the spiritual eastern culture, seeking meditation and enlightenment through the teachings of the Maharishi. Disillusioned with the Maharishi, years later John Lennon said, 'There is no guru. You have to believe in yourself. You've got to get down to your own God in your own temple. It's all down to you, mate.' Ever a guy to hit the nail on the head.

The new generations were now well into the wave of change and had been publicly speaking out against the patterns of society and governments for some time, notably with the 1960, march to ban the Hydrogen Bomb, when at least 60,000 people had gathered in Trafalgar Square in London to demonstrate, the largest public protest of the century at that time.

The shift in consciousness began to accelerate in the 1960s, carried along by a power surge on the incoming wave. The doors to the Age of Aquarius were truly opening quickly. However, the expression of the outgoing dark wave in this period was that America was still at war in Vietnam (1959 to 1973), with major troop deployments arriving in 1965, but leaving in a hurry ten years later, on April 30th 1975.

The Point of No Return

In response to the intensifying dark wave of Vietnam, the Universe threw the Jimi Hendrix Experience at us and that short period of Jimi's presence on the world stage between 1966 and 1970 changed everything forever. There was now no going back. That was the very point in time where the old consciousness would never be able to reassert itself again at the same level, the level at which humans blindly followed without question. The time of independent thought and questioning was emerging in the mass conscious-ness. That doesn't mean the old patterns would not continue to try and express themselves again and again, they would, but from this point on, the resistance to those old patterns started to grow. The power of the incoming wave was now beginning to outweigh the power of the outgoing wave of the Age of Pisces.

A Searing Display of Aquarian Light

Hendrix exploded onto the world stage like a shooting star blazing across the heavens; he arrived like a comet seen for the first time but never forgotten and celebrated thereafter. He came bearing unique gifts and talents, an illumination pouring from the core of his being, not only through the way he played guitar, but through his whole persona. The leading guitarists of the day stood aghast at his ability when he burst onto the scene in England. The light, energy and power, which radiated from the man and his music left a lasting mark on humanity in only a few short years before he left the planet. He didn't need to be here any longer than he was to enlighten a multitude of souls; to excite a whole genre of music; to awaken a fire of change, which opened the minds and consciousness of a whole generation, and beyond.

Playing as a virtual unknown in New York, Chas Chandler of The Animals brought Hendrix to London in Late September 1966. Within two weeks he was in rehearsal with his new band 'The Jimi Hendrix Experience'. Within the month he had recorded his first two songs, one of which, *Hey Joe,* was released December 16th 1966. Two months later this unknown artist was at number 4 in the British music charts. His following record, *Purple Haze* reached number 3. Also in June '67, Jimi returned to America to play the Monterey Pop Festival where he is introduced by Brian Jones of the Rolling Stones as, 'the most exciting performer I've ever heard.' After a superb performance Jimi smashed his guitar in an act of wild frenzy. His career would go super-nova after that and the release of his first two albums, *Are you Experienced* and, *Axis: Bold as Love* shot to the top of the charts. Two years later, at Woodstock in August 1969, where Hendrix was the headline act, he played his searing rendition of, *The Star-Spangled Banner,* which of course drew all manner of criticism from the old school conservative folk who were not ready for this lightening assault on the National Anthem. Jimi, of course, was only bringing the new light to an old tune in an arrangement, which would speak to the people of the day. This performance of *The Star Spangled Banner* is one of the most studied pieces of musical film ever and is an absolute testament to Hendrix' genius. The man and his music have remained symbolic of the social and conscious change, which began in the 1960s and continues to this day.

Hendrix was the first musician inducted into the Native American Music Hall of Fame. He had both Tsalagi (Cherokee) and Nahua (Aztec) ancestors, as well as African American ancestors. A fusion of great mystical cultures in his genetic make-up created the most amazing virtuoso: he could play the guitar both left and right handed and even strung the wrong way up, not to mention with his teeth and behind his head. His mode of expression was a world first.

Jimi's energy, power and light were a portent of the spiritual light, which is available to all of us at this time of ascension. He surfed onto the world stage on the most influential wave of Aquarian Light yet seen. His words from the song *Voodoo Child* at the head of this chapter were prophetic, but also have great meaning. When you connect into the energy within that music and those words, they say: I am passing through here at great speed. I am laying down an energy, which those of you who are ready will pick up on, connect with and which will move you into change, but you won't be able to keep up with me, because I am passing through here very quickly, so that I can get on with the next chapter of my own mission of growth, teaching and sharing the energy. So, you better get a move on, catch up … *If I don't see you no more in this world, I'll see you on the next one, and don't be late!* These lines, if nothing else, are the anthem of the Aquarian Age. They are saying, what you experience now in your present life is nothing, it's only the beginning. Open your mind, there is no end, you are eternal. Connect with the, 'all that is' and live your life without fear and if you lose it, don't worry, because I'll see you again. We will all see each other again in the next world. Awaken. Don't be late.

It doesn't matter that Jimi chose to leave the planet when he did, his work was done. The energy and passion he left behind awakened people and left a huge, lasting mark on modern music. Thirty years after his passing, young people still yearn to be able to reproduce the energy and sound, which came through him, and the vast majority can't. They never will be able to either, for that was Jimi. The energy expressed through his consciousness was unique and that energy was transmitted into a waiting world through his medium of expression, a voice with the flexibility and range of a musical instrument, and a musical instrument radiating energy like nobody had ever experienced before. It is true that today, there are many great virtuosos of the electric guitar, but the mark of a true master is the effort put in to produce the goods. When you see Jimi's work, not only did it blow everyone away, but it was effortless. When you do it without effort, that is the Spiritual Force working through you. That is when you are delivering your message from the heart. That heart was illuminated with the driving expansive force of Aquarian Light. You can see the spirit expressing itself through the human. You can see God bringing the light of change to humanity.

It doesn't matter that the message didn't awaken everyone on the planet, because many scenarios are being played out in different arenas of learning. Not everyone is at the same point of evolution, and they don't need to be. For everything is unfolding exactly as it should. But change has to be served in a major way into the mass consciousness and Hendrix's Light heralded the point of no return for a changing world-consciousness.

The Turning of the Tide

The period 1967 to 1970, was the last great wave of the high tide of that period, and as we have seen, the energy of those three years created a change in human consciousness, which was to be a permanent feature. It was a point from which it was not possible to slip back for those who were awakening. In comparison, the 1970s, were almost like a rest period, as the tide began to recede, but at the same time consciousness was continuing to unfold beneath the surface. That tide went out quickly and we entered a period of slack water between an outgoing and incoming tide; a period of waiting for the tide to turn again.

When a tide is in, at high water, when it is washing upon the shore, this is a period of yang, active masculine energy. When a tide is out, calmness falls across the beaches and tidal reaches of the planet and a period of yin, passive, feminine energy can be observed.

Waves are an ever-present feature upon the body of the ocean, served upon the shore by the tides. The tides come and go in a twelve hour cycle, but moving forward by approximately an hour each tide. A perpetual forward motion. As well as the daily cycles, there are also monthly cycles in which the moon brings the tides from low (neap) to high (spring) and back again and then there are seasonal forces like the equinoxes, which bring even higher and lower tides.

Observing the Law of 'As Above, So Below,' Universal tides will also be affected in the same way by outside forces of a greater magnitude than the moon, and probably also subject to certain anomalies such as passing through force fields, like the tachyon belt, for example, or leaving an Age and entering a New Age. After the high tide of 1967–70, the tides began to become more frequent. Things began to speed up. Time now presents the illusion of moving faster — but, in reality it is consciousness that is accelerating.

Another Stage in the New Dawn

The energy of the 1960s, had begun to open our minds and the 70s had been a period of consolidation and to a certain degree, inner silence, but as we enter the 1980s, the incoming light of the Aquarian Age was about to reveal its most powerful gift of transformation and liberation yet.

'When the power of love
overcomes the love of power,
The world will know peace.'

Jimi Hendrix

7

The Birth of the Age of Healing

Jesus said,
> 'I have cast fire upon the world,
> And behold, I guard it until it is ablaze.'

The Gospel of Thomas

In the calmness of the 1970s, something was gestating very quietly. A lady called Mrs. Hawayo Takata began to attune people with the Reiki Light that she had worked with for so long. Like Hendrix, she was a pivotal key in the birthing of the Age of Aquarius. Apart from initiations behind closed doors in mystical traditions or religious orders, this was the very first moment in the whole history of humanity when one ordinary person began to empower another ordinary person with the ability to open others to spiritual light in the wider context.

The Birth of the Age of Healing

During the late 1970s Takata taught and initiated 22 Reiki Masters who began at the turn of the 1980s to spread the Reiki Light by teaching their own students. Like a domino effect, the Reiki Light began to move across the world, coming to Britain around 1988, the year we can say is the Birth of the Age of Healing; the year the healing of humanity begins proper. Acceleration followed that initial outpouring from Takata, which will be recorded as the point at which the Aquarian Light began the first real phase of its work — the opening of humanity to a potential that it was largely unaware of. Twenty years earlier, in the 1960s the new generations were breaking the mould of the old school by dropping out of mainstream society and experimenting with mind expansion, but in the 1980s the individual began to

become truly empowered. What touched and stimulated Takata in those moments to begin the process of passing on the knowledge, knowledge she had
held for some considerable time? When light touches you, it brings guidance
with it. It awakens desire and it pushes you forwards. Takata was pushed by
the Light of Aquarius to begin the process that would open millions to their
own healing path; to their path of self-empowerment and inner illumination.
After those first Reiki Masters were created we then experienced an acceleration of the next incoming wave. Within no time at all, hundreds of people
were carrying and spreading the Reiki Light, and all from the one source.
The energy of the 1980s was all about the new inflowing tide, which would
drive Reiki forward and give birth to many other new modalities of facilitating healing and transformation, opening and enlightening the consciousness
of thousands of people worldwide through the next decade and beyond.

In the nineties, the surging, uplifting waves of the incoming tide began to
gain momentum and by the time we hit the millennium, who knows how
many people had been awakened into the new light of self-healing and helping others to heal? It was certainly in the millions. We do know that the
Reiki Light was the first Light, which opened the doors to this new age, and
when a door begins to open with a Divine power behind it, then there is not
much you can do to stop it. Those who were ready for change were attracted
like moths to the light and those who were not continued to dwell in the old
energies. What we are now beginning to see is a separation of consciousness
within the people of earth; a widening gap between those who are awakening and those who are still dwelling in the undertow of darkness; those who
allow the light to awaken their hearts to freedom and those who continue to
allow the fear in their hearts to control them. As we progress, this division in
humanity will accelerate and intensify as those who are awakening find the
courage to step out of the world of illusion and into the world of truth. The
increasing light will illuminate the truth in every situation. You will see this
very clearly as hearts begin to open. You can already see this very clearly in
the number of people who no longer vote for politicians. These people see
truth at a new level and no longer want to be a part of that old culture,
which no longer represents their values. We are not quite at a point where
we can see a clear alternative path, although that alternative is gestating and
awaiting birth.

Throughout the nineties, many other forms of healing were created,
invented, channelled or rediscovered from various parts of the world. The
Reiki Light was the catalyst that would reveal many other forms of healing
light. Awakening accelerated and healing was the next phase, as the new
streams of energy and light were calling. Each and every soul who took an
attunement was helping to raise the vibration of humanity as a whole. As we

move into the new millennium, new energies are now being served once more for the people of earth. Reiki has been the most amazing tool in beginning to open humans to their deeper selves, and will always continue to be a great door opener for those discovering themselves and the healing path for the first time. That is its purpose. However, there is absolutely no comparison to the new streams of light now entering earth.

Reiki is essentially a tool for self-transformation and healing, but it has limitations, which are to do with the difference between energy and consciousness. Reiki allows you to work with the energy structures of the subtle bodies, but it does not have the power to open the deeper consciousness, due to its vibrational rate. When you think about this logically, it makes perfect sense. Using a motoring analogy, would you put someone in a Formula One car to learn to drive? You could do, but I bet they would come off the road a few times before getting the hang of controlling that amount of power. Reiki is specifically limited by the universal consciousness so that you can learn the ropes of energy work without getting into too much trouble. What would happen if you took an attunement and all of a sudden your consciousness opened to a point where you could see the past, present and future? What if you could suddenly see every lie your friends told you? What if you could suddenly see the cancers eating people alive, and you knew that they didn't know? It would be too much to bear. A friend of mine opened very quickly after a motor accident in this way. In fact, he kept seeing the motor accident before it happened, but hadn't realised that it was himself who was in it. This was the Universe trying to get his attention. Energies began to unfold very quickly within him after this and he was regularly seeing the imminent deaths of some of his friends. Indeed it was too much to bear and he had to walk away from his particular gifts for a while. So, God opens the door for us in a gentle way by presenting something like Reiki, but for those who are truly ready, the next phase is already being served.

Changes on the Planet

As we hit the millennium there were signs of change everywhere, not just in the awakening human consciousness, but particularly so on the planet. Changes in weather patterns were now big news everywhere. If you study the Precession of the Equinoxes you find that the twenty five thousand year cycle produces one complete cycle of the, 'earth wobble,' allowing the tip of the earth's axis to describe a complete circle in the heavens. The wobble allows earth to experience periods of warming and cooling as it constantly changes its position by a few degrees in relation to the sun. Of course, those with little vision and even less of a desire to find out what is truly happening, listen to very limited scientific opinion, which is only part of the story. The major focus of the story from the media is that carbon emissions are responsible for the earth warming up. Yes, clearly man is contributing to global disaster in many areas, but the really big changes are coming because the great picture of evolution is unfolding and *part* of the answer can be found in the heavens above us. The planetary changes are being experienced through the surging, uplifting, incoming waves of Aquarius as the earth moves into a new position in relation to the sun. In the very near future you will find many new theories being put forward and many will have aspects of the truth within them. This is the period of discovering the Truth. We will no doubt need to find and understand many small parts in order to grasp the big picture, but the changes are most definitely unstoppable, as is the energy of the Aquarian Age. Changes are being served upon us at every level. We must learn to welcome and adapt to them, work at learning to accept and understand them, whilst at the same time modifying our behaviour towards the Earth Mother.

Don't panic at the changing weather patterns; embrace the change. You can't stop it and you can't control the power of nature, which man in his arrogance mistakenly thinks he can. The globe has warmed before and it has cooled before. The magnetic poles have shifted and reversed previously and they will again. Mountains were once the ocean floor and you can't get much more of a reversal than that. Everything goes in cycles and cycles will repeat themselves in the future. Eventually the sun will go super-nova and the earth will be vaporised. And, do you know what? It's all part of the plan of evolution.

However, the eternal spiritual being, which inhabits and expresses itself through humans will have evolved and moved to a higher expression of itself by that time, and just like all the animals that have become extinct. There will not be a need for human beings any longer, so they will become extinct. At least the animals will have a better chance then. Also, by that time, we will have understood much more about the power of mind and its creative possibilities. As the mystical traditions have told for many centuries we create our own reality, so the sooner we choose to create a superior reality, the better. The Aquarian Age is bringing us that power and understanding and as the light continues to illuminate us, we will learn what we need to in order to continue our successful evolution.

The Shifting of World Energies

The axial shift of the earth is also responsible for moving the hot spots of yin and yang energy to new locations around the world. For the past five thousand years the spiritual centres and power bases for illumination of consciousness have been in the east. Spiritually, the peoples of these countries grew enormously at a deeper conscious level and this gave rise to the development of the great religions, the Indian Mystics, Tibetan Buddhism and the great libraries of knowledge, the Chinese five elements, acupuncture and the great temples, monasteries and centres of spiritual learning of the east. The natural energies allowed the people of those continents a choice. The spiritual energies provided the possibility of illumination provided that the consciousness of the individual was so attuned or awakening to seek it out. Thus, we observed the growth of a deeply connected spiritual people with great patience and pride in the amazing legacy of texts and knowledge that have been left for us. Just look at the radiant vibrational colours of India compared to the dull colours that people wear on the streets of the west. The vibration of colour is instrumental in constantly raising the consciousness. If there is vibrant colour around you, then it is reflecting into your energy system constantly.

Five thousand years ago, the great continent of North America was virtually empty except for the indigenous tribes who dwelt and cared for the paradise of which they were custodians. It was a new land, untouched in any measure. However, in the developing west, such as Britain and Europe, we were learning industrial skills, as we began to construct cromlechs and stone circles. In the west, we were still functioning very much from the left hemisphere of the brain, acting out the yang aspects of conquering others in our old pattern of subjugation, domination and greed. However, this left-brained activity spawned great advances in technological achievement, especially, in the last three hundred years or so of the industrial and then technological revolutions. But, as the axial shift of the planet continued to wobble around its pre-destined course, the energies of yin and yang began to relocate.

From the 1960s through to the 80s we saw spiritual forces in the west accelerating the awakening process through the incoming Light of Reiki. Where did that Light first emerge? One could argue that it was half way between east and west, as Takata lived in Hawaii. In reality, once she had lit her students' lamps, the light spread west into America, then crossed the Atlantic to Britain and Europe. It then spread to all corners of the world. We can confidently say that Reiki is one of the signs from Heaven of the birthing of the Age of Aquarius. Major steps of burgeoning spirituality were being taken as many people were reaching out and bringing in to their lives, not just Reiki, but many of the old practices from the east. Humanity was reaching eastwards for the ancient knowledge. In comparison in the east, we see growing industrialisation, as the focus of yin and yang is switched from one area of the globe to another. In the east there is now a hunger for material wealth and mainstream spirituality is becoming submerged. Instead of chasing understanding and inner peace, the new guru in China and India is the dollar. The new guru in the USA, Britain and Europe for the most part is the upsurge in spiritual awareness and personal growth.

The New Wave of Healing and Healers

Ordinary people have sought the spiritual Light of Reiki as it calls to them. You are seeing more and more ordinary people awaken to the fact that healers have a lot of answers, which modern medicine does not. More people will turn to healing and healers in different forms for answers as the new age unfolds. Eventually healing and vibrational medicine will overtake conventional medicine, as the public begins to learn how to take back their power and accept responsibility for their own wellbeing, understanding more about nutrition, what the body truly requires for health and a general change toward healthful living. As consciousness illuminates through the incoming light of the new age, ordinary folk will again learn how to access and trust the power of the intuitive ability, which they have lost. More importantly, you will see an upsurge in common sense. Ordinary people have lots of it and where there is a lot of common sense and a little logic, answers to many problems that might elude a powerful intellectual mind can be found. The most powerful shift of all is that people will discover the courage to take a different course. As the light continues to emerge into the world, it opens the heart, where personal courage is seated. The courage to change one's mind, and thus one's path, will be opened from within, bringing changing values into our world.

Changes on Every Level

In the west, the awakening brought by the incoming spiritual consciousness is accompanied by the growth and development of intuitive gifts. These enable healers increasingly to understand the human condition, as they learn to see and perceive through the various levels of illusion into a higher truth. The deeper you see, the more that Truth is revealed. The real problem is that hardly anyone, relative to the size of the present community on earth, sees the truth of the unfolding bigger picture. Nobody sees the waves of change and the changeover of power, which is taking place on all levels. It is now acknowledged that the growing industrial power of the east has outstripped the west. China and India are rising at an incredible pace. Foreign governments and individuals hold a greater stake in the financial and property sectors in the west than at any other time in history. The stake continues to grow as they invest in industrial, service sector and financial might. The Chinese, for example, have been buying American Treasury Bonds for years and now have around the equivalent of the national debt. This is the same as the bank owning your house when you take out a mortgage. You live in the house, but the bank owns it until you have paid them back. Essentially this means that the politicians over the years have sold America to the Chinese from under the noses of the American tax payers. By the same token, the Arab States own great chunks of Britain. If you mishandled your own finances in the way that your elected politicians have handled your national birthright, you would be in the bankruptcy courts in no time. But nobody saw the Truth of what the politicians, and those in power, were doing. They were doing what they have always done, that is tell lies and create a screen of illusion in their selfish pursuit of ever more power.

At the same time, there is nothing to worry about, for things are unfolding exactly as they should, for if those in power did not behave in such a way then the collective consciousness would never discover the untruths and illusions that have been perpetrated. So, a bit at a time, those in power undermine themselves in the face of an incoming light that will reveal all. That guy Jesus had something to say about it, too.

> Jesus said,
>   'Know him who is before your face,
>   And what is hidden from you shall be revealed to you:
>   For there is nothing hidden that shall not be manifest.'

> *The Gospel of Thomas*

He was dangerous, that Jesus. If you were a bad guy, he knew it just by looking at you. The way that kind of spiritual light works means that 'you know that he knows,' because it is revealed to you through the feelings in your own heart. When you lie in front of anyone who has this kind of inner vision, they feel it immediately because they are connected with your heart, but then, the Truth of the situation illuminates your own heart and you can feel the untruth of your words or actions. So, the people in power at the time needed to get rid of him, because he knew too much and that inner knowing made them feel uncomfortable for all their scams were visible to him. There would be panic amongst their ranks and questions being asked as to how they might create his removal. History shows that Pontius Pilate tried very hard to arrive at a vindication of the charges against Jesus, but eventually he was one against many and the weight of opinion placed Pilate in a position where all he could do was make the gesture of hand washing, which displayed to the people that he was having no part in the condemnation of an innocent man.

Politicians in general, as well as lots of other folks who play the manipulative power game in our present age, don't really know that they are lying most of the time because it is just the way their world works and is an engrained habit for them. They are so accustomed to playing the self-serving card in the game of life that they rarely consider there is anything else to aim for. Boy, are they going to be in for a surprise. What we will see as the Aquarian Light surges forwards and illuminates everything and everyone it touches in turn, is that the bad guys won't be able to lie to you anymore because that light will begin to burn holes in them when they do. And, suddenly, they will find themselves confessing and asking for forgiveness.

As the light touches your heart and begins to illuminate it, you can feel the difference between good and evil. That feeling is called your conscience. One of the dictionary definitions of conscience is 'sense of right and wrong.' You can actually substitute the words good and evil for right and wrong, for that is what the true meaning is. A pure act of evil is when someone tells you something that is not true. That is how simple it is to understand evil. When your leader says to you that 'the people of that nation over there are going to kill us all, so we need to kill them first to protect you', that's a pretty good example of an act of evil. The killing part is a natural follow-on from the first lie. You get hooked in with that, which gives them permission to continue with the illusion. All the other lies that come after are just a continuation of the flow of evil energy that was allowed to manifest. You fall for the first lie, then the rest is history, it just keeps rolling out, century after century. Easy, isn't it?

Entering the Golden Age – A Commentary in the Moment

As we are in the final process of editing this book, the banking collapse of October 2008 has just happened in the USA and across Europe. The politicians are, at this moment, being hailed as heroes for bailing us all out. The truth is that those same politicians supported the illegal activities of the bankers before the whole house of cards came down. You will notice that bankers are not being fired for incompetence and the politicians are being fielded to the media rather than the bankers. The whole debacle is an illusion of smoke and mirrors. The politicians are now telling us that they can fix the problem that they themselves have created, and the collective consciousness of the general population seems to believe it. The whole process is merely moving from the lies they told, which created the problem, to the lies they are now telling to convince that the problem can be resolved. Politicians are not accountable for their actions, like the bankers do not appear to be accountable for ruining the banking business.

Let us look at another aspect of this issue. Banking is collapsing because it is fundamentally flawed and built upon lies. A bank note should bear a promise that the bearer of the note can redeem the value of the note from the issuing bank in gold. If the money in your pocket is no longer supported by gold, then the promise it bears is an empty one. In Europe, they introduced a new currency a few years ago called the Euro. These notes do not bear any promise at all and so we must ask ourselves by what means they are supported? Is our paper money of today just another illusion? In the late nineties, the United Kingdom Chancellor actually began to sell off the Gold that had supported British Currency. This is like selling off the bricks beneath your house. Once the foundation has gone, the house will fall down. Surely we should be asking is this not an act of treason?

The next part of this illusion is how spiritual groups and individuals are viewing the banking collapse. The internet is rife at present with misguided pleas to support the markets with positive affirmations and visualisations of the stock market indices rising rather than falling. These financial well-wishers have completely misunderstood what the universe is doing. As the light of the new Age of Truth accelerates and begins to expose and tear down all that is unwholesome and wrong in our world—in this instance the financial systems—they, with a distinct lack of spiritual insight, are trying to rebuild and perpetuate the old model. Those who claim to be walking the spiritual path are constantly talking the talk about entering the new golden age, speaking of the changes that will come, and the minute something happens to tear down an edifice of evil, they are the first to band together and attempt to rebuild it. When all the prophecies say that everything will change, they mean everything. How can you ascend if you are so attached to an old paradigm that you can't let go?

The new waves of light are awakening people to Truth. You will see the growing common sense of ordinary people as they distance themselves from the sleaze, dishonesty and malpractice of the old ways. If you are prone to fear, you might see the economic changes as very scary, but those who are prone to fear will not dare to look at the truth of the situation anyway. Fear prevents them from doing so. Those who get scared easily are strongly governed by the old Piscean energies—the energies of belief systems and structures in which nearly everyone gave away their truth and power to people who took it as quickly as they could in order to empower themselves, at the cost of those who were weaker. A pretty good example of evil in action, don't you think?

Don't worry about fear. The incoming light will help you understand how fear controls you by allowing you to feel the fear. If you do not feel it, then you cannot learn how to dissolve and rise above it. You cannot learn how others use it to control. Using fear as an instrument of control is like using it as an instrument of torture: it is an act of evil. As you learn how to let go and embrace the changes, you will become masters of your own destiny, masters of freedom. This series of books will lay out guided techniques to help you to raise your vibration, shift your conscious perception, see through the lies and illusion and find the courage to embrace change and truth. Then you will begin to create your own destiny, rather than be at the mercy of systems of control, like the fear a falling market or a collapsing economy can instil in you. To enter the new age successfully, you must learn to let go of all attachment, embrace whatever change is forthcoming and learn to trust in Universal Consciousness.

8

Science and Medicine – The New View

Jesus said,
> 'No one Lights a Lamp and puts it under a bowl.
> Nor does he put it in a hidden place.
> But he sets it on a lamp stand in order that everyone
> who goes in and comes out
> May see its Light.'

The Gospel of Thomas

Entering a new age involves a complete shift in the individual consciousness of those who are able to respond to a changing time. As consciousness shifts so new patterns of imagination and thought emerge. In this incoming period people will learn much more about how to create creation, or how creation is created as a result of our thoughts, feelings, needs, wants and desires. As we unfold into higher vision and perception, then some of our older institutions are doomed to restructuring on a grand scale. I say doomed, for that is what many of those in the positions of the old power will consider is happening. They will consider that the world has gone mad and that we are all doomed if we continue to turn towards other forms of science and medicine.

God-Power and Man-Power

There are two kinds of power: the power given from the God-consciousness for those who use it wisely to uplift others; and the power exerted by those who misuse it to control others. The problem with wielding the second kind is that you can only do so by disempowering others. We might say it is a kind of stolen power. The misuse of this kind of power corrupts your truth and integrity. The other kind of power though, cannot be misused, because if you try to use it to disempower others, then it is taken away from you again. That's a pretty foolproof way of learning how to use it. We could call these two kinds of power God-power and Man-power. Where there is man-power there is *always* misuse. If we look towards the most powerful institutions on earth, such as Government, Science, Medicine, Business and Religion, we can find corruption. Perhaps not blatant corruption in some cases, although it is there, but more a kind of corruption in terms of lack of truth, through fear of truth and because it is endemic in the model. Developed over hundreds, if not thousands of years, the corruption is considered nothing out of the ordinary. People will tell you, 'this is just the way it works.'

The study of medicine and science has to be a good thing, until you reach a point where the students and academics disregard areas that they do not wish to research. Suddenly the area of study becomes incomplete. When you view a subject purely from a mechanistic and physical viewpoint, discounting any mental, emotional or spiritual aspect of the content, then you have a drastically incomplete model. It is like designing the internal combustion engine and then saying that there is no possibility of discovering a fuel to burn in it. What you end up with is an incomplete model.

In science and medicine today, we have a structure that is terrified of acknowledging that there might be a world outside of the five senses. Yet quantum physics, another branch of science, has developed to the point where the scientists are seeing their own experiments paralleling thousands of years of teaching of eastern mysticism, which acknowledges that indeed there are many levels of reality, not just those available to the five senses. Because of quantum physics, which is not new by any stretch of the imagination, there is great hope for the future that all sides of science and medicine may put their different world views aside and come together to pool knowledge and resources for the benefit of all. However, the first step is to begin to acknowledge the world of potential outside of the five senses.

While we are on the subject of science, and playing for a moment with words, the word conscience can be taken in two parts: con and science — con-science. Right now we might say that parts of science are indeed a con, because scientists have the truth of quantum physics as a result of their own experiments, but continue to trot out what they know are untruths, because the old model does not work with the new knowledge. There you go again … another act of evil. However, the truth of what we are seeing is the speed of change needed to keep up with the light of the new age. When the Light of Aquarius illuminates the minds of the scientists to the point where they break the paradigm of their own structures wide open, where does it leave them? In a place where they have to stand up and face the truth and that means facing humanity and saying, 'we were wrong'. Wow, can you imagine that happening? I'll tell you what you need in order to do that, and we've already covered it. You need courage to speak the truth. You need courage to stand in the face of everyone who is not ready to face the truth and when you know that something is not right and you continue to put your voice to it, then that is an act of evil. But it will happen. Courage will be found, for the light will reveal it as it opens people's hearts to truth.

You Can't Test or Prove God

One of science's problems is that it always has to prove something for it to be acknowledged and then accepted. This is the pattern of the old wave still strongly in action. It will eventually be the downfall of all structures, which continue to deny the higher conscious faculties of the emerging few against the dogma of the unenlightened many. Science is eventually going to have to concede that when you start to create with higher consciousness you have to enter a level of trust. God will not be tested. Higher consciousness will not be tested. You have to trust that something does what it does without being able to prove it, for as soon as you try to prove it, it won't work. That is how God teaches you trust and when you trust what is coming from your internal guidance and your heart, then it always works. Science as we understand it today is going to hit a brick wall. What will happen is that as the wave of higher energies envelops the earth, certain scientists will start to become more intuitive. Unable to continue to deny their own deeper truth, they will then begin to form into groups with like-minded souls (like attracts like), and a new science will be born. It will not be important to prove something, but it will become wonderful to observe something working and then accept it unquestioningly. That process will never lead to us *not* asking how or why something does what it does, but we will be more relaxed and accepting about it. It is merely a case of learning to trust.

So much good work is thrown out by science today because the present, limited systems and minds can't prove it. Also, science's dog eats dog system has a terrible habit of destroying the lives of its own great researchers because one scientist can't reproduce what another scientist can. Can they not see that it is their own mind, which creates the limitation when they can't reproduce something? When you look back at great discoveries and inventions, many times you see that the answer came to a person intuitively at some level, often in a dream. It is all based on 'seek and you shall find'. Those who consider a possibility are the ones who are open to receive the results of that possibility. Those who are rigidly sticking to functions at a physical and mechanistic level of reality are only seeing a tiny part of the picture. If you approach your work with an air of expectation, then the chances are it will happen. If you approach your work to try to prove someone else's work doesn't function as claimed, then your expectation is likely to be fulfilled and your experiment won't produce the fruit which, of course, you don't want it to produce. Essentially, you usually get what you expect. Trying to disprove something that is claimed to work is a negative approach and thus, rather than creating, one is destroying.

This is perhaps the greatest limitation of science today, along with the ego-driven selfishness of individuals who can't find it in themselves to celebrate the work of their colleagues. Let's now look at science briefly in a slightly different way.

Spiritual workers are learning or have learned how to play with some of the Universal Laws. One of these Laws is The Law of Attraction, which has been brought forward for mass awareness through the teachings of Abraham as introduced by Esther and Jerry Hicks. The only reason it is here now is because many are ready for it. The Universe is bringing in that light through Esther and Jerry to help those who are awakening to the opportunity of learning how to play with the laws. I work with and teach The Law of Reflection along with other Laws of Evolution, which, when you under-stand and apply them, begin to allow you to evolve your consciousness. Like Esther and Jerry who have been given The Law of Attraction to bring to humanity through the teachings of Abraham, these Laws of Evolution have been brought forth through myself. They unfolded through my own guidance as I was ready to understand them. Before the Laws are given, we have to learn how to use them through experience and as our knowledge accrues from the experiences, then the clarity and understanding of the Law is imparted to us so that we can then teach it. When you absolutely know how the Laws work and you can connect at that level of consciousness, then truly you begin to create reality. The Law of Reflection also begins to reveal other aspects of deeper Laws which pertain to the creation of reality.

Here is an example of how reality works. Consider that scientist A is working on an experiment and something deep inside is guiding his every move. He lives and dreams the process of what he is trying to prove. He puts his heart and soul into it and then one day in the lab, it happens, his experi-ment is a success. Why did it happen? Simply because he believed that it would! He created success from the knowing in his heart that he was going in the right direction. Something within him was guiding him to that conclusion and he absolutely trusted the feelings of what he was trying to create. Therefore, he created it.

Now, this might be an earth shattering discovery and other scientists might also have been working on it. So, immediately within the scientific community there might be a great buzz, but also a disappointment because someone else has found the answer first. The first reaction of the community is to see if they can reproduce the experiment, but in reality, what they are often doing is trying to disprove the experiment. In their working model of science, the successful experiment of Scientist A must go through the phase of being reproduced by others for the work to be accepted. However, the one thing they can't reproduce is the self-belief, trust and absolute inner knowing of Scientist A. They cannot possibly create the same energetic or spiritual conditions for the experiment because they can't put Scientist A's energy of belief and love into their work. So, unless the experiment is based purely on mechanistic or physical processes, it is impossible to reproduce.

The trial can be approached in two ways: with excitement, belief and the desire for it to succeed; or with the desire for it to fail.

Scientist B tries to reproduce the experiment and fails. Scientist A repeats his success. Scientist B repeats his failure. What is happening? Scientist A is infusing his work with the energy of expectation. Scientist B is infusing his work with the energy of doubt. Scientist A is working at the cutting edge of creation and bringing all the tools of the creation process to bear in his work. Scientist B is also bringing all the tools of the creation process to his work. The difference is that one is trying to create success and the other is trying to create failure. Both scientists achieve what they are trying to create, therefore, both are successful.

Can you see how easy it is to create successful reality when you know how the Laws of Creation work? We all create reality at every moment, but are we creating what we desire and desiring what we create? Or are we creating what we don't want through a lack of focus and understanding of the Universal Laws pertaining to powers outside the five senses? Well, this whole creation thing is another story, and not for this part of the book, so we'll move on.

The ancient books and texts are there to be opened. If you think that the be all and end all is to be found only on the cover, then you will not find what is hidden within the book. How many times have people held up their hands and said that someone's theory appears to be right after all? Unfortunately, this often happens long after their fellow scientists have had their careers destroyed by their peers and have passed into obscurity or death. Human's can be a very sad species, cruel beyond belief and if you have a system that is set up to allow that cruelty, then for sure, someone will be the victim of it. That's not progress.

All Truth goes through three stages,

> It is Ridiculed
> It is Violently Opposed
> It is agreed to be Self-evident.

Schopenhauer...

The whole of the scientific model functions from an ego-centric viewpoint. Who, in their right mind would want to work within the constraints of such a model, where your successes stand every chance of being ridiculed and derided by your contemporaries?

The Awakening

It is unfortunate that those who arrogantly cling to the life raft of a dying age will eventually go down with the shipwreck of that age. It is not so much an accident though, as part of the Divine plan as we move from one wave of energy to a higher vibrational wave. Just as the spiritual aspirant goes through trial, tribulation and trauma as they are challenged by the inner battles of learning on their path of evolution toward enlightenment, so the whole of humanity is now being challenged to awaken to that same path. Science and medicine are good and they have many good people within their structures, but their whole system is governed by a hierarchy of fear and repression. But the good news is that it's all going to change and many fine hearts and minds will be liberated, if not in this lifetime, then the next. The Age of Aquarius is an irresistible force.

Healers and Medicine

I have seen many healers seeking to be recognised by mainstream western medicine, trying to acquire positions in hospitals. For the most part they are derided for their gifts, skills and efforts to shed new light on old problems. Those people whose consciousness is still aligned with the dying, ebbing undercurrent of the old Piscean wave try to keep them out or control them. If you are open to see, you will find there are the most wonderful and amazing practices from the ancient world, which are completely ignored, or again, derided by the medically arrogant. Thousands of years of study and practice of the subtle energy arts and sciences are completely ignored. Think of acupuncture from China and Ayurveda from India, for example; herbalism from many continents and more recently Homeopathy from Hahnemann in

Germany and Flower Remedies from Edward Bach in England. Bach was, in fact, a medical doctor, pathologist, bacteriologist, surgeon and homeopath, before turning his attention to subtle energy. You could even say that Hahnemann and Bach were opening to the stimulus of Aquarian Light, for they are both looking at cause and not effect. We have seen all this wonderful knowledge not only ignored, but turned away as having no value, so don't think for one moment that your healing will always be welcomed by the old school. The time is coming, for your work is unfolding now, the incoming light is opening and training you, but the rightful place for your work will not necessarily be within the cloisters of those old structures.

Certainly, there are individuals in medicine today who are open to change, but you need to understand that you are dealing with a collective consciousness which, if it so chooses, will crush the individual who supports your effort and crush you underfoot without a second thought. In recent times we have seen this collective consciousness ostracise and destroy the career of its own leading research doctors over the MMR vaccine. What was their crime? Daring to suggest something, which was alien to the interests of the medical model. The people at the top were not necessarily interested in the Truth, they were interested in protecting their model, the model, which protects them and their interests. Another little act of evil. Do you really want to be a part of that culture, which will soon be in its death throws?

Ultimately, ordinary people will choose what they want. The old wave will try to control and limit you as a healer, but eventually the people will turn when they realise who has the real answers. However, let us not be too hasty and completely rule out modern medicine. Great work has been done to develop drugs, which help many ailments. When you break a leg you don't want a homeopath, you want a hospital to fix it. You might then want a homeopath or an essence therapist to support you at an energetic, pain or emotional level while the physical repair work is being done. What doctor these days is concerned with subtle energies? Very few probably; it is virtually impossible to bring up the subject as it is outside the scope of the model. Perhaps a few more doctors are interested in the emotional aspects of caring and healing, though. The fact that most serious illnesses, cancers and energy depleted states such as ME come from an emotional or spiritual root, or are based on bad lifestyle choices through lack of education, should concern all doctors. But the model is set up right now to treat the symptom and not the cause. Lifestyle and emotions, let alone a holistic view of the person, really don't enter into the equation.

The limitation of the present medical model is that it is almost exclusively concerned with issues at a physical level. Areas of expertise are in what might be described as advanced plumbing and joinery. If you need a heart bypass, call the hospital, they are brilliant at it. If you want a new hip joint, call the hospital, they'll turn your life around. However, if you have a major energetic problem with your crown chakra you will end up in a psychiatric hospital where they have no idea whatsoever about chakra problems. A blown or leaking crown chakra will give symptoms, which could be described as acute anxiety and extreme terror, but will be seen by psychiatry as psychosis or manic depression, a complete mis-diagnosis. A problem with a crown chakra such as this can often be repaired, depending on the process used, in as little as an hour to a maximum of around three weeks. However, psychiatry will approach the problem by prescribing a series of debilitating drugs, which will absolutely not solve the problem, but will most certainly compound it.

Psychiatry is never going to make any serious progress until the psychiatrists can see into the subtle energy system and work with higher light to bring about repair processes to those energy structures. Unfortunately, if any psychiatrist wanted to go down this route, they would be laughed out of practice, because the only way to develop these skills is to learn how to be a healer first. Anyone can do it, you just have to practise. The collective consciousness of the psychiatric model of medicine does not want to open it's mind to this possibility, therefore, unfortunately, there is little hope of any progress. Let's face it, the drugs they have at present, for the most part don't help, but suppress other aspects of the brain/mind continuum and the subtle energy system as a whole. Suppressing something is not going to fix it, it is going to compound the problem and create often, very nasty side effects.

Many of the answers are out there, some have been out there for thousands of years, but if you don't want to look, then you are not going to find them. If you do not desire to enter into self-development, then you are already entering into limitation. Even as a wild guess, without looking at any figures or diagnoses, I would say that if you brought advanced healers or lightworkers into psychiatric hospitals you would find that at least 50 percent of the patients had nothing more wrong with them other than energy system issues, which could be repaired in no time at all. Once the energy work is entered into you can then consider life-style issues and mental and emotional patterns. At the same time you can begin to rebuild the patient's confidence by explaining what has gone wrong and why. A little at a time with the right support and guidance, time would then heal the rest as they regained their confidence that truly the issues causing the problem had been resolved.

As healers of the future we have to take a new view of what we see. If the old paradigm is too entrenched in its own blindness and lack of desire to open the doors of possibility by considering that there is more to life than a mechanical problem, then it would take an overwhelming amount of energy to begin to change that paradigm. We cannot afford to waste that energy on trying to fix something that is perhaps beyond fixing. I am sure that many of you at some time have had a piece of household equipment or perhaps a car that has just reached the end of its days. For all that you loved it, you have to realise that no amount of money or expertise is going to put it right once it has worn out. You have to bite the bullet and retire it to the recycling plant. That is where our medical model is right now. You and I can't help them fix it because their minds won't open to the possibilities that we can offer. You must consider that the fear within the model is probably overwhelming. That old fear of change, again.

Find the Courage to Stand in Your Light

Therefore, I say to the healers and spiritual workers of this time, do not give your power away, but learn how to stand in the full glory of it. Do not bow and scrape to align yourself with doctors and the accepted medical model of today, because you will be buried beneath the fear of the old wave and seen as unimportant and ridiculed behind your back, if not directly to your face. Don't try to align yourself with crumbling structures of a fading age, but stand firm in your own truth, brandishing your own courage, and trust that you are working with light because you have been called to do so. You have been called to bring something new to the world and the world is waking up to what you have to offer.

Jesus said,
>   'No one Lights a Lamp and puts it under a bowl.
>   Nor does he put it in a hidden place.'

Your light has truly been lit. You are now beginning to carry the light of which Jesus spoke. Okay, so it might take a few years for you to develop, and you may not develop to the level of light that Jesus was carrying, but believe me, your light is of the same light that He carried, and He said, do not hide it.

>   'But he sets it on a lamp stand in order that everyone
>   who goes in and comes out
>   May see its Light.'

I say to you now, put your light where it can be seen and align yourself with the God-consciousness, which is awakening within you, trying to guide you and speak through you, for then you will truly be Known. Stand in your own light so that the world might discover you. It is time to form a new model. Prepare to stand and be counted as you create an alternative model for the choice of the people as they awaken and desire to seek their own answers in this new age.

There is ultimately only one light and we are merely working with different facets of it as we learn to carry ever more of that light. Do not resist what is irresistible, but learn to ride the Wave of Time as it comes to uplift you into the next age, that of the all-seeing Light of Aquarius.

As this new age unfolds you need to understand that those who can only function through the five senses are limited in their ability and will eventually be seen as the undeveloped species. Like Neanderthal man, they will become extinct. If you cannot open your consciousness and function intuitively at some level, then you will be seen as incomplete, handicapped or challenged in some way. Those who are taking the trouble to work on developing themselves through the use of spiritual light are preparing to be the leaders of the future. They will be the ones who develop their consciousness to a point where they will be in tune with the unfolding reality of the Aquarian Age. As they pass out of one life and forward into the next, they will continue to accelerate and to lead by example.

Standing in Your Power

When individuals take back their power and begin to ask for help and guidance, the universal consciousness always responds. The new light of this age is about opening consciousness and developing individuals so that they can help uplift their fellow man out of the collective poverty consciousness we all presently dwell within. We are leaving the age of structure and entering the age of free flow. Those of you who can allow your consciousness to flow freely and be guided by your intuition and your heart, will be the people the universal consciousness will guide the seekers of answers towards. Therefore, do not fear if you are not recognised by the governing bodies of the old school, for you are the light beings of the new wave. You are the hope of the future. Learn to stand in your power, stand in trust, truth and integrity and you will see how the universe supports you.

The New Medicine

Ultimately, two models of medicine will be recognised and will work side by side. There are so many aspects to helping people and they don't all need a medical doctor's degree. In fact in the new age a degree will mean nothing in the healing arts. You will be recognised by your actions. It is impossible to give an award to an intuitive worker because it is impossible to judge their ability. Ability will be in the realm of knowing through illumination by the light. Therefore, you will be Known by your Light. People will be guided by their own Higher Consciousness to the Light that will help them. That's how it's been working for me for 20 years. No advertising, they just came, and still do. Who sends them? How do they find me? Universal Consciousness sends them and I'll explain how that works later.

Jesus said,
> 'When you Know your Selves,
> Then you will be Known.'

In the future, when you go to your enlightened doctor, he or she will assess your case quickly and then refer you to one of two particular aspects of healing medicine. The first will be the healers who deal with you holistically, looking to help you at a mental, emotional and spiritual level. Or, the second avenue open to the doctor will be to fix the physical things that need fixing at a mechanical level.

In the majority of cases the first port of call will be an intuitive healer, who will help you get to the bottom of understanding the problem and how it has developed within you, in fact how you have attracted that difficulty and what you are trying to learn from the situation. It may be that you have the power to heal yourself if guided. This is self-empowerment and it is incumbent upon all healers through the Universal Laws to help to empower you. If intervention is required, you will then be referred back to the doctor and he or she will then refer you to the hospital consultant. The consultant will ensure that you are working with all the other healing specialists for your mental, emotional and spiritual wellbeing before carrying out any physical work, so that he/she knows that whatever is performed at a physical level will be healing before the knife is even put in. You will already be in the healing process before the operation.

As an example, my Mum had to have some major surgery a few years ago and prior to going in, she had an appropriate amount of healing. After the operation, she felt no pain and her recovery was rapid.

Doctors are from time to time rightly struck off the register of medical practitioners, but there is also a growing core of enlightened doctors who are being removed for their forward thinking views. There are even some who find that the system so stifles what they feel they need to offer humanity that they have no alternative but to resign from medical practice to become free of the system in order to heal. Some of these doctors have trained in Reiki or other spiritual practices and understand the value of intuitives and healers, but ultimately their hands are tied by convention. Eventually, visionary people will step outside convention, for it strangles the baby of initiative at birth and the energy of the Aquarian Age will not allow that to happen. Those structures will crumble and fall into the past, where they already belong. The enlightened doctors will form new cooperatives as they find the courage to step outside of the existing model.

The other major lesson of Aquarius is that people will be awakened specifically to help other people. They will know it in their hearts. I see it every day in my work. Some of those people will be the doctors of the future and their hearts will not allow them to become trampled by a system that is closed to empowering and uplifting others.

Considering the New View

Take your time. Think things out. As the Buddha said, 'Don't believe anything. Not even anything I tell you.' I had been saying something similar to this for years before I heard that the Buddha had said it before me. So what? The important thing is not who said it first, but that you understand the true meaning of it. It means go out into the world and have your own experiences, then you will know your own truth. If it is the same as mine, or the Buddha's, then fine, if not, then that's fine too, for it is your truth. We can only walk the path in our own truth in the moment and when that truth changes, you let it go with grace and adopt your new truth. That is what the institutions find so difficult, admitting that their truth does not work any longer. They can't seem to find the courage to let things go. For example, in the case of the MMR vaccine, it is more acceptable to our present model of medicine to continue to vaccinate children with a potentially life-destroying product rather than face the truth that perhaps it needs review. It shows a lack of integrity and an inability to face truth. Another little act of evil, then.

You will come to these realisations as you continue to walk the path and as the universe reveals to you the things you need to know in order to unfold your own life. When you prove something to yourself, then it is your Truth and you can work with it. Just because it has been given to you, does not mean that it has been given to others, also. But, you might be able to help others attain that Truth for themselves, with your guidance. You are here to evolve and learn. As you evolve and learn, so you can help to uplift others into their own Truth.

Those who are awakening are *all* the teachers of the future. You are *all* at the leading edge of the game. At some point, God will force you to step up, if you don't do it by yourself and He won't let go of you until you do. He has an amazing way of applying pressure: you won't believe it until you have experienced it.

Understand right at this point that the new light is expressing itself through you. If you are reading this book, then you are already on the path and in the light of the new age. Don't ever look back, you cannot afford to waste that kind of energy. Only look forward and learn continually how to become the next thing that the God-consciousness wants you to become as it pours the light and guidance through you. This journey is for individuals expressing themselves in the way that the light is opening them. Each person will have to take responsibility to be an individual by finding the courage to stand in your own power, the power, which is being given to you by the incoming light.

The light is here for all, but the resistance entrenched within powerful structures will try to maintain a stance, which is unthinkable in the face of changing reality. You can't tell entrenched people this, for they won't believe it. We are faced with no choice other than to follow our own path and as we do that, ever more people will awaken and join in the march towards freedom. Eventually, those who continue to fight the change in universal consciousness will fall by the wayside. They will become extinct. It is not because they will be fighting the new thinking as minds become illuminated; it is not because they are fighting a changing paradigm through their resistance to opening their consciousness. They will become extinct because they are resisting the will of God and if you resist that growing inner light of truth strongly enough, He takes you out of the game for a debriefing.

Watch and learn.

9

All We Need is TRUTH

Jesus said,
> 'The Pharisees and the scribes
> took the keys of knowledge,
> and they hid them.
> Neither did they enter,
> nor did they allow
> those who wished to enter.
> But you, become prudent as serpents
> and innocent even as doves.'

The Gospel of Thomas

There are always waves within waves. The trick is learning to see them. Usually, you can't until they have passed, then you begin to pick out the patterns. Once you learn to do this you can find your place in time and space. It helps you to understand why you are here now. All people who are here right now have chosen to be here at the cutting edge of a new age and that means they have entered the earth realm at a time of great excitement. All you have to do is learn how to see and understand it. I hope in this first part of the book I have helped you to do that. Let's wind up this first part by reviewing what we've learned alongside a view of what is happing today.

The Age of Pisces was the Age of Belief Systems. You could almost call it the Age of Blind Faith. You were told what to think and when to think it. It was the age of the growth of religions and the indoctrination of minds by governments based on illusion, delusion and misinformation — and in some cases just plain lies.

The Age of Aquarius is the Age of Knowledge, Truth and Freedom. If we consider that the Second World War was the last great battle of the patterns of 'Fear of Change,' we are deluding ourselves. We are still perhaps a hundred and fifty years away from crossing the cusp into the new age proper. There is a long way to go and the forces of light and dark will continue to slug it out for a while yet. This closing Age of Pisces has an awful lot invested in controlling the people of this planet. Every structure is tied up with the subjugation and domination of humanity. You might think you are free, but try stepping outside the system: it is very difficult to do. We are all locked in like hamsters on a wheel in a cage. But don't let that worry you, for there are freedoms within the cage. You can either be paranoid and collapse under the pressures of the regime, or you can pretend that it isn't there, and then it won't trouble you. It is far better to acknowledge the imperfections, but then create your own reality and the way you want to feel within the systems that we have.

Battles to Come

There will be many more great battles. Look who has most to lose and that is where you will see the panic and fear of a changing time. If you look around you today, you can see the fight everywhere, although, Truth is being revealed already in many ways. The century we have just left was a great time for old scriptural texts to be rediscovered. Quantum physics is showing us how to attain the God within us. The spiritual teachers and motivators of our age are already well ahead in connecting with the God-consciousness within. Quantum physics and the spiritual teachers together are treading the same boards. The Truths of the cruelty perpetrated on innocent people by organised religion is being revealed. All these things challenge the so-called truths, which were served up over the past 2,000 years. Despite having to defend themselves against the indefensible, religions are not going to fade away quietly. They will fight to preserve what they have and the most valuable commodity is the power they wield through their indoctrinatory belief systems. Facing their own Truth will be only one of the battles. However, if religions began to look at their commonality instead of their differences, and looked back to the sources of their teachings, they would all see that for the most part they propound the same message. I am sure there is a role for religion in the future, but it might be very different from the one it is playing at this present time. There are many lessons for religions to learn.

The Greatest Lie Ever Told

Perhaps the greatest lie of all was perpetrated by those who said that unless you followed their teachings, you would go to hell and there would be no place in heaven for you, 'Come to us and we will save your soul,' was that lie.

In fact, at one point in history, if you didn't believe what you were told, there was a good possibility you would be put to death. The only problem was, that they—and we are speaking about the Church of Rome—didn't know how to save your soul, and what's more, they knew they didn't. Even before this church emerged, the learned carpenter, Jesus, had told us that the knowledge was already so well hidden that is was to all intents and purposes lost. Nobody could enter the kingdom of Heaven. This is why he came at that time, to reveal the Truth of the situation and bring the teachings out into the open again.

Quite simply, the saying at the head of this chapter means that those entrusted with the Keys of Knowledge, which would unlock consciousness and transform humanity were so unwise that they failed to enter the kingdom themselves, and also denied the Seekers of Truth the pathway to enlightenment.

Jesus was telling his followers two thousand years ago to begin to look carefully at their lives and learn to distinguish between truth over illusions and lies. At the same time, He encouraged innocence of purpose, for it is those who are free of guilt and who live as a seeker of truth who will find their way into the kingdom. The light which comes forth in this new age will help to illuminate that hidden path of inner guidance. Unless religious teachers and organisations repent and apologise to those they deceived and betrayed, then ultimately they will meet their demise. That Truth is now coming out and more and more people are awakening to it and asking questions. Blind faith in the church is no longer an excuse.

Thanks to someone who had the foresight to bury the teachings in a jar in the desert in Egypt—before they were destroyed no doubt—we now have those keys to the kingdom again. It might be interesting to note that they were discovered in 1945, a year after, according to my calculations, the doors of the Age of Aquarius began to open.

Jesus said,
'He who finds the inner meaning of these logia
Will find Life independent of death.'

As the incoming waves intensify, the Aquarian Light will help reveal the truth of the hidden messages within the rediscovered teachings. Those who are awakening at this time have little to worry about, as many teachers are amongst them to guide and uplift into higher vision and perception of the changing realities. As soon as you begin to seek an answer, you are always guided to a teacher who can help you. But, we must not be complacent, and it sure helps if you make an effort to do some work on yourself. However, many will not be ready to awaken yet, as it is either not their time, or they are too entrenched and attached to the old world that is melting away from us.

It is interesting to note that the Church of Rome does not recognise the Thomas text. We are back to that lack of courage to face the truth. If an organisation that size, with representatives in every corner of the world, were to work with Truth, boy could they do some good for humanity. But they would rather continue to perpetrate the Great Lie. When will the courage emerge?

Democracy at Work

As we enter the 21st century we also see the illusion of the freedoms given by the democratic leaders of the so-called free world. Countries, which are supposed to be a beacon of these freedoms, the USA and Britain in particular, are introducing acts such as the Patriot Act (in the USA) and the Anti-terrorism Laws (in Britain). This kind of legislation enslaves people more than ever. Still there is the dark wave of resistance to letting go and the continuing need to control through the slavery of mind and physical movement based on the lies and illusion of Weapons of Mass Destruction. And, to finish this period of illusion off what better way to introduce the free world's great model of democracy and freedom by force onto a country and culture like Iraq, in the name of setting the people free? Do you think the people of Iraq think that this great model of freedom from the west is really all it's cracked up to be, when this example of democracy has brought death and carnage to ordinary people like you and I, as they go about their shopping in the market place? I think that before you go preaching to another country about the right way to do things, you should be able to demonstrate a working model of peace and harmony within your own borders.

People are beginning to see through the illusion of the age of lies. Minds are awakening. The heart chakra is beginning to develop and as it does you will begin to see Truth. The heart is the organ of Inner Knowing and with its awakening you begin to develop Inner Sight and Inner Knowing. The heart is the Eye of Truth. As the spiritual light of the new age enters your heart, you will begin to see Truth where once you were the blind victim of illusion. Prepare to see Truth.

Jesus said,
    'I have cast fire upon the world,
    and behold, I guard It
    until it is ablaze.'

The Gospel of Thomas

Are You Ready for the Shift?

Evolution is a process. It can be a natural process, brought about by the shift in natural cycles, or it can be brought about in many other ways, for example by following a particular path and learning what you need to learn in order to transcend your present vibrational position. The latter is a choice, the former is being thrust upon the world, for now is the predestined time for it to happen. Evolution will open you to new perceptions, it will awaken that fire within you that Jesus speaks of, above. The incoming waves are bringing about a conscious shift in humanity across the board. If you submit to the energies of change, then you will go through it. If you fight the energies of change you will struggle. Not everyone will be ready for the shift, but for those who are, the particular messenger who arrives will speak with a resonance that will be received at a level, which will change their lives forever. When the heart is ready to perceive Truth at a new level, then you will hear the message. It doesn't matter who brings it, or in what form it comes, all that matters is that your heart is ready to receive it and respond to it. Many messengers have been awakening in recent times. Their time is here to deliver the individual message that has been illuminated within them by the light.

Ghandi brought Light through his passivity and patience. Einstein brought Light through his vast open mind. Martin Luther King brought Light with his dream of freedom. Hendrix brought Light through a phenomenal ability to create new sound. Billy Graham brought Light through his passion. His Holiness, The Dalai Lama does it with his compassion and lightness of heart. The commonality in all these people, and thousands more who are less well known, is their passion and self-belief, their Inner Knowing that they have power and they are connected. They know that they can change things and make a difference in their lifetime. The reason we are awakened by their message is that their qualities connect with us on a fundamental level of inner consciousness. It is the passion of the messenger and the Light within the message, which opens our heart to Truth. As the heart opens we begin to see and feel the confidence and self-belief within the messengers and it entreats us to look deeper into their work and into ourselves. The Light draws us in and we become illuminated.

I mention these outstanding people, but the many messengers who are not so well acclaimed, have the same qualities: the passion, the knowledge that they have a message to bring to humanity, the confidence and self-belief that they can help people to change their lives for the better. In our quest for spiritual evolution, it is important that we search those people out and hear their message. We have to find the ones who resonate with us, who are on our wavelength of light, so to speak.

All we Need is TRUTH

It is not that we need a new message or a new Guru, all we need is Truth.
Truth can come in many different forms and from many teachers. The way
in which the Truth has been presented over the centuries has depended on
who has brought it into this world. The same Truth is available in a form to
suit everyone. Although we have had great and revered Gurus in the past, the
present day teachers are very much ordinary people helping ordinary people,
bringing the Truth in their own individual way, based on their own experiences. I find it quite amusing when a client calls to speak with me and the
first thing they tell me is that they are nervous because I have written a
couple of books and been on the TV. They build up their own image of
who I am. In reality I'm just an ordinary guy who works for a living — I just
happen to work with the teachings of the evolution of consciousness. It's a
long day, usually at least 12 hours, and I have the weekends off. I'm very
approachable and friendly and come from an ordinary background. I am one
of the new teachers sent in this time and we have to be able to relate to our
contemporaries. I seem to have an ability to blend with all kinds of people,
from whatever background. In times gone by, those seeking evolution of
consciousness may have been the privileged or the wealthy, seeking out the
sages and gurus of the east. Today's seekers, awakened by the new age light,
are ordinary folks from around the corner. So, guess what? God illuminated
ordinary folks as the teachers too, so everyone would feel comfortable and
get on with the job. He's a clever dude that God, He has it all figured out.
Perhaps what is more amusing than clients feeling nervous, is that if I choose
to call someone for a reading who I don't know, I'm just as nervous as the
client. You know, people the world over are just people. We are all more or
less the same, chasing the same things in life and all we want is a bit of peace
and some food in our bellies.

It is great to be able to sit with a group of people and help them find the
answers they are seeking, but teachers need to constantly remind themselves
that they are not above the student. On one level we are all equal, but by the
same token the God-consciousness ensures that you understand the difference between being equal in the eyes of God, and having a higher vibration
than your contemporaries. We all have a different vibration, based on our
evolutionary position on the path. You must always truthfully acknowledge
where you are vibrationally. If you don't then lessons will be sent to you. By
the same token, it is not about being above anyone or better than anyone, it
is about honouring your place on the path. The only reason students will
seek you out is because of your vibration. God will guide them to you as He
illuminates the radar in their heart and points it in your direction as the
teacher. If you are fortunate enough to have walked the path for a time and
you have experience to share, then share it in an appropriate manner, hon-

ouring yourself and your students at the appropriate level and with integrity and truth.

The teacher should not set themselves up as a Guru, but be available to facilitate those who seek their message. The process is one of uplifting others. The ultimate Truth is not beyond any of us, but it may be a difficult and lengthy journey of unfolding. Any teacher who has walked a path, which has helped them to perceive at a higher level has something to share and when you begin to earnestly seek, you will find the person who has the right message to share with you at that particular time; the teacher who will help you move forward.

Some people, like those famous people above, are born with amazing gifts and talents. The gifts emerged and unfolded in a natural way, all by themselves. Each individual blossomed into their ultimate expression and they did what they came here to do. Will you do what you came here to do?

The Prime Limiting Factors to Evolution
Many of you reading this book will also have the most amazing gifts and talents. Even as you read these words I know that some of you won't believe it. I can almost feel you saying to yourself, *'that's not me'*. You are only saying that because you have not been trained to believe in yourself; to know the God within you; to know that you are what we call God. You are the power of creation and you are creating every moment of every day. At some level you will be full of fear and doubt, as we all are because we are all here at this time to learn how to go beyond fear and doubt. You all have it in you to unlock the most amazing hidden resources because at the core of you is the Light of God. God is within you and without you and you are as God. In his own image are you made. The only thing, which separates you from the God-consciousness within are a few energetic barriers. What we call the Prime Limiting Factors to Evolution. As you learn how to transcend these barriers, you will discover the inner power and the creative force. The only difference between you and the great people we have mentioned is that they had already walked the path that you are learning to walk now. So, when they came into this lifetime they were already awakened by a great spiritual light, which was burning within them. They couldn't be who they were, though, without having done the work on themselves in previous lives. I say again, if you are reading these words now, then you have worked on yourself spiritually in previous lives. The vibration of the book would not call you otherwise.

In this lifetime you have the same opportunities as they had, but like them you have to learn how to go beyond those Prime Limiting Factors or blockages, which prevent you attaining the next level of your own perfection. If your gifts are not opening by themselves, then you will need a little help from others to unlock them. Those of you who are drawn into the worlds of healing and helping others are the lucky ones, because you are connecting to people in an area of humanity which is fast evolving. Those who work with energy and light are in the vanguard of human evolution already. You all know that anyway.

The Laws of Evolution
Later in the book we are going to look at the absolute laws which govern the evolution of human consciousness, but I would like to give you a brief introduction here.

The First Law of Evolution – *You Cannot Walk the Path Alone*
One of the most important Universal Laws is that mankind cannot make it alone. The most important thing that you can learn right now is that you can't do it by yourself. This is because we all come from the same source and we are all one. The illusion that we are individuals or individuated is exactly that, an illusion. Yes, we are in separate bodies at present, but as our consciousness rises, it begins to touch into the oneness that we are all connected too. It is only those barriers that are keeping the illusion of separation in place. I know that it can be difficult to get your head around at first, but the more you work on it, the more you begin to see, feel and understand it. The Ascension Process is a process of coming back together; of returning to unity. How can you walk the path alone if we are all connected? You can't do it. It is an impossibility!

The Second Law of Evolution – *You Must Learn to Reach Out for Help*
Most people will continually struggle through life rather than reach out for help. This is old programming. Think back to those war years when it was unseemly to appear weak. That was an era when the mental and emotional programming of, 'make do and mend' and, 'roll your sleeves up and get on with it' were needed in order to survive. But the programme stuck. Parents pattern children with their own life experiences. In turn they were patterned by their parents. Add to this the patterns of society's structures of the day and it is amazing if you ever get to think your own thoughts. But times are changing.

'Whoever enters the way without a guide
will take a hundred years to travel a two-day journey!'
  Jalalludin Rumi

It is time to learn that you can't make it alone and you will have to learn
how to reach out and ask for help. That can be a tough lesson in itself. By the
time you get to the end of this book you will understand why. When you do
learn to reach out for help you might just find that your messenger or
teacher will be shown to you in a flash. I have seen God bring instant rewards
to people who seek help time and time again, but that help will not come
until you learn to ask. It is a Universal Law. Seek and you shall find. Ask and
it will be opened to you. Once it is opened, then the work begins. As soon as
people let go and submit, stop holding out and thinking they can do it all
themselves, many apparently insurmountable problems can disappear almost
overnight. That's how fast God works.

  When you learn this Second Law and begin to Reach Out for Help, you
might just find that your own hidden and amazing gifts and talents begin to
emerge.

Old Souls

You won't have picked up this book without the old energy of previous lives
calling you back home again, or the new energies of Aquarius now entering
and awakening the seeker within you. It will be calling you to remember
who you are, and calling you to awaken again and take your place on the
continuing wave of progress towards perfection. As in previous times on
Earth, we are again journeying together, sharing the light and information,
which will guide us on our paths towards completion. Drink from the
fountains of knowledge, which call out to you wherever they may be and
continue your journey.

10

The Great Insights for Humanity

Jesus said,
> 'If they question you,
> What is the sign of your Father in you?
> Say to them:
> It is a Movement with a Repose.'

The Gospel of Thomas

Since 1999, The Guides have shared much information on many things concerned with unlocking the evolution of human consciousness. But perhaps most important in this amazing arsenal of skills, abilities and tools given, is the knowledge of what they call The Great Insights for Humanity.

Without a knowledge of the Great Insights, it becomes almost impossible to understand how to unlock your evolution and ascend into the Aquarian Age of 5th dimensional reality. The Guides try to present these insights in a very grounded, common sense way suggesting that everything should be kept as simple as possible at all times where evolution is concerned. A simple, straight forward, practical understanding of how light works with you as it brings change will unlock your understanding of exactly what is happening at any time you might be experiencing difficulty. This is so important to know, because all true transformation is difficult as it involves part of your personality dissolving to reveal a different, inner you. With the right guidance the process can bring much needed understanding and relief, helping you pass through the difficult phases with the knowledge of what is happening within you.

The Great Insights will help you to understand where we are in our time and space, where we are in the Ascension of Man, where we are in association with the Mayan Calendar and more importantly, where we can be if we know how to apply the rules of the game to our own lives. The Keys to

Eternity are with us, they are on offer now, and what you need to understand is that for most people the journey into a fully realised state is not a quick unfolding process, but a steady, one-step-at-a-time process where you can feel the shifts and the growing inner knowing month by month. The Keys of Transformation, when applied correctly will unlock you continually. Many people truly seek spiritual evolution and enlightenment, but continually stumble because the steps they try to take are too big. Anyone, following the guidance in this series of books will attain tangible shifts in consciousness on a regular basis. It is that inner knowing when you truly make a shift that allows you to feel and 'know' that you are indeed on the right path and this then brings the confidence and enthusiasm to take another step. If you are working with processes that do not allow you to experience the shift, then you are most probably not having a shift. That is how simple it is.

At the head of this chapter is a saying of Jesus, which describes the nature of a spiritual shift. It describes what I have just explained above. When you truly make a shift or evolve, there is a movement with a repose. This means that when the God-consciousness moves within you to reveal the next layer that needs to be understood, you feel the movement. You have the inner knowing that something has moved. Once you have been moved at that inner level, then everything settles into repose, or allows you to feel normal again, but with the perfect inner knowing that at some level you are not the same any longer.

In book two of this series, we will introduce you to a range of The Great Insights for this age, providing simple explanations of advanced energetic scenarios, which are interacting with you as Universal Consciousness unfolds through each acceleration period. In the following chapters we will reveal the first two of The Great Insights for Humanity. We hope you enjoy them and that you find they lend great understanding to our entrance into this New Age.

II

The Great Cycle of Time

The disciples said to Jesus,
> 'Tell us in what way our end will be.'

Jesus said,
> 'Have you therefore discerned the beginning
> since you seek after the end?
> For in the Place where the beginning is,
> There will be the end.
> Happy is he who will stand boldly at the beginning.
> He shall Know the end,
> and shall find Life independent of death.'

The Gospel of Thomas

Where did eternity begin? That's a pretty big question and not one that can easily be answered by mere mortals. The more you apply your mind to it, the deeper you enter the consciousness of all that is and then, the more over-whelming the imagery becomes. As you look ever deeper, the process expands your heart and crushes your mind as you enter the fear of dissolving everything that you are, in order to enter that space. The result is speechless-ness, as when you touch things, which are much greater than your capacity for understanding, governed by the limitations of the human mind, you eventually have to let go of attempting to understand. Comprehension of these bigger questions becomes pointless for a couple of main reasons. Firstly, when you touch the vastness of the consciousness, which creates Universes, it is impossible to explain it to others, words cannot paint such a picture. Comprehension comes by way of the experience as it unfolds over time. Secondly, once you experience such a thing, the imagery and under-standing is too great to hold within such a small kernel as a human life. You must let it all go again, as it only gets in the way. It hinders your progress, but having touched it, you then have the knowledge of it. You have the knowing that you have touched something great and the nature of the fundamental experience remains with you.

We may not be able to determine a beginning to what we call eternity, but certainly at some point there was a beginning to our present Universe. Something moved as a thought and the creation of the present Great Cycle of Time Began.

The Great Cycle of Time

The Big Bang – Unity Expands into Separation

1. Consciousness Streams Forth and Creation Begins.

2. Gases Combine and Form Stars.

3. Solar Systems and Galaxies Form.

4. Earth is Born. Life begins on Earth.

5. Man appears on Earth.

6. Man begins to Evolve.

7. The Creation Point

8. Man begins to Create with Conscious Self Awareness.

9. Jesus Casts Fire upon the World.

10. 1000AD – The Maya Prophesy The End Time.

11. 1940s – The Doors to the Age of Aquarius Begin to Open.

12. 1960s – The Calling Begins – Consciousness begins to Seek Unity.

13. 1988 – The Age of Healing is Born.

14. 1999 – The Age of Evolution is Born.

1. **Consciousness Streams Forth and Creation Begins**
   A Great Cycle of Time is the period from when the original thought chose to move from Unity into Separation. It is the period from the birth of a Universe to the moment where all the consciousness, which expanded into Separation eventually returns to Unity once more. Physical creation may continue on its course of evolution, but the consciousness, which was the original stimulating force for that creative

process returns to the core, or returns to itself to once more experience itself as Unity. The Journey of Consciousness through a Great Cycle of Time is like throwing yourself off a cliff with the knowing that you will not hit the bottom, but arrive back in safety at the place from which you leapt. It is a journey requiring great courage and self-belief and it reminds me of a lone yachtsman that I once saw. In order to keep himself fit and strong through the long days at sea, he would dive from the bow of the boat into the ocean and then swim alongside as fast as he could, as the yacht overtook him on the wind. In a precise moment, he would then locate and catch a rope trailing from the stern, to haul himself back aboard. This act demonstrates tremendous courage and self-belief, as to miss that single moment of catching the rope would spell certain death as there is no second chance. As you watched the wind carry the yacht beyond your singular world, it would be a matter of hours before you would cease to exist.

When consciousness expands into separation, it is a similar journey. You leave the mother ship of unity to travel alone on a journey of discovery until a point where it is time to be called back. At that point, you must learn how to find your way home again to unity. Original Unity is the seed, which is God or God-consciousness. At the moment God chooses to experience separation, it is like He jumps off that cliff, knowing that in billions of years time, He will once again arrive back at Unity. Essentially, the only way God can experience Himself is through separation. One of those sparks of God-consciousness is at the core of your heart, learning the way back from your present state of separation, to unity.

2. **Gases Combine and Form Stars**
   At the moment of creation, many forces become active. Imagine the male and female waters of life mixing together in a storm of activity to create new life through the formation of an embryo. Then, imagine that same process on a universal scale, as gases swirl and form into star nurseries, giving birth to billions of suns.

3. **Solar Systems and Galaxies Form**
   Gases gestate, giving birth to the fiery creations of solar systems and galaxies in many forms, although, the spiral galaxy is a very common form. You can observe it happening today through the amazing photographs of the Hubble and Spitzer deep space telescopes. Creation continues to create. It is an unstoppable, ceaseless, endless force unfolding throughout eternity, but the only version of it we know is that of our own universe.

4. **Earth is Born. Life begins on Earth**
At some point in The Great Cycle, the Earth is formed and eventually, individual life forms develop within the waters and then upon the land. Sea creatures, trees, plants, invertebrates, mammals, birds, etc.

5. **Man Appears on Earth**
From the moment of the original streaming forth of consciousness from Unity into Separation, some kind of evolutionary plan has been unfolding through this continual creative process. Over billions of years, life forms have morphed and adapted in a constant stream of evolution. Necessity being the mother of inventive evolution. As the planet changed, the life forms either adapted or became extinct. At a certain point in time, the animal we call man began to develop.

6. **Man Begins to Evolve**
Man was and is an animal, a mammal to be precise, along with the apes, the whales and many types of small fury creature. As The Great Cycle of Time continued to unfold, man evolved through various stages, but things would not change dramatically for man until a certain intervention took place.

7. **The Creation Point**
At some point, possibly between 10,000 and 20,000 years before Christ, the seed of the God-consciousness was implanted into the very core of the heart of man. Biblically, this point is known as the creation of Adam.
From the birth of the Great Cycle of Time, consciousness had been streaming forth and creating creation more or less to its own plan, or some higher plan that we are not aware of. The created forms evolved following some pre-determined course, but lacking in one major aspect, 'Self Awareness'. Consciousness merely created creation in an ongoing stream until the Core Consciousness within the heart of Unity reached down and touched mankind with the spark of Self Awareness. God placed an aspect of Himself into humans.
This is the bit, which Darwin missed, although, I do believe that he tipped his hat towards Creationism towards the end of his work on evolution. But this is also the point where the battle between the Creationists and the Evolutionists come together, but nobody seems to have seen or understood it even though plain common sense bears it out when you look at the history of life on earth.
One day, when opening myself to Universal Consciousness to find an answer to something I was working on, I was taken on an amazing jour-

ney and shown this act in some detail. Even before I began my out of body journey, Guides kept repeating the words, The Creation Point. In my ignorance, I thought I was looking for a point in a chakra where it would be possible to access stronger creative energies. Naively, I was thinking of art and artists and how they might be able to access the Creation Point within themselves and thus produce their best work at all times. As I was taken further and further from my physical body, I began to travel down wormholes through space and time. I arrived suddenly in front of the scene where God created Adam. This was the Creation Point. The point in time where Creation began to take a different turn. The vision was not given in any great biblical way, but in a very practical demonstration of the introduction of conscious Self Awareness, or to be more precise, the planting of the seed of God-conscious awareness within humanity. Although, I only witnessed this for a few seconds, the intensity of the energy was such that I returned to my body instantly and was so ill that I had to lie down for a couple of hours. It took me several days to recover my composure completely, such was the tremendous energy of this overwhelming scene I had witnessed.

So, what I was seeing was not God creating Man, as man was already in existence, but God implanting the seed of Himself into man and the start of the journey of man learning to become God again, or learning how to return to unity. From that moment on, mankind would begin to co-create with the seed of the God-consciousness at the core of his being. To this present time, we might say that mankind has used this power of creative Self Awareness to create an awful lot of destruction rather than to create creation, but he is still learning. As we move into the light of 5th dimensional consciousness as we enter the new age, ever more people will truly learn to create creation, rather than destruction.

8. Man Begins to Create with Conscious Self Awareness

The power is given to create with and man can choose what he wishes to create—war or peace, love or hate, good or evil. This is the nature of duality, it is two sides of the same coin and all you have to do is choose how you wish to create. The light at the centre of the heart illuminates man and allows him to express himself as a creator God. The greater consciousness at the core of all things does not judge, it merely allows each being, which is experiencing separation, to experiment with the forces of creation to a point where they begin to create creation, rather than creating destruction. When the individual reaches the awakening stage in their own evolution, creating creation becomes a natural part of their existence. Once the awakening begins, more power is granted, but if the individual then regresses at any level, then lessons are sent very quickly from the core of unity to help them learn how to stay on the path. The power can also be withdrawn. And so it is, through this inter-action between God at the core of all things and the awakening God within the core of the heart of the individual, that he or she begins to learn how to find their way back to Unity.

The first signs of man's attempt at creation were indeed extremely grand expressions, such as the Stone Circles, Cromlechs and such sites of the British Isles and Northern Europe. The Pyramids of Egypt and then later, Central America. The Temples, Libraries, Societies and cities of the Middle East, the Mediterranean and the Far East. Truly great works of structure and endeavour in the Sciences, Mathematics, Schools of philosophy, etc.

9. **Jesus Casts the Fire of Evolution upon the World**
The God Apollo was the symbol of the light of God-consciousness above the Earth, before it had descended into humanity. The coming of Jesus, at the birth of the Age of Pisces, was the symbol of the spiritual light descending into Earth. Another way of looking at this is that Jesus arrived on the scene as it was time to illuminate the seeds that had already been planted at that moment called The Creation Point. In this saying of Jesus, 'I have cast fire upon the world, and behold, I guard it until it is ablaze,' He is stating that He has come to Earth on this mission to begin the process of illumination. It is like the warming of spring calling to the seeds in the soil to begin to reach up from the darkness. Jesus' arrival starts the process, He is the messenger of the new Age of Pisces and the fire He is casting will gestate through the period of Pisces, roughly 2,160 years, and then begin to illuminate at the dawn of the following age; the Age of Aquarius. As that time comes, there will be a quickening. Awakening will happen very quickly and we have already been witness to this through the speed with which healing has opened and spread throughout the world since 1988.

10. **1000AD – The Maya Prophesy The End Time**
About half way through the Age of Pisces, a thousand years after Jesus and a thousand years before the present, the Mayan People are learning how to expand their consciousness and bring forth information about the changes to come, such as The Great Cycle of Time. They create a calendar of time naming the end time as the year 2012 in our present day calendar. This symbolises the end of the age of what they term, The

Sixth Sun, or the end of a cycle. We would begin to understand much about the calendar through the work of such visionaries as Ian Lungold and Carl Johan Calleman, who did great work in unlocking the secrets within. As our own consciousness awakens, we become naturally inquisitive to the vibrations of such messages, as the mind tries to get us to investigate what is being presented to us as the truth of the age and what it means for humanity.

11. **1944 – The Doors to the Age of Aquarius Begin to Open**

We have discussed this in detail in Chapter 3, *Perceiving the Dawn*, but as a quick reminder, my own calculations and sensing point to a date of around 1944, as the point where we begin to move into the new energies of Aquarius, but the period required for the doors to become around half open is in the region of 216 years. Once the doors are open by about a quarter of this figure, 54 years, then the energies are beginning to bathe the planet quite strongly and this would be around 1998/9, exactly at the point of the birth of the Age of Evolution. Anyone can see the huge shift in human consciousness since the 1960s, and those who are tuned in and working spiritually, will most definitely be able to appreciate the changes even in the past few years since the turn of the century. We only need to give recent history a cursory glance to see that great change is with us, and if we look a little closer, we can see that the change is accelerating very quickly.

12. **The 1960s – The Calling Begins –**
Consciousness Begins to Seek Unity

The first real signs of Aquarian energies are beginning to be seen as Universal consciousness calls to mankind from the core of Unity, stimulating the fire, which Jesus cast about, awakening the seed of the God within. As the seed hears the call, it begins to send impulses into the individual, which encourage them to seek answers. They begin to question who they are and why they are here. They question the structures around them, their parents and many things, which do not seem to make sense to the awakening heart. They begin to seek ways of expanding the mind, often through hallucinogenic drugs and meditation in this period, but also experimenting with different cultural attitudes. Individuals begin to drop out of, 'normal' mainstream society and begin to create alternative life styles. The Calling has begun and the growing light within causes many souls to become restless as they put their feet on the path towards home.

13. **1988 – The Age of Healing is Born**

Reiki very much leads the way in the healing revolution. Within 10 years it spreads world-wide as a phenomena as individuals learn how to use power to help unlock others. By the end of the 1990s, new practitioners were being created every week. From simple and humble beginnings, Reiki begins to awaken other streams of healing energy within individuals and many other forms of healing develop. By the turn of the century, there were hundreds of new and different spiritual and healing practices, all focussed on helping the individual to heal and change.

As unfolding consciousness continues to illuminate, it ascends, it begins to connect with higher vibrational information. The individual discovers that although the human entity is still in a state of separation, the consciousness begins to touch into unity. The individual begins to understand and experience that consciousness is not defined by the body, that it is everywhere in time and space and that the being occupying the body can access things beyond time and space. Consciousness becomes a tool that you can use to change your life, to awaken and transform. Every photon of illumination connects you into a greater picture of reality. You begin to go beyond the limitations defined by centuries of programming. The mould begins to dissolve as your consciousness becomes ever more unlimited as you learn how to work with energy and light.

14. **1999 – The Age of Evolution is Born**

In line with the Mayan Prophesies, the Universe begins to accelerate rapidly in 1999. So quickly in fact that it catches many people unawares as the vibration shifts to a place so fine that, although, people perceive that something is happening, their consciousness is still too rooted in the old world to let go enough to perceive the new world — the world beyond healing, the world of Evolution of Consciousness.

Many people are beginning to channel in the coming years and the development of the world wide web ensures that information is spread around. Although, there is much information being channelled to describe the ascension, there is little information in terms of how people can find practical solutions to help them ascend.

Entering 5th Dimensional Conscious Awareness

Those who are truly up to speed are so linked into the Universe that shortly after the turn of the millennium they are leaving healing behind and beginning to work with evolutionary techniques. These people, although not many, are riding the Wave of Time. They are unfolding in the moment, ready to let go of anything and everything that they are in that moment. They are responding to direct guidance from Universal Consciousness and their work is ever changing, in line with the vibrational changes of Universal Consciousness.

Prior to 1999, Universal Consciousness went through one complete shift every 20 years. In 1999, the Universe changed gear and accelerated and at this point, Universal Consciousness went through a complete shift once every 360 days, or near enough once a year. Those who are vibrating at that cutting edge then found that they could not work the same way for more than a year in succession. Guidance and Universal Consciousness would force them to let go and change, or should we say, let go and await new instructions. In 2012, the Universe will change gear again and then we will attain a conscious shift **every 20 days**. This is why it is so important to work as hard as you can at this time to accelerate your vibration to the maximum you can hold. There is no time to lose, as when we hit the 2012 acceleration, those who are on the Wave of Time will be gone. They will be resonating at a whole different level to the rest of humanity.

You might even consider that this is the case now, and to a large degree it is true that the world of those who are awakening spiritually have left the physical world behind in many ways. I am sure that many of you can identify with that through the friends you no longer resonate with. But this shift will be different, for nobody has experienced what will be coming and therefore, we will have a lot of learning to do when the wave hits us. This is why it is important to be up to speed, for when you are up to speed, you can receive the guidance more easily and clearly and adapt to necessary change more readily.

Since 2004, there have been accelerations taking place each year, which surge consciousness forwards. This is a time to begin to let go of everything that you are, but especially let go of thought, as thought is heavy compared with intuition and intuition is the level of consciousness desired for entering 5th dimensional conscious awareness. When you can enter this level of vibration, you begin to create all manner of new things, which the earth has never seen before. Every process that I work with has been created in such a way. By means of being able to open the mind, expand it, then lose the mind, the Universe stimulates the intuition into, 'new thought' and new thought does not have the boundaries and limitations of the old heavier world. We are straddling two worlds and we have no idea how the new world works, therefore, we must lose all our structures in order to enter the new world with a mind open to absolutely any possibility, as anything is truly possible. So it is, that I have been able to bring so many practical world first solutions to the spiritual arena. When guidance comes to me in visions or when I work with clients and students, my consciousness views them in 5th dimensional reality. It is a strange phenomenon because as you view the vision, like watching some movie of a person's energy system, it makes perfect sense and you can identify with everything that is happening within their consciousness, but when you try to then put this into words or pictures it is not possible because we don't have the language to describe 5th dimensional reality and we certainly can't draw pictures in so many dimensions. It's a lot of fun.

The options are there for you too, but what you have to understand about this journey is that it is all consuming. It is not a game, not something you can enter into lightly, as once you step through the Universal doors that I have learned how to open, then the Universal consciousness at that level will be waiting to play with you on a grand scale. That always means accelerating you at some level. Acceleration can be a difficult ride to stay on, as it sometimes turns you inside out, while you are trying to figure out what on earth is going on. Anyway, the answers are there for those who truly seek them.

Returning Home

The Great Cycle of Time is a map of consciousness, from the outpouring at the birth of a Universe to the point where the chosen subject, in this case humans, has the seed of God-consciousness firstly implanted into them, then secondly, awakened, so that they can learn how to return to the core from whence they came forth. We are now at that opening doorway, where the God-consciousness within our core is beginning to illuminate as it is being called back home again. Just like the Prodigal Son, we will return.

It is also important to understand that ascension is about allowing the consciousness to ascend, not the physical being. The more we can assist our consciousness to transcend the earth bound shackles, we reach a point where we truly understand the truth of reality and we are ready to ascend by letting go of earth and its lives. We have choices to come back and assist others, but would we really want to? When you truly discover that place of life independent of death, do we really continue to desire to enter this reality?

12

The Wave of Time

Be the change that you want to see in the world.

Mahatma Gandhi

We have talked of waves and tides, but there is one wave, which is so important to you right now that you wouldn't believe it. It is the wave, which determines your absolute success in this lifetime. If you don't learn about it, your potential could be severely limited.

The Guides began to connect me into The Wave of Time shortly after the turn of the century, around 2002. They began to show me the vibrational speed within my clients and how this related to the speed at which Universal Consciousness was unfolding. Over a period of a few years the Guidance revealed more and more about this concept. A little at a time it taught me how to help people accelerate their vibration to the point where they could ride The Wave of Time.

The Wave of Time is an energy, which affects you every single second of your life and it influences every atom of your being as it washes through you. When you are in harmony with The Wave of Time, your life unfolds in an incredible way. You are guided every second and you begin to live at a much faster pace within. Let us just say that you begin to live with a fire burning in your heart. You come to life at a higher register.

At this moment in the Ascension there are two groups of people who are awakening, those who are absolutely driven to do everything in their power to ascend, regardless of whether they understand the concepts or not, and those who think they are ascending, but in reality, are not. The difference in the inner illumination of these two groups is phenomenal. Those who are really taking things seriously and pushing the boundaries of who they are and what they can achieve through seeking to understand how the bigger picture works, will benefit immediately and enormously from these insights. For the second group, they will find that the light within the concepts helps to pull them out of the illusory states that can prevail as you work with energy, illuminating something within, which then helps them to discern a true path.

Going Beyond Acceleration

It is most important to understand The Wave of Time and how it works as it is probably the singular most important concept of this New Age and you will understand why as you begin to move through these teachings. How we would summarise what this concept means is like this. As we reached the late 1990s, those who had awoken to the healing path were accelerating at great speed ahead of those who were not yet awakening. We might say that the healers of the day were light years ahead of their contemporaries in terms of their vision, perception and vibration.

In 1999, Universal Consciousness changed up a gear. Things began to move much faster. At the same time as accelerating, the vibration became much finer. As the acceleration continued through to around 2007, everything was moving very quickly. Most awakened people were aware of this acceleration and spoke openly of it. But during this shift the leap forward in vibration began to leave everyone standing. In 2007, there was again a surge forward and because the vibration was so fine in what the Universe was unfolding around people, they could not detect it. Although, the first riders of the Wave of Time had opened quickly in the 80s and 90s, the acceleration was so rapid from 1999, that most of them began to slip off the crest of The Wave. Once you slip off, it can take quite a time to realign yourself with the cutting edge of creation.

The big problem is that because the vibration at this point in the New Age is so fine, the majority of the awakened ones cannot perceive it any longer. They have become attached to what has gone before and the Universe has moved on without them. This is your wake up call. The energies of the healing rays are still there for those who need them in order to begin their awakening, but the energies of the new age are evolutionary in nature and are very, very different from the healing energies of before. It takes quite a stretch to be able to attain this speed of acceleration and then maintain your position on The Wave.

Creating Creation

In the beginning there was nothing,
Then a breath of God rippled the void,
And the Universe was a thought, thinking.

And the ripple created The Wave.
And The Wave moved forwards,
And settling itself into a motion with rhythm,
It began to create creation.
And, as The Wave passed by,
It left creation in its wake.

Dave Ashworth
23:41pm, Jan 19th, 2009

The Wave of Time demonstrates how the universe moves and creates itself. The Wave of Time is a Wave of energy, which constantly moves forward into the void. The void is the potential of the uncreated future. The Wave of time constantly creates the future within the void so that we can experience it as we move forwards.

Imagine that there is nothing in front of The Wave, but as it passes any given point in space and time it leaves in its wake the forms it has created. The Wave continues to move forward — forever — creating creation.

The Wave will never stop moving forward. The Wave will never stop creating. There is only ever one Wave in a single Great Cycle of Time, but it repeatedly rolls over the same space as it constantly surveys its own creation, whilst laying down the next image of creation.

Imagine a vertical cylinder with a Wave running around its outside. As The Wave moves round the cylinder it continually passes the same point, over and over again. Another way of looking at this is to imagine that it is the cylinder, which is revolving and The Wave that is stationary, like a barograph, which is a weather recording device with a pen, which records changing phenomena as the cylinder revolves.

The surface of the cylinder represents everything in creation, a kind of map of creation consisting of our world, our solar system, our galaxy and the whole of this particular Universe. Every time The Wave passes over this map of creation, it paints creation anew. If you imagine the cylinder turning at 100 revolutions per minute, The Wave would be passing over every millimetre of the cylinder 100 times every minute. It would, therefore, be recreating creation a hundred times a minute.

Wave of Time

Single Point in Physical
Time and Space

Wave of Time

Single Point in
Physical Time
and Space

Russell Scientific Instruments Ltd. United Kingdom

In reality, The Wave is washing through creation countless billions of times per second. It is moving so fast that it is recreating creation everywhere during every breath you take. The Wave is just a blur in time, or even a blur in eternity. However, every time it passes the same point, it is carrying different energy, new information and painting a new and different picture of creation for us to experience. Imagine that The Wave was like the wind and it was passing around the world several billions of times a second. Imagine this wind was so fine that it could penetrate anything and in every pass it flowed right through every atom of your being. Imagine the wind passing through the mind, thoughts, emotions and feelings of every single person on the planet.

The Fundamental Plane of Eternity

To understand how The Wave of Time suddenly speeds up, we need to examine The Fundamental Plane of Eternity. Imagine that The Wave rides on top of something very smooth, like a sheet of glass, but more flexible — a sheet of clear acetate — something that can ripple and vibrate with ease. This sheet is called The Fundamental Plane of Eternity. It has no beginning or end, it just is. The Fundamental Plane of Eternity acts like a support structure and an accelerator for The Wave at the same time.

Wave of Time

The Fundamental Plane of Eternity

The 'Plane' has its own rhythm or resonance, which powers or drives The Wave. Imagine the image of a Space Shuttle being launched from the back of an aeroplane. The aeroplane provides velocity, height and forward momentum. The height provides less gravity and therefore less resistance, so when the space shuttle fires its own engines it is already moving very fast in a zone of very low resistance. Shall we say, the aeroplane 'supports and enables' the space shuttle.

In the same manner, the Fundamental Plane of Eternity 'supports and enables' The Wave of Time. The Fundamental Plane is already vibrating and moving at great speed and thereby constantly assists The Wave in gaining momentum. The Plane provides a foundation and a platform to support and assist The Wave.

At the predetermined points in what you might consider universal time, as mentioned above, the Fundamental Plane changes gear or changes its resonant frequency. It suddenly begins to vibrate much more quickly. The result is that The Wave of Time begins to speed up too. However, there is a catching-up process, which must occur as The Wave tries to attain the speed of the Plane. You can understand this a little like a gear box in a motor car. When you change gear in your car, the car does not suddenly leap forward from 35 mph to 75 mph in a single second, there is a progression. When the Fundamental Plane changes gear, it does it instantly, jumping from one vibrational frequency or speed to another, but The Wave enters a progression until it catches up with the vibrational speed and rhythm of the Fundamental Plane.

When the Fundamental Plane of Eternity shifts to a higher speed, the effect is so dramatic that it begins to impact the consciousness of humanity instantly. Those of you who are already awakening and, therefore, vibrating faster than the greater mass of people within the collective consciousness will have a deep inner knowing that something is happening, but you might be unaware of exactly what it is. When you are fully connected with the truth of what is taking place, you can often figure out what the Universe is doing as it's consciousness ebbs and flows through the birth pangs of this New Age. Your higher vibration allows you to become a part of that high speed resonance. Shall we say that a higher vibration creates a lack of resistance, which allows you to sense the change in speed more easily. In essence, you become aligned with universal consciousness as it changes by the second. This is called, 'Riding the Wave of Time.'

There is also an accelerating pattern to the speed change of the Fundamental Plane. The most recent accelerations were in 1755, and 1999, and the next will be in 2012. You can see how the time interval between each shift in the Fundamental Plane is diminishing dramatically. This gives you a sense of how fast things are moving.

Rhythm, Speed and Information

The Wave has, for the most part, three components. It has speed, which as Universal Consciousness speeds up as we move into the New Age is accelerating by the second. Every revolution or pass, which The Wave accomplishes initiates a slight increase in speed. Every time it washes through creation it is travelling and, therefore, creating, a little faster than its previous pass. The speed of The Wave gives it rhythm and stability. You could say it is like a pulse or heartbeat: something with a steady rhythm. The Wave also carries with it information. This is the information it uses to create creation.

Rhythm: We might describe the rhythm as very smooth; the energies and information within The Wave are also relatively smooth. Every time The Wave passes through the same point in creation it washes over it without any struggle, hardly causing a ripple. We might say that creation itself has a resonance or rhythm caused by The Wave constantly passing through it, like the heart beat. Therefore, when the next Wave comes through, it is like a very fine vibration overlaying a very fine vibration. There is almost no difference between following waves. As the incoming vibration is moving ever-so-slightly faster, shall we say an almost infinitesimal amount faster, the existing ripple of present creation blends effortlessly and seamlessly with the new, incoming Wave of creation. Everything is smooth and synchronised, yet every atom is empowered and renewed with life countless times each second with

the passing of each Wave. Have you ever watched a high speed four-colour printing press delivering the printed image at the end of a complex process of many synchronised interactions? It is a similar picture. Creation constantly delivering an image of perfection.

Speed: As we have said, The Wave of Time is constantly accelerating, but the increase is so small that it is incomprehensible. However, at certain predetermined points in time, through what you might call history, The Wave goes through an acceleration process, suddenly speeding up dramatically, almost as if it has changed gear. This is the great work in the Mayan Calendar, which describes these phase shifts in Universal speed.

Information: Let us say that The Wave of Time is instructed or programmed as it continually moves forward. The information, which The Wave carries falls into two distinct categories, from two sources of instruction. The first source is from that which we might call God or the Original Thought, which created both The Wave and creation in the first place. The second source is you.

The first impulse or ripple, which gave birth to the all, is constantly repeating itself, like an instructing mantra, within the framework or energetic structure of the Fundamental Plane of Eternity. We might even say that the Plane is just a manifestation of the God-consciousness, that they are one and the same thing. From the Plane, the God-consciousness constantly reminds The Wave of the eternal plan, which is, 'creation and eternity'. So The Wave constantly carries out its prime function, which is creating creation within eternity. Brilliant and simple, isn't it?

You are the Creator

The second source of information comes from you. Each time The Wave washes through you, it collects an electro-magnetic imprint of everything that you are. In particular it reads your *thoughts, emotions, feelings, desires, dreams, needs and wants*. It gathers an imprint of every whiff of energy, light and darkness that you are composed of and are processing within every nano-second of your existence. As you think your thoughts, experience your emotions and feelings, feel your desires and dreams and consider your needs and wants, The Wave records this information and then paints that image of your reality back into creation at the very next pass. That is how you create your own reality. You think it and The Wave paints it for you.

Oh, it is such a beautiful picture. If you could only see how it worked. Well you can. The more you read this, the more you will understand it and the more you understand it, the more you will see it. The more this will then

help you to perceive and understand how you are the creator; how you help to create the reality that you experience.

Let us Summarise

Every single time The Wave passes a particular point, countless billions of times per second, much faster than the speed of light, it recreates the whole of eternity with two components. Firstly, the original thought of the God-consciousness, which is eternity, followed by the original impulse, which is creation. You could describe this aspect as a self-fulfilling prophecy. There is no beginning. There is no end. There is only eternity, which is constantly being created as such. Secondly, The Wave creates what we, the humans, perceive and express as our reality. The Wave is constantly creating what you are experiencing and desiring in every single second of your life. This is how you consciously *and* unconsciously create what you perceive as reality. Anything you choose to think, be or do is reflecting back to you billions of times in the next second of time. At any moment, you can sow the seeds of change, by changing your *thoughts, emotions, feelings, desires, dreams, needs and wants.*

(As I was writing the above and being shown the images of how things worked, I asked Guidance to explain how The Wave can travel faster than the speed of light. Their answer was that the speed of light is controlled by the laws of the physical universe, but The Wave of time exists outside the physical laws and so they do not affect it. Even though it is outside of these laws, it is active within our dimension, or to put this perhaps a little more accurately, the driving force of The Wave functions beyond our reality, but at the same time it influences everything within our reality.)

As you read this, The Wave is passing through you and creating in the very next second what you are experiencing as you read it. You are the creator. You can create whatever you want. At this very moment you have the ability to influence the image of perceived reality in either a negative or positive way, depending upon your thoughts and viewpoint. If you consider that what we are telling you is rubbish and you dismiss it, then you will impact creation in a negative way, or shall we say, fail to accommodate the potential in the void. But if you are excited about the possibilities this imagery offers you, then you will change reality in a positive way. You can see from this explanation what people mean by positive thinking. Whenever we hold out a vision, or a visualisation of something positive, then by Universal Law, you will paint that image into this reality.

Consider this for a powerful scenario. Imagine a situation where everyone on the planet changed their thought patterns at a pre-determined time and continued to do it for a number of days. You would change the future

dramatically as the new thoughts were gathered up as an instruction to the Universe of how you wanted creation to be. Billions of times a second that new thinking would be painted into the picture of eternity over and over again, becoming stronger and more resilient by the second. Then the modified picture of the present second of reality is gathered up again and again and repainted in its modified and strengthened form. So it goes on, pass after pass after pass, The Wave relays the image of creation just as we choose to think, experience, feel, dream and desire it to be.

The Law of Reflection and The Wave of Time

If your main programme is that of anxiety, depression, fear, limitation and poverty consciousness, as the wave passes through you it collects that imagery and then lays it down again in the following second so that you can experience what you are currently processing and creating. Creation reflects the image of your truth for you to experience. Or, we might say The Wave paints your canvass with what you are choosing to experience. This is the Universal Law of Reflection in action.

If your overriding conscious programme is that of joy, hope, expectation, love, unlimited possibilities, then The Wave creates it in front of you. Creation is a blank canvas lying just one micro-second in front of you. It is awaiting your inspiration, desire and intent. You can paint whatever comes into your imagination and the more trust, truth and intent you put into it, the more powerful becomes the reflection of the reality you create.

The majority of the collective consciousness of humanity is programmed with the darkness of original fear, closely followed by the negativity born of self limiting fears. Therefore, fear is the current overriding reflection of what is being created. However, the New Age will begin to bring up the fear so that it can be examined, dissolved, released and replaced with the light of unlimited possibility. It is a big job, it will be a long process, but the moment you accept that you create your own reality and also have a simple under-standing of how you effect that process, then the speed of transformation for each individual can be quite dramatic as you apply yourself to change.

Changing our world might seem like a daunting task, but like everything else on the spiritual path, it is done by tackling it one-step-at-a-time. Changing the fundamental programme of humanity is done by each indi-vidual finding the courage to step out of the collective consciousness and begin thinking for themselves, rather than thinking with the pack. The next most important act is taking responsibility for your 'Self' and your life by choosing to change your thinking. As you choose to change your thinking, you become an active creator and your evolutionary path has commenced. There is no point looking at the big picture where humanity is concerned because you can only truly change your Self and when you do that you will inspire others to do it too. This eventually leads to a domino effect and that is how the world will eventually change from an overall negative programme to an outstanding positive force to create a lasting new reality.

As Ghandi said:
Be the change that you want to see in the world.

Learning to Ride the Wave of Time

In its simplest form, learning to ride The Wave of Time is about learning how to consistently raise your vibration. It is a simple process, but it does take time. The key is to keep taking small steps and appreciating the results. As we work through this book and also in other places in our websites, we explain and teach you how to do this. The opportunities are there in front of you. The void is that uncreated potential awaiting your thoughts of change.

Riding the Wave of Time

The Fundamental Plane of Eternity

You begin this journey of spiritual evolution exactly where you are at this point, somewhere behind the crest of the Wave of Time. But each small increase in vibration will begin to pull you up the back of The Wave, towards the crest. This is a journey that you can take. Anyone can take it. All you need is desire to be in that place, coupled with a little determination.

If you are happy where you are right now, then that is fine, but if you are serious about your evolution, the questions you should begin to ask yourself are:

Are you ready for Truth?

Are you ready to Reach Out for Help?

Are you ready for Challenge?

Are you ready to learn how to ride The Wave of Time?

PART TWO

The Chosen Ones

13

The Fundamental Questions of Life

Jesus said,
>   'He who drinks from my mouth
>   shall become as me;
>   and I myself will become him,
>   and the hidden things shall be manifested.'

The Gospel of Thomas

When you are born into a human life, I should imagine it is very rare that somebody tells you who you are and why you are here, why you have come to earth in this incarnation at this particular time in the unfolding of eternity. Therefore, there comes a time for many people when they stop and ask themselves the two most fundamental questions of life which, we all need to know. The first question is: Who Am I? And the second question is: Where Am I Going In Life?

Who Am I?
Most of us don't really know who we are, most certainly not at a deeper level. We are only awake at a fraction of our potential level of 'knowing'. We all have the most amazing array of untapped gifts and talents lying beneath the surface, awaiting discovery. Self-discovery is a permanent pathway of evolution. There is always another level of your Self to discover until you discover the ultimate layer, which is known as the Real Self. It is through discovering these various levels of your deeper Self that you will eventually emerge to stand in your own light and power. Don't expect it to happen all at once, it usually doesn't. However, you can expect it to unfold through every ounce of effort you expend in asking the question. The Universe will always come to your aid when you truly and sincerely search for the answers

and each answer you find will endow you with more knowledge about your inner Self. As you discover these hidden gems about you, then you begin to become more powerful. As you become more powerful, then you will be able to learn how to use that power to make mistakes with. As you play with power, the Universe will give you a good smack on the back of the head every time you get it wrong. Like a child playing with matches, every time you misuse the power you get burned in some way, as the instant karma comes back to you. Eventually, through trial and error, you learn to truly stand in that power. As you learn to stand in power, then more power will be served on you.

If you think that you don't have any hidden gifts and talents you are deluding yourself. We all have them. They are seeded into us and reveal themselves at every level touched during our unfolding process, as we search to find out who we are. They are the gifts we were given in order to walk this life with ease, but most of us have never listened to what is going on at a deep enough level and so we never discover the gifts, or the ease with which we can walk through life if we use them. In some cases, the gifts are blatantly obvious, but we deny them and avoid using them. We make life as difficult for ourselves as we can.

Where Am I going in Life?

This is the second fundamental question. Where am I going in Life? Sometimes you look at people and everything just seems to unfold for them. You know them, they are the ones who don't seem to have to make any effort at all, but everything goes their way. The ones who could fall in that proverbial bucket of manure and come out smelling of roses. Well, there is a reason for that. They have learned plenty through many lifetimes and in this one they are being given a kind of reward, like being given a day off work for achieving great sales, for example. They get an easy life. A life to enjoy without effort. There is no point looking at them in envy, because they are enjoying the fruits of their labours. If your life is a bit tougher, then in this life you are here to do some learning.

We all have a purpose or a mission in being here on the earth at this time. For some, that mission unfolds and is shown to you as you progress in your self-knowledge. Others are pushed, almost mercilessly, through difficulty after difficulty until they begin to see their mission and understand what it is they are meant to be doing.

Richard Bach in his book *Illusions*, poses a little question to find out whether your mission on earth is completed. The answer is that, *'If you are still alive then it isn't.'* And, he's right. If you are still here, then you better get your head into gear and start working at life, because that is what you are meant to be learning about. You should be asking yourself 'what am I supposed to be doing?'

Finding Direction

How can you find the answers to these most fundamental and important questions? Who am I and Where Am I Going in Life? There are many ways to begin your investigation.

Astrology

Certainly, in the beginning, I found working with an astrologer very helpful. She identified aspects within me that I was totally unaware of, but it gave me a starting point to who I might be and what I might be capable of. I would say that there is a good chance that I wouldn't be doing what I do today without that help. That first astrological chart was so scary, it took me weeks to read it, and it was scary for two main reasons. The first was that I didn't want to know the truth, although I didn't realise that at the time, but began to understand it later. The second reason was that the two aspects of the chart seemed completely at odds to me. On the one hand it was so accurate in the way it described me as the person I knew, but on the other it also described a person who was full of mystical gifts, abilities and power. This other side of my personality was completely alien to me, but as time unfolded that chart proved to be absolutely right and those gifts and abilities emerged. In the early days of working with the chart, I had reasoned that if the astrologer was so accurate in describing the aspects of my personality that I knew, then surely there must be something to the aspects that I could not recognise.

When you are ready to learn, God will connect you with someone who will show you where the path lies and each person who comes into your life will have a piece of the puzzle you are looking for. All you have to do is work with what they give you. Work with what they reflect back to you. Keep looking and turning over every stone in the search for truth.

As a starting point on your journey of discovery, if it appeals, then look for an astrologer and commission a natal chart as a guide. When you receive your chart, you will find lots of aspects of your Self you recognise, and probably a fair few that you don't. If you let others read your chart, they will often feel that some of the aspects that you don't recognise are really very accurate. When my first chart was done, I showed it to my cousin, who knows me well and is very intuitive. Her comment was, "It's like this person has known you all your life."

When you receive your astrological chart, read it over and over. Pull it out every few months and look at it again. As your consciousness and self-knowledge develop, and your vibration begins to shift, you will be able to perceive more of the hidden aspects of truth about yourself that the astrology has revealed. As this happens, you begin to become more connected with your inner self. You begin to see that the aspects, which at first you may have been blind to, are now connecting with you in a way, which you can understand. As you begin to 'connect' with the chart, this shows development of consciousness.

If you find there is something you don't understand in the chart, work with it. Keep asking the Universe for clarification until you do understand it. If you just leave it, you will never learn. You must pursue unanswered questions doggedly until you find the illusive answers you seek. It doesn't matter if it takes a long time to get there, but don't leave any stone unturned. I have had a number of charts done over the years to gain different perspectives and interpretations of the fundamental data from different astrologers and I go back to them all from time to time just to see if something jumps out, which might need attention. If it does, then I work on it.

Numerology

As well as astrology, you could work with a numerologist. Numerology is another way of finding out more about yourself and the practitioners of this art, like the astrologers, will all have different gifts developed to different degrees. They will each be able to bring another part of the puzzle to you, by revealing aspects of yourself, which you almost certainly will be unaware of unless you haven't already done a reasonable amount of self-investigation.

Consider this too: you will be moving into an area of terminology, which may be unfamiliar. If you consult a couple of different people, they might interpret a single aspect different ways. One way may be easier for you to grasp than another, so it pays to have some different angles to approach the same subject. Each will add something unique to your quest.

You might also consider psychic readings, angel readings, crystal readings or the age-old Tarot as a form of unlocking the hidden truth about your life and mission. At the beginning of your search many will find an unquenchable appetite develops where you need to touch so many different things and when that burning inner desire is ignited and you learn to follow it, then you will always find another piece of the puzzle.

What is Your Origin?

We are eternal spiritual beings inhabiting a temporary physical body. We are just here having a physical life experience, but it is all part of the unfolding journey of evolution. The physical body we understand because it is a very visible part of our world and very similar to many other animal species in its form and function. We can clearly see a relationship between ourselves and the animal kingdom. However, the spiritual aspect of who we are might be very different from person to person. Your eternal spirit might have inhabited lives other than within a human. The spirit might have had multiple experiences in any number of realities and dimensions, including the animal kingdoms.

Some people feel that they don't belong on earth. They have an overwhelming desire to 'go home' or 'not be here'. Some people feel that they are very different to others, or that they don't fit in. Some people feel that they are here from some higher calling, as if they have descended into an earth life to bring something to the earth or its people. If you feel you don't belong here you may well be right. A little book, which might help you identify who and what you are is called *Earth Angels* by Doreen Virtue, which explores many aspects of personality to help you understand strange inner feelings or drives about how you fit in to this world.

For example, I used to find one of my clients had energy, which was very distant, almost not there sometimes. On reading Doreen's book, I realised instantly that she was what Doreen called a Star Seed, a person with the spirit of a being from many light years away, experiencing life on earth in a heavy body. The girl was not used to being in a body so heavy. Just reading that book brought me huge understanding of many other aspects of people's lives, which I had seen and perceived many times, but without really taking the time to go deep enough to understand.

For example, I had often been aware of nature spirit consciousness within people. I could spot the consciousness of a faery or an elf residing in a human being a mile away. Whilst on holiday once, I was having a massage and I noticed that, although the girl was present in the room, her consciousness was drifting out of it. I said "Where are you going?" Startled, she said, "What do you mean?" "You are floating out of your body." I replied. "How do you know that?" she asked. "Because I can see your consciousness," I said. She continued. "I know. I've always had great difficulty staying in it. I don't understand it. It is like I go out into the universe." We had an interesting conversation, whilst I looked into her consciousness and explored who she was, where she was from and why she was here on earth. Within a half hour, she had the first vision of her life that made sense and as a result was instantly more comfortable with herself. So many questions were answered for her that it gave her whole life a focus it didn't previously have.

As someone with gifts to both unlock and manage events around spiritual evolution in the individual, the Universe sends me the people who are naturally awakening so that I can help them understand what is happening as their lives often begin to develop unusual patterns through the awakening process. As I look deeply into them to find the answers, what is often revealed are previous lives as Healers, Spiritual Teachers, Shamans, Mystics, etc. Many of these people have a great depth of wisdom, yet often don't understand it in the context of this present life, as the wisdom was based on what they knew in others lives, but as you teach them what they need to know at this moment in time, then they begin to connect with who they are at a deeper level with an understanding of the ancient aspects of themselves, which they have incarnated with in this life to help them complete their mission.

My particular brand of wisdom is deep and searching. It is a wisdom coupled with the power of penetration, which can plumb the depths of time and space. My partner Denise also has much wisdom, but it is different. She has such a wonderful connection with the earth, the creatures, the flowers and nature in general, but the trees in particular. She often brings me out of the deep places I go to, by teaching me to see and hear what is going on with the animals and trees. I always considered that she was an elemental at her core, an elf in particular. When we went on a mission to Delphi one time, she sat beneath a tree at the Castalian Spring, whilst I was busy with my own work at the spring itself. When I returned, she had had the realisation that she was indeed a tree spirit and it was tree wisdom, which came through her. So, Denise seems to have both Elf and Tree Spirit in her make up.

There can be many reasons why you don't know who you are at a deeper level and I find this a common problem with clients in general and true seekers of truth and evolution in particular. This is what is called an identity issue and is relative to their connections with the earth through the base chakra. When you can see issues of this nature in a client, explain it to them in terms they can relate to in the way it affects their life, then bring about changes to their earth connections, this is when their life truly begins to open up.

Working with Energy

The above suggestions are a short introduction to just a few ways that will help you on an intellectual and intuitive level to make a start in connecting with your Self and identifying and discovering Who You Are. This is merely a process of starting to fill in the blanks, if there are any and revealing the deeper layers, of which there will be many.

Summary

The first steps on your evolutionary path should be:

Learning to connect with who you are.

Learning to understand why you are here.

Keeping an open mind about everything.

Knowing that you are on a personal mission of some sort.

14

The Secret Agenda

Reality is merely an illusion,
albeit a very persistent one.

Albert Einstein

This book is filled with the Light, which triggers Evolution of Consciousness therefore, I naturally assume that you are drawn to Evolutionary Light or spiritual matters in general if you have been drawn to this book. The Light is the reason you have picked it up in the first place, not just because you fancied the title or liked the look of the cover, but because like attracts like and indeed Light attracts Light. Maybe you are being drawn to Evolutionary Light for the first time, or perhaps you are an established healer, practitioner or facilitator for change and you are ready to seek the next frequencies of Light that will illuminate your journey. Whichever it is, the Light, which Universal Consciousness is placing in the words of this work will help you open up even more. The God consciousness is always trying to guide us to a vibration that will trigger the next part of our evolutionary journey.

How do I know that the book is filled with Evolutionary Light? Because I know how Evolutionary Light works and how you access it. I know where it comes from and how to use it. Guidance has been teaching me about evolution, as opposed to healing, since the late nineties. In this instance, I have been prompted by the Universal Consciousness to write a book, so that the same source can infuse your life with light through the words and message as you read. The only reason this is being done now is because God reckons you are ready to receive it. That doesn't necessarily mean that you will understand it all just yet, but that is not important. What is important is that you are touched by the light, which will then begin a process. When God first reckoned I was ready to be touched by the light in the late 1980s, I didn't have a clue what was going on, but the times, they are a changing. There are many more awakened people, lots of books and knowledge and a lot more help and answers than there were back then. What you will discover as you touch into works that carry spiritual light is that often all you need to do is own the book and its vibration brings change to you over a period of time. Also, you find things that you don't understand, but as the light works with you and your vibration increases, then you attain the perception, which brings the understanding. Often, when you pick up the book again, months or even years later, you have a different awareness of what it means.

Are You Special or Different?

Cast your mind back for a moment to a point where you were first drawn towards spiritual matters, the unusual or esoteric in some form or other. Perhaps you will have had the awareness to know that there was something different or special about you. You may well have been very 'connected' as a child, perhaps with powerful gifts such as psychic ability or some kind of higher visual acuity. This might have been an ability to see subtle energy, auras or nature spirits, or even just a Knowing about who was coming to visit or what was happening in the lives of those around you. Perhaps you noticed a pattern where people who were troubled always sought you out for help. It is entirely possible that you lost that depth of connection as you grew into adulthood. It is entirely possible, too, that you began to fear your vision and closed it off, or that people continually ridiculed you for talking what they perceived to be nonsense. Perhaps they accused you of making things up. To prevent being admonished you learned to be quiet, you pushed the gift or ability away and closed it off. But some of you will have continued to remain connected and kept quiet about your Inner Knowing. In fact, some of you will have thought that everyone sees what you can see.

You may have been drawn to spiritual matters in your twenties, some as you step into your forties and others even later. As your intuition tried to open up and speak to you, you will have learned how to ignore it or *not* listen to it, making excuses for its guidance like, 'I'm just making it up' or, 'it's my imagination'. It doesn't matter when you were originally drawn to light, but the time period in which it happened for you is significant. The significance is that the time period is *this* lifetime. The question is, how far have you taken your initial attraction to spiritual matters, energy or light? How much have you listened to and acted upon that inner voice, which tries to guide you? How much have you ignored that inner knowing or that feeling that pulls you in a certain direction? And, before you say anything, I have heard all the excuses. Yes, all of them. Yes, I know you are too busy. Yes, I know you can't afford it. Yes, I know you have responsibilities. Yes, I know that you think people will laugh at you. Yes, yes, yes.

Do you mind if I go to sleep for this bit, because I *really* have heard all the excuses. However, what I can tell you is that even if you have been walking the spiritual path, or have been working as a healer or therapist, I would bet anything that very few of you and I mean almost none of you, will be working anywhere near your potential at this present time. Now, that is a bold claim to make and I make it because my own Inner Knowing and Higher Guidance tell me that it is so. As I have worked with hundreds of you over the years, I see the potential and I see the gap between what is and what could be. As you read through this series of books you will begin to understand how and why I know these things, and you will also begin to understand exactly where you are in terms of the evolution of your own consciousness. Most importantly, you will begin to understand why you are not at the cutting edge of a changing time—yet. It is called Self-denial.

Although, some of you will have taken your attraction to the esoteric to a point where you work full time with energy and light and earn your living by it, there are still questions, which need to be asked.

Do you really know why this attraction is there?
Do you really know what is expected of you?
In fact,
Do you really know what you agreed to do prior to
taking this incarnation?
And,
Do you know who you agreed it with?

The Secret Agenda

When you first begin to be attracted by any form or source of Spiritual Light, particularly healing, crystals, essences, divination, etc., there is, believe it or not, **A Secret Agenda** being played out within your life by God. Well, it isn't really a secret, it is just that you don't see the message until you have been taught how to interpret it. It's like learning another language really, the language of trust and feeling. In fact, another reason it's not a secret is because you agreed it before incarnating. But you know how it goes, just to make life interesting you get to lose your memory when you arrive on earth, and nobody packed the mission statement to read when you got here. It's a bit like losing your bags when you go on holiday, which can be a major inconvenience. In fact, some people never see the message at all, because they are always looking in the wrong direction, even though all the signs are pointing the way, while others can actually be looking so hard for it that they can't see the wood for the trees.

As you grow from a child into adulthood, you are taught many things by many people: parents, aunties, uncles, extended family, teachers, friends, etc. You learn all about the physical and practical world around you and how to function in it. Most of the lessons are really based on survival. You are essentially taught to survive and prosper in the world. This teaching is based on human experience. Those of you that are a little bit different, a little bit special, also need a Spiritual Teacher, Mentor or Guide to show you the other side of the coin, so that you can understand concepts, which are different from what is considered to be the norm in our prevalent left-brained thinking and functioning society. How many of you were taught spiritual matters by your teachers in your formative years? The best you might have experienced was probably Sunday School or General Religious Studies in school. That is not so much spiritual as religious teaching and the two are completely different. If you did have spiritual guidance in your formative years; then you are one of the lucky few who had a head start.

A troubled Life

Do you know how much trouble being special causes people? Well, I know what you are saying to yourself, we are all special and in one way you are right: we are all individual and unique. But some of you are just a little more special than others. Some of you have been sent here on a mission and you don't know it, because nobody ever told you. That is why you needed a Spiritual Teacher in your formative years. Those who are special often have a very difficult life. Something within them is trying to point them in the right direction in life, but because there is no training they don't hear the messages. So, most of you will be fumbling along through life, experiencing anything and everything that can go wrong, and usually does. That's all part of learning the lessons. When you are experiencing difficulty it is only the Universal Consciousness, which is trying to tell you that you are going in the wrong direction. How could you know this without having a Spiritual Teacher or Guide? But, hey, I'm telling you, now, and you know what? It's not too late.

You people who are special are actually on two separate missions, not just one. The first mission is to learn how to awaken your Self within and the second is then learning how to awaken those who are waiting for you to awaken them. In reality, this total awakening process may span a number of generations and lifetimes, and to some degree in the past, it didn't matter how long it took as long as we were all moving towards the goal that some refer to as Self Realization, or realising a state of an awakened Self. However, time is currently intervening in the plan and the mission needs to speed up a little. In fact, it needs to speed up a lot because we are approaching what is known as the end time. So, even though this might sound the craziest thing you ever heard, a lot of you people reading this and being awakened by its vibration, are the spiritual teachers of tomorrow. You might be sixty years old already and I'm telling you that you are going to be a spiritual teacher and you are thinking of hanging up your mountaineering outfit. Forget it, there is much work to do and no time to do it in.

You Know It Within
Those who have this 'Special' quality that I am referring to actually know it. They have a powerful Inner Knowing that they are different, but do you know what these people do with that Inner Knowing? They continually deny it. They don't believe it. They don't take it seriously. They say to themselves, 'Does everyone not feel like this?' But an inner voice continually tells them that they are special. In fact, it tells them more often when things in their lives are very difficult. It tries to remind them that there is 'another way'. The inner voice constantly repeats, 'But you know you are special.'

These special people, like most of humanity, are caught in the trap of what they think is reality. They base this image of reality on what they have been taught by their parents and peers who act out society's 'reality picture' based on their own experiences of life and what their peers reflect to them, in turn, from their experiences. Every time the inner voice speaks to them, they deny it. They make excuses for it. They ignore it and as a result, they *always* suffer for their ignorance and lack of trust. Only a generation or so ago, there were very few spiritual teachers and very few who were awakening, so there was nobody to teach you to see reality differently. There was nobody to teach you how to listen to the inner voice. Nobody learned the language of God. Nobody learned how to hear the guidance of the God-consciousness within

To understand the Secret Agenda, you have to awaken to a different level of conscious awareness. I won't say higher consciousness, just different. You have to enter into a different level of Self Belief. There are many paths you can travel and many teachers to encounter who will help you attain the level of awareness you need in order to understand who you are and why you are here. As you walk this path, then you will begin to understand that the Secret Agenda is not so much a secret after all.

The Aspects of Knowledge

If you are reading this book right now then something extraordinary is happening in your life. There is no way you can be reading this book if you are a simple, ordinary human being. You are something quite special. This book is here to help you discover who you really are and to help you play your part in the grand universal plan, which is rapidly unfolding. This period of human history on earth is called The Ascension Period, as well as, the birth of the new Age of Aquarius.

If you are reading this book it is because it's time for you to know something of the higher realities, which are guiding you. It is time for you to realise that you are here for a reason. You are on a mission. I am not going to tell you directly or in detail what mission, because each of you will unfold unique and individual gifts, which will allow you to play your part in The Ascension.

However, I am going to guide you in how to discover the pathway for yourself. I am going to empower you with Truth so that you can begin to understand who you are and why you are here at this amazing time of human history and earth changes, bringing the shift in human consciousness, which has been prophesied for centuries.

There are three aspects of knowledge, which will give you what you need to know right now in order to understand the first part of who you are and why you are here. They are:

The Calling

then

The Message

then

The Keys

Summary

You should be learning to acknowledge and accept that you are special.

You should be listening to, and acting upon, that inner voice.

You should be actively following your heart and seeking out teachers.

You should be learning that your journey has barely begun, even if you have already been on your path for a number of years, I can tell you that it has barely begun. By the end of this book you will discover that there is so much more to discover in unravelling this mystery; that two things will happen:

The first is that you won't believe what I'm telling you.

The second is that you will have that inner knowing that tells you that you can't afford not to believe it.

And that will be your dilemma because the fire that will be awakened inside you as you work through this book will begin to reveal the nature of the illusion that you live within. However, your mind and its constructs try to deny the truth of the reality, which is holding itself out to you and you will prefer to continue to bow to the illusion. For it is the illusion that you relate to and know and the illusion that controls you.

The illusion is your reality and in order to move into truth, you will have to learn how to let go of your present reality, which of course, is the illusion.

15

The Calling

Jesus said,
> 'I have cast fire upon the world,
> And behold, I guard it until it is ablaze.'

The Gospel of Thomas

The End Time

There is a timeline in operation, which spans aeons of time. The timeline is so vast it is almost impossible to comprehend. It is the timeline of the process of creation, but within the larger concept of eternity. So, let us say that there is eternity, but within that framework there is a parallel process called creation. Creation began, whenever it began. We don't really need to go back that far to understand what is happening now. But as a matter of interest, the Maya created a calendar, which maps the whole process from what is termed the beginning of time, millions of years ago, to the end of time. The period of time that we are in 'now;' this time slot between 1960 and 2030, is one in which huge changes for human consciousness were foretold. The timeline throughout history can be seen and understood if you care to study the Mayan Calendar and if you are to gain any understanding of what you are a part of, then I suggest you should. All the major changes of humanity can be outlined against the patterns in the calendar and the period we are really interested in is the year 2012, for this is when the end of time is predicted. Don't panic; this doesn't mean the end of the world. It means the end of a time period.

Let us narrow the timeline down a little further, to between 1985 and around 2015. That is only thirty years, well within a single life span. This time slot is a period of great acceleration of the energies, which bathe our planet, our lives and particularly our consciousness. This is a time where human consciousness is awakening. It is the time when it was always predicted that human consciousness would begin to enter a period of transformation, the beginning of the transition into fifth dimensional awareness. Many of the people who are alive at this time have not only chosen to be here now, but have actually been sent as envoys and ambassadors and particularly as teachers, to those who are awakening. However, because we lose soul memory when we incarnate, we don't recall why we are here. Many of those who have come as the teachers of the new age still do not recognise their mission.

The Calling
The secret agenda is that you have been called. What this means is that you have been called to awaken beneath the flood and influence of the waves of new light, which are coming to earth in this period. Since the mid 1980s in particular, many new frequencies of light have been bathing the planet and awakening those who are a part of this advanced guard, who are here to learn to understand how to change the perception of reality.

The Calling

Your Name has been Called in Heaven.
You have been called to Awaken.
You have been called to Evolve.

You have been called because it is Your Time.
Time for your Heart to Open.
Time for your Consciousness to Transform.

Such is the nature of The Calling.

Misunderstanding Your Healing Path
When you discover healing you might labour under the misapprehension that you have found something new and exciting, which of course, healing is. You may think you are following a desire to learn something new as you are drawn to working with people in an interactive or energetic way. In reality though, you didn't find healing, you were guided into it from the light within you as that light began to awaken to The Calling. Your new found, exciting 'thing' was put in your way so that you could fall over it. And, if you missed it the first time, it would be put there again and again until you eventually awakened to the reality that you were being drawn or guided into

something, which you desperately need in your life in order to fulfil your mission successfully. The emerging light 'within' you was attracting something, a tool in fact, to bring you into contact with both energy and light from 'without.' A tool that would begin to open your channels and begin the birthing process of a Teacher of Light. A Teacher of Light is many times removed from a healer. Your vibration needs to reach a certain 'pitch' before it develops a momentum whereby your consciousness then enters a process of continuous change. At that point, you can wear the mantle of a Teacher of Light. For now though, it is important to understand that the healing path is just the first stage of your awakening. It is the kindergarten of light.

Your Name Has Been Called

What is actually happening as you stumble into healing is that your number has come up in Heaven. You have reached the top of the pile and your name has been called. You are being reminded what you agreed to be a part of. For some of you, this will be a repeat path of previous lives, where you have learned much about healing and bringing energy and light into the lives of those around you.

Well, what am I being called for specifically, I hear you ask? You have been called because it is your time for the Evolution of your Consciousness. It is time for your consciousness to awaken into the coming light of the new age, to awaken to a point where your hidden gifts and talents are about to unfold. You have been called because you agreed to play a leading role in The Ascension of Human Consciousness. You came here to lead the way in the opening and emergence of a new humanity. You are a trailblazer, a pathfinder for others. Does that sound a bit over the top, a bit grand, perhaps? Well, it isn't. It is just the way it is, so get used to it. The only difficulty in preventing you becoming a world beacon for change is your own lack of self-belief and your inability to see this picture. Strong words, but that is the truth and this book is about revealing the truth.

Now do you understand why you feel special? It is because you have been called. You have been infused with the light of God at your centre so that you absolutely know that you are different and special. That special feeling within makes it hard to deny it to yourself. You have been called because it is your time, more than at any other time in any other life, in the history of humanity, to begin to emerge into light. This is the time where humans may just, with a bit of luck and guidance, approach becoming human, and then proceed with some alacrity to becoming Gods incarnate as they learn to allow that seed of the God-consciousness to illuminate within and radiate from them. They may just learn to allow that light of God-consciousness to flow through them and outwards into the world around them, in turn illuminating and transforming everything it touches, revealing truth over illusion. If you think that this is a little fanciful, then you could be in for a surprise. That light is awakening within you even as you read these words, for that is why they have been written, to radiate that light towards you, to call you even more to your awakening. It is all part of The Calling. Even now, as you are reading this, I can feel the old patterns of denial that have been there for centuries and countless lives. I can feel you wanting to turn away. I can feel you wanting to put the book down. I can feel you failing to acknowledge who you are and why you are here. When the light touches you, the first thing you feel is fear; that is why you want to turn away. That is the programming, which you feel. It has been there for so long that your natural patterning is to deny the God within you, to continually 'allow' your patterns of unworthiness to define your life and dictate your future. The lack of self-belief in who you are is painted throughout every atom of your being.

You Can't Pretend You Didn't Hear

The problem with being called is that you can't ignore it. What happens is that the light within the core of your being begins to awaken and expand. It begins to push and speak to you. It begins to show you the sham and lies of what you perceive to be reality. And, if you do choose to ignore it, you become painfully debilitated. You can even lose your life. The pain, the illness and the possibility of death are all differing reflections of the extent to which you ignore what is going on inside of you, reflections of the denial that you offer to that God-consciousness awakening within. Once you have been called; that light is emerging and nothing will interfere with it, except complete and utter denial. But, even that doesn't stop it, for if you deny the emerging light of God within you to your utmost, then you get taken out of the game, debriefed on the other side and sent back in again, like a soldier having his wounds patched and returned to the front line. That's where you are, on the front line of a changing reality and you have been called to learn how to help change it for the benefit of humanity.

The light, which is presently attempting to illuminate you against all your opposition arguments is the emergent light of God. It is the fiery seed of the Christ Light, which was sewn into the hearts of humanity two thousand years ago when the teacher walked the earth.

Jesus said,

> 'I have cast fire upon the world,
> and behold, I guard it until it is ablaze.'

The Gospel of Thomas

Don't think that you can deny it all the way to the death of your physical body, because you can't. Okay, I'll rephrase that. You *can* continue the denial all the way to the death of your physical body, but it doesn't end there because it is the spirit and consciousness, which is being illuminated, not the physical body. If you choose denial, then the spirit will be reborn into a new physical body in record time, for there is no more time to lose as we prepare to enter the end period of time.

So, ask yourself, do you want to go through pain and suffering and learn how to do it all again? Or do you want to get it as right as you possibly can in this amazing time of acceleration? You chose to be here at this time, so sit up and take notice. Join in the Ascension and enjoy the ride. The choices are yours and in terms of your evolution the choice to get on with the work is a most important option.

The Message

The problem with Evolutionary Light is that once it has been ignited within you, at your time of The Calling, it just keeps on coming, you cannot ignore it. What is worse is that when a messenger who has been guided to deliver the message to you has done so, you can't pretend that you didn't hear it. You know, when God says that time is running out and you need to wake up, then He sure throws everything at you so that you hear the message. And, if you have been given the message, like you are being through this book, then He knows that you have heard it, so the only person you can fool by pretending that you didn't hear it, is you.

There are many teachers and messengers delivering different aspects of the same message in their own interpretive and individual ways as received through their own guidance. The God-consciousness will speak through them all in its own special way so that their message is individual to them, so that it represents that spark of individuality that God is trying to illuminate the world with. Although, much of this book is directly guided, there is also the essence of my own individuality within it. God is trying to use my personality as a lamp to attract those seekers who resonate with the message as radiated by me.

If I don't put the message out there, more or less word for word, whilst also allowing my individuality, not ego-self, but individuality as illuminated by the growing inner light, then I'll be in big trouble, and I don't want to manifest M.E. or cancer, thanks very much, and then have to go through the process of learning what part of the denial process allowed me to manifest it for my education. So, when that voice speaks with guidance from within, I act immediately. When the fire is ablaze and comes through me and says, 'don't pull any punches Dave, tell it as it is,' then I use the words that are coming through and I don't pussyfoot around or substitute the words for something a little more modest. You will find that in the new reality, which is emerging, some of the old sayings like, '*if you can't stand the heat, get out of the kitchen*,' don't work any longer. For, when you have been called, you can't get out of the kitchen and believe me, God's kitchen can be as hot as hell.

In this time of acceleration, there cannot be just one teacher, for there is too much work to do in too short a time. Look what happened the last time we only had one teacher. Once he was gone, his teachings became the subject of a 2,000 year power struggle by men of darkness. That does not mean that everyone in the church is a bad person, far from it, but the Truth is that its foundation is built on lies, deceit and murder. When you work with the level of light that is now incoming, there is only truth or lies, only good or evil; only black or white. There is nothing in between that is acceptable and the new frequencies will illuminate truth in a way, which will expose the lies.

The new energies of the incoming age, which are already with us, will sweep away anything unwholesome or deceptive, for the light of this age will reveal truth at every level by revealing the lies that hide truth. Citadels built on lies will crumble beneath the Light of Truth, but you can expect some major battles to be fought on the way.

The situation is this. Until your consciousness reaches a certain vibration, you can't hear or perceive the spiritual or evolutionary messages for yourself. So, what the higher consciousness does is send a messenger. Within that messenger's words, whether spoken or written, is placed enough light of the correct level of vibration to trigger some movement in that light at your centre, light which is already trying to emerge within you as a result of The Calling. The Calling lights that lamp within, so to speak. All these processes are to ensure that you hear the message when it comes. As the light within begins to move from the vibration delivered by the messenger, the awakening continues. It is like planting seeds of light within and awaiting their emergence from the heart. As those seeds emerge, so your vibration rises, your perception changes and you begin to be illuminated by the message.

In this instance, the light in the words of this whole book are the message and the light is both written and unwritten. Once you have read the words, the light within them ensures that you absolutely know that they are speaking to you. God is looking on, from within your heart and He knows you've got the message, therefore, it is impossible to lie or deceive your heart in any way.

Time to Acknowledge Your Truth

It is now up to you to take responsibility. It is time for you to acknowledge that you always knew that you were special; that you always knew that there was something different about you; that you always knew that you were here for a purpose. It is now time for you to take responsibility to find out who you are. It is time to take action.

The Illumination

Think for a moment how you feel when something new and exciting comes into your life. The excitement fills your body and mind to overflowing sometimes. It can be all consuming. You can't stop talking about it. Have you ever asked where this excitement comes from? It comes from the God-consciousness working in your heart. When you perceive the right thing for you, the illumination in the heart goes into overdrive so that you cannot mistake that you are connecting with something important for your own self. So, when something attracts you to it in a magnetic way, it is really the God-consciousness within your heart, which is pulling you towards that something. For example, if you are drawn to a particular book, or crystal, or course, or teacher, this is God guiding you from your own heart to find what He wants you to find. He wants you to find the key to your purpose and He does this through inner illumination. The inner illumination fills you with that spirit of purpose, that drive and desire to be or do something, to be or go somewhere, to connect with someone.

When you awaken each morning, look for that feeling of illumination within you.

God is working within all of us constantly, trying to guide us to what we need to find. But in your case, because you have been called, He is working extra hard to ensure that you get everything out of this life, which you are supposed to. As individuals, we are only a tiny percentage awakened when compared to God-consciousness itself and so we sometimes have difficulty in figuring out the direction we should be going in. However, as His Light pours into you from many external sources, He continues to awaken you a little at a time to new opportunities, always trying to bring you to the next thing you need. You will find that these new opportunities begin to help unfold your consciousness.

To be fair, it is a joint process, but if you don't take responsibility, especially when you have been told, then God often takes a hand in things to help you. And as the old saying goes, God works in mysterious ways. Some of the ways he chooses might not be that palatable or comfortable. In fact, you would be amazed at the difficulties He can create to help you find the right path.

Called to Awaken to *Your* Evolution

This is not a lifetime to sit back and take it easy, this is a lifetime to work hard and accomplish what you have come here to achieve. You have been given amazing gifts and talents to work with, but as yet they will not have awakened fully. The level to which they have already unfolded depends on how much action you have taken so far. Even if you have taken action and have already attained powerful healing abilities and achieved a higher vibration, you still have a long way to go. In fact, I might even say that if you are an advanced Lightworker, you might just about have your feet on the first rung of the ladder and as such, it is now incumbent upon you to take even more responsibility for your evolution than someone who is only just starting out on the path. Why should I say this? Because the only way you attain any measure of power is when it is given to you to work with and if you have power to heal, facilitate, guide or teach the lives of others through the use of higher gifts, then those gifts have been given to you for that purpose deliberately and are only given so that you can learn how to use that power appropriately. When you do learn, you are given ever more power. There is no limit to the power you can obtain for your work as you constantly step up through allowing your perceptions of what you consider to be reality to fall away, ever revealing different aspects of the illusion. However, though that power is given, it can also be taken away again in an instant and this is a lesson concerned with understanding the difference between ego and power, which we will touch on later.

If at this time you carry a reasonable measure of power, then you have already learned some of the spiritual lessons of our time. As time moves forward and changes, the lessons will change. For example, it is no longer appropriate to seek an eye for an eye. That is the mentality of another age. If you are carrying powerful healing light, it is incumbent upon you to begin to research the new streams of light, which are being beamed into the planet right now. The new light is here in order to begin to speed up the evolutionary processes of all those who have been called. As a practising healer, at some point you will need to take responsibility for teaching and guiding others. The learning is never over and the lessons, you may find, become ever more difficult to grasp as they turn your mind inside out, so that you can learn to perceive differently, in fact, in some instances, so that you can learn how to dissolve the limitations your mind creates. This is because your consciousness must change before you can see the lessons. If some of the things I say in this book don't resonate with you, then consider that it might be because your consciousness cannot yet see this level of Truth. It will come.

To put this into context, the Disciples asked Thomas what Jesus had said to him when he took him on one side. He replied that if he told them, they would take up stones against him. What that meant in those times was that they would stone him to death. What Thomas was really illustrating was that the Disciples' perception was not yet evolved enough to understand the truth. If he told them the truth, then they would probably consider it a blasphemy and stone him to death. Truth is truth, but you can only perceive it as you learn how to see through the illusion as your vibration moves upwards.

The path of evolution is a path of great responsibility, responsibility to yourself. You are called to open yourself to light and by so doing open yourself to your deeper Self. How many of you are really awakening as quickly as you can or should? How many of you are grasping the nettle and moving forward in leaps and bounds, embracing the reality, which is presenting itself to you and learning how to see the lesson in it and then going beyond that level of reality? How many of you think that things are going swimmingly, whereas in reality they are quite sluggish, if not completely stuck? How many are in denial and have continued to work at the same level for years? If your work is not evolving, if your work is not changing; if *you* are not changing, then you are stuck. We are going to find some of the answers you need to know in order to reveal where you are on your path of awakening.

I have been teaching how to know where you are on your path for many years and I am constantly amazed at how little attention people pay to learning lessons and evolving. They talk the talk, but very often do not walk the walk with any determination or clarity. The question you must always ask yourself is, 'Am I doing enough?'

The Illusion
The reason you have been called to work with energy or light is that these are the only tools, which will unlock the evolution of your own consciousness. So the call to healing is really an illusion, a little trick to get you playing with energy and having fun with power. Everyone thinks that they have become a healer so that they can help others and then they revel in the

power and adulation that it brings to their lives as they experience success. Come on, wake up. This is only the beginning phase. The phase when light touches your life and awakens the Ego-Self so that you can discover how it sabotages you and how strongly you are attached to it. As you begin to climb the spiritual ladder into ever-higher Truth, you begin to see the illusion and how it works. Being granted the gift of healing is not so that you can focus all your attention on others, it is so that others can be brought to you. You learn about your own shortcomings as your clients reflect your issues back at you. It is just a little trick of the light, which is played on you by God, just another part of the illusion. How does it feel when you discover that things are often exactly the opposite of what you think they are? The trick is that you can't see the reversal or understand it until your consciousness reaches a certain level. That is why so many people continue to stand in denial; because they can't see Truth. The teachings of the great Masters were always in metaphor because you can only understand them when you can experience the level of light, which unlocks the metaphor. Light is a key and the level of your vibration turns the key in the lock of truth.

The Healing Addiction and The Trick of Power

The reality is that power is addictive and so God, in His mysterious way, fools you into thinking you are powerful and you can do this amazing healing work, when in reality it is all an illusion. The only person who heals is the person receiving the energy. But you say, 'but I have seen amazing results from my healing work.' Yes, you have, but do you really think the resultant healing was accomplished by you? What you did was facilitate energy and light, no doubt with all your skill and ability. You stood as a channel so that your client could receive Divine assistance, through your vessel and through your practised skills. But they only received on the level at which they were ready to receive, ready to let go and move on. They sought you out because they were guided to you, because they were ready to let go of a certain level of conscious patterning. You allowed the Light to flow to them in order that the letting go could take place, based on their own inner agreement with God. That person had reached a level where they were ready to move forward and so God guided them to a healer so that energy and light could pass to them in a process, which brought two, or more, people together. This is a part of the universal plan, which is about bringing people together. The other part was to experience the exchange.

What God is really doing, a little at a time, is taking you out of the mundane world of illusion and lies and placing you in the dynamic world of Light and Truth. Once you are in here, He can then reveal his subtle subterfuge. However else would He get your attention other than to allow you to think you were powerful? He uses the addictive properties of power to fool you. How clever is that, to use illusion to draw you away from illusion?

Summary

The Calling is a process of being awakened from within.

You are Called when it is your time to evolve.

The Calling ignites the God-consciousness within.

Then the light begins constantly to emerge.

Once you have been called, you must take action.

You don't have a choice.

God tricks you with power so that you can discover your ego.

God uses illusion to draw you out of illusion.

16

The Chosen Ones

Jesus said,
> 'Happy are the monakos and the chosen
> for you shall find the Kingdom
> Because you are from the heart of it,
> you shall return there again.'

The Gospel of Thomas

If you are a healer, you are now learning that your mission or journey in life is *not* that you have been called to the healing of others, it is that you have been called to evolve your own consciousness. Healing others is merely the path by which you attain your own salvation through the reflection of your-self in those with whom you work. You have been called to healing by default, called because it will give you the tools to find your Self. You have been called to healing so that you can work practically with light and, in turn, so that light can work with you. All your work is an exchange with your client. You both benefit. Your client is often your teacher, they present with the issues God wants *you* to learn about, both for your own experience and as a reflection of some aspect of you. This is how God teaches you, through the mirror of others. All your clients are sent to you by the Universe. Don't ever think it is otherwise. We might add that there is an exception to the client always reflecting your issues and this is when you go through a conscious shift as a result of the work you do with your clients. As you go through a conscious shift it is always accompanied by a learning experience, a raising of perception. When you learn to see something at a higher level and change as a result, the Universe often brings you a series of really easy cases as recognition that your shift has been noted.

You have been called to your own healing path. The healing needed is your own. You have been called and now stand with that light burning within you. In some instances it tries gently to coax you into life and in others burns a hole right through you as the fire, which Jesus tells us, 'He guards until it is ablaze,' begins to illuminate your inner being, in order to encourage you to act. Are you going to sit back and allow this amazing opportunity for evolution to pass you by? Or, are you going to grasp the nettle and face anything, which the God-consciousness brings, in order to help you learn?

The Age of Evolution is Born

We have mentioned healers awakening to their evolution, but you may have been drawn to this book even though you are not a healer, but you will most certainly be drawn to esoteric things. In addition to the healers who have been awakening since the 1980s, many others are now awakening, too. These people are not necessarily called to the healing path in the same way. In 1999 The Age of Evolution entered our world and evolutionary light began to pour forth into the lives of those who had been chosen to awaken more quickly. Those who are awakening now will learn to walk the path differently. They may find themselves becoming spontaneously awakened to a point where their intuition is wide open, their knowing, radiant with the light of truth and purpose. Certainly, many of the clients and students who have been sent to me are from this group. When touched by the appropriate level of light, they can then literally open as much in a few days as a healer who has served a long apprenticeship. Of course these newly awakening people do not have the experience of the healer, but you may be surprised when I tell you that what is unfolding right now does not demand that they do in order to heal, serve or awaken others. The way the awakening process is now working brings so much insight with it as it helps you access 5th dimensional consciousness; that you do not need the same level of experience to interpret what is happening with a client. The illumination brings all the answers to you. I know that many healers will not understand this because they are not vibrating in this energy or light yet, but be certain, this level of inner illumination is currently pouring into many who are now awakening rapidly. We will all witness and experience a great shift in emphasis in the immediate future.

There is, however, a common purpose between the healers who have been working for some time and those awakening in the evolutionary light of this moment: they have the inner knowing that they are here to help others. In fact, in the latter group, it seems to be a sharper knowing than in the healers and this is because of the differing nature of the light that has awakened both groups. As the healers awakened, slowly and with a strong desire to keep learning more, they progressed in stages and were allowed, because of the timeline of this period, to discover their own mission in their own time. The latter group, awakened by evolutionary light, are infused with the inner knowing immediately and with a sense of urgency. Indeed, there is no time left. Humanity is already lagging so far behind the leading edge of The Wave of Time that many will find it a great wrench to catch up.

The Chosen Ones

The Secret 'Heavenly' Agenda is no longer a secret. You have been told what it is and why you are here, and also what is happening to you in this time. Now that you know you've been Called, the best option is to sit up, take notice and get on with the job.

When you have learned to see or perceive into the deep consciousness of other people, you can see their level of connection into the Spiritual Realms. Many people have very high connections. Some are connected into the Realms of Guides, some into the Angelic Realms, some into the Arch-angelic Realms and some into the realms of Christ consciousness. Believe it or not, some are even connected beyond this. However, when a person has a connection into the Christ consciousness, they absolutely know it at some level. You cannot have this connection without knowing it. Many people at this time have been given this connection, or shall we say have evolved into it through working hard on their evolution in previous lives. This does not mean that the connection is switched on all the way up the spiritual channel and into these high realms, but it does mean that you have been given the option of attaining Christ consciousness anytime you are ready to walk that path and open those doors. You are only given this connection when you have been 'Called to Evolve' and when you have been Called there is a name that you are known by in the higher realms. That Higher Consciousness knows you as The Chosen Ones. We would like to elaborate on this further.

Jesus said,
>   'I will choose you, one out of ten thousand,
>   and two out of ten thousand,
>   And they shall stand boldly, being a single one.'

The Gospel of Thomas

The Accelerated Masters and The Chosen Ones

Two individual aspects of humanity are being called to evolution at this time. Both groups have done much work in previous lives in preparation for the teaching of these times, not necessarily knowing what that work was ultimately for. The Higher Consciousness calls them The Accelerated Masters and The Chosen Ones. Both are given equal resonance, reverence and illumination within this time of acceleration, although, The Chosen Ones are a little ahead in terms of their spiritual connections and vibration. Equal resonance means that each group will be bathed in the same levels of light, allowing both equal opportunity and possibility of attainment. The light will accelerate both groups towards a common goal, but based upon their ability to reach within themselves to find the courage to continually go beyond their present limitations.

Accelerated Masters will have more to learn than The Chosen Ones, as they were not previously as advanced in terms of their evolution prior to the end of some of their recent incarnations. But shall we say that time is now so short, as we open into Aquarius, that it is a case of all hands to the pumps. This is not a latter day fix of an unfolding problem, it was always planned this way. This is why we mentioned the fact that many teachers are needed in this time period. Shall we say, of the Accelerated Masters, that God is attempting to push them so fast that they will need to learn the lessons of two or three lifetimes in one. He is bringing them forward at such a speed that they are literally skipping a couple of lifetimes of learning in order to be at the cutting edge of the opening of this period of light.

The Jesus Connection

The Chosen Ones have a direct connection into Christ Consciousness. Those who have this connection absolutely know it. They will perhaps feel that Jesus is with them, or they will know that they are somehow very special, or that something special or unusual is within them. They may even have had visitations from Jesus. The inner knowing is the Christ Light awakening and emerging within them that enables them to feel this way. However, these people often strongly deny this feeling or knowing, as this presence within often causes great feelings of unworthiness. Humanity, with its present programming, finds it difficult to step out from the crowd and acknowledge the truth within. They prefer to continue with the tribal instinct, to be the same as others. This is partly a protection device from times when they stepped forth into public ridicule and even death as a result of acknowledging their inner knowing. There are strong memories of painful times within them, so there is a strong desire to keep their heads down this time around.

Both Chosen Ones and Accelerated Masters often have difficult lives or perhaps did not fit in with others as they were growing up. They knew they were different, but often think that perhaps everyone feels or thinks this, though it is not the case. However, as we have said, having the connection into the Christ Light is one thing, having it fully illuminated and switched on is another. Shall we say that there is virtually nobody at this time who has attained the fully awakened connection, but it is coming in this time of Ascension. The Chosen Ones are here in particular to lead the charge, uplifting others into the changing consciousness of the new age. They are here to teach those who are ready to evolve and especially to assist the Accelerated Masters to attain a similar connection to their own, in order that more teachers can be prepared for the coming time.

Everything offered to The Chosen Ones is being offered to the Accelerated Masters. The Chosen Ones, as they awaken will understand their role in uplifting and then leading others as guides and teachers. The Accelerated Masters, because the Universal energies of the new age will be pushing them hard, will need to learn how the spiritual laws work in their lives. They will face a number of internal battles as they learn to overcome their programmed desires to dominate or control others. It is a learning curve, that is all, on the path to enlightenment. Many of The Chosen Ones have already walked this path and learned many of these lessons, therefore, more power can be granted to them more quickly. Power is only ever granted once you have truly learned the lessons associated with Universal Laws.

In this period of acceleration in general, all levels of spiritual connection will be amplified, all levels of attainment pushed. The God-force will be relentless in recruiting and awakening as many as possible to the roles, which need to be played out in unfolding the consciousness of humanity into its expression of true evolution.

Developing as a Leader

If you feel that you might be A Chosen One, or an Accelerated Master, because this description resonates deeply within you, don't think for a moment this puts you above anyone else. They might sound like grand titles, but all they mean is that, at a soul level you have been offered the opportunity to put yourself forward as a candidate for evolution. If you are then chosen and this only happens when you are truly ready to learn the bigger Universal lessons, then a great responsibility will be placed on your shoulders. If you are chosen, then you have agreed to develop as a healer, teacher, guide or facilitator first, but then a leader, as you learn the evolutionary lessons, which are sent to you. No time frame is given, but it is expected that you will continually seek the pathway into higher consciousness and step into the role, standing above the crowd to lead others from darkness into light. As your own evolution begins to unfold, then you will be expected to uplift others in a selfless manner, for the agreement is that you will work towards the salvation of humanity through the evolution of human consciousness. As you gain experience, knowledge and power, you use that enhanced ability to uplift others through sharing that knowledge, empowering your fellow man with the gifts and knowledge that you have obtained. This is like taking your students and enabling them to be as you are, pushing them so hard that they become as you, pushing them so hard that they become greater than you. You are here to bring out the best in them, even though they might exceed you.

Jesus said,
'You will do works greater than I.'

It is only through selfless sharing and uplifting with knowledge and power that humanity will be saved. Because we are going to be moving much faster than we are at present, great power, but also great responsibility will be given to individuals. Your lessons will reflect back to you as you make mistakes with power. It can be like being on a battlefield, constantly dodging the bullets, but finding that every single one hits you, because you can't learn fast enough. You will find yourself begging for some respite, but you didn't sign up for respite, you signed up for evolution.

We mentioned that The Chosen Ones often have very difficult lives in their early periods. This is because of the magnitude of the lessons, which are brought to them. As the Accelerated Masters begin to unfold, they may indeed also find that their own lives become very difficult, for they too will need to learn the same lessons.

In the saying from the *Gospel of Thomas* at the head of this chapter, the word *monakos* is used. I would like to give you Hugh McGregor Ross' explanation of this word from his book *Jesus Untouched by The Church*, as there is a direct link between what Mr. Ross says about monakos and the guided information I have both seen and been given on the term Chosen Ones.

"Three times in the Thomas Text Jesus employs the rarely used Greek word *monakos*. It does not translate into English. The nearest is the rather unsatisfactory word 'loner', in the sense of the nineteenth century American phrase, 'Go west, young man'. In South Africa, then they were called Pioneers, and were whole families. It implies foremost an independence, with perhaps something of an adventure about it. It means one who is willing to go forward on his own, who can become detached as a liner loosens its moorings to set out on a voyage."

Hugh Ross

Based on Hugh's description, especially of the liner setting out on a voyage or journey, a single entity travelling alone, seeking its own destination, my own identification and description of *monakos* would be, 'on a mission', for that is what it is like when that light is burning from your centre. You eat, sleep, live and breath the search for whatever it is that you are searching for and, of course, the answer is alignment with and attainment of the Christ consciousness. We might not realise this on the earlier stages of the path to unity, but this is the ultimate destination of everyone's journey. As I have said elsewhere in this book, you can only make that journey alone, for this is where your individuality and uniqueness comes into play. No two people can ever unfold the same Truth at the same level of understanding in the same moment, for our perceptions are all different. The destination is the same for all, but the journey by which we attain it is unique and the timeline for our unfolding is based so much on our ability to enter the inner world of our Selves. It is perhaps unfortunate that so much of modern life is out-wardly focused, teasing us away from the journey, until that moment when God calls and says, 'it is your time.'

Understanding Jesus' Teaching

At this point, we need to look at the words of Jesus' teaching at the head of this chapter, repeated here for ease of reference.

> Jesus said,
> > 'Happy are the monakos and the chosen
> > for you shall find the Kingdom
> > Because you are from the heart of it,
> > you shall return there again.'
>
> *The Gospel of Thomas*

As I was working with my clients in the first few years of the new century, occasionally, as I was connected very deeply within an individual's consciousness, the Guidance would speak. It would say, 'This is a Chosen One.' I would ask, 'What is a Chosen One?' and they would reply, 'You are not ready to know'. The answer is always all around you, but it is that your vibration is not yet at the right level to perceive it. One day, I read the above teaching of Jesus in the Gospel of Thomas, which I had read many times before, but this time, I was ready to perceive and the light came through immediately.

At the beginning of the Gospel of Thomas, Jesus says, '*He who finds the hidden meaning in these logia (words) shall find life independent of death.*' I cannot tell you what the experience is like when you suddenly perceive the hidden meaning. There is such an instant level of inner knowing that you are suddenly raised to a place where you perceive and feel the truth of all that is. There can be no mistake, no doubting, just acceptance and thanks pouring forth from every cell of your being, for the momentary illumination. This process is called 'confirmation'. When The Guidance told me I was not ready to know what The Chosen Ones were, it really meant: 'soon you will find the answer you are looking for and it will come in a form that will present 'no doubt' for you that you have touched truth.' However, the truth can then often raise more questions than it answers.

To understand the saying we have to look at it carefully. Forget the word Monakos for a moment. We know what it means, but just drop it from the teaching and you are left with,

Happy are the chosen

The next line says,

for you shall find the Kingdom

Whoa, slow down, now that raises a big question. Does it mean that some people will *not* find the Kingdom? Well, it sure does, most certainly in this lifetime. Take a look around you, how many people are awakening. You don't have to look far to be able to work out how many are in such a deep programme that there is not much chance of awakening any time soon. However, to take this a step deeper, many people have not come through to this lifetime with awakening as part of their mission. They are on some other learning experience, therefore, we don't need to worry too much whether they will awaken in time to catch this particular Ascension. The Third Book of Revelation will also explain more about this and there is an extract at the end of this chapter. We are now coming into the realm of understanding a lot more about humanity and evolution and how that fits with the Ascension. In this time of acceleration, as we have already seen, there will be a split between those who awaken and those who become too rigid and fail to awaken. Those who awaken will at least attain the path at some level.

The Ascension is a great uplifting wave of consciousness and, as any surfer will tell you, sometimes you just can't get up enough speed to catch the wave. Those people will not find the Kingdom in this particular cycle of time, as we shift from one age to another. They will not be able to let go sufficiently from everything that they are attached to and, therefore, will not attain a fast enough vibrational speed to break away from the old patterning, which holds humanity prisoner at this time. However, great hope and assistance is constantly being held out by the Universe.

The saying goes on ...

> Because you are from the heart of it,
> you shall return there again.

Next question. Is everyone not from the heart of the Kingdom, then? The Answer is, no, they are not, but The Chosen Ones have been there. They have also chosen to return to help others, because they are from the heart of the Kingdom, they shall return there again, because they have the knowing of how to get there.

The Great Cycle of Time
In the Great Cycle of Time, we explained the unfolding process from the Unity of consciousness, moving into Separation and then back to Unity again. This explains the answer to this question above. The Chosen Ones have made that complete journey before. They have emerged from God, learned how to attain Christ Consciousness and returned to Unity. They have sat on the Right Hand of God. That is why they have been chosen to be the guides and facilitators to those who are awakening in this period of entry into the Age of Aquarius, during this present Great Cycle of Time. But in order to do this, they must come to earth as ordinary people and be seen to grow from ordinary roots, learning how to become God, so that all may be able to recognise and associate with them, having observed their journey.

The Second Coming of the Christ Light

We are in the period of the second coming of Christ, but it is a different age to when He first appeared. His method of arrival will not be the same. When Jesus arrived at the dawning of the age of Pisces, He brought the light of spirit into the earth plane for all to experience. He was the sower of the seeds of light, casting them upon the world and guarding them until they were ablaze. Those seeds are now germinating and emerging in so many of you. His coming at that time was the first act of bringing Heaven to Earth. Heaven is now sewn into earth in many humans. The nature of His coming this time will be through the lives of ordinary people, for Jesus was a carpenter and an ordinary person until his own transformation in the desert over forty days and nights.

He will not come as one man, but emerge in many men and women simultaneously, for the man was only a symbol of the consciousness. His words and teachings were the Christ-consciousness speaking through the man. The man was just a man, the consciousness that he radiated was that of God or Universal Consciousness. God, Jesus or the Christ Light, whatever you want to call it, is now emerging in men and women the world over and at some point those who feel this will have to acknowledge it as that light burns in their centre, for otherwise there will be denial.

There will be a mass awakening of the Christ Consciousness within ordinary people. It is said that the crucial number will be 144,000 who will be illuminated enough in order to radiate the awakening light to others. As we need to ascend quickly, we will need to experience a lot of transformation. Now, Jesus once said something to the tune of, 'I could transform the whole world in three days, but few would survive it.' What he was referring to here is the intensity of his light to transform original darkness. As the darkness within becomes illuminated, then you begin to transform, but also, as the darkness becomes illuminated, the fear within that darkness is illuminated in overwhelming proportions. That process is often too much for the human form to bear and thus you would not survive it.

The light is emerging from within, rather than being cast upon you from without, as Jesus did with the disciples. But the fire within is burning away the limitation to your recognising it for what it is. A little at a time, we might say, Jesus is igniting that light within many, but especially The Chosen Ones and Accelerated Masters and as that light radiates from them, so it will awaken all those who are ready to be attracted to it, to open to it and to receive its rays.

The Chosen Ones are also what some will call The Christed Ones; those who have agreed to carry that light with all it entails, to be awakened by the Christ Consciousness from within, so that they might assist and uplift humanity out of the darkness of ignorance and into the light of truth. Out of poverty into truth.

If we take another of Jesus' sayings from The Gospel of Thomas, it reiterates everything that we share with you here.

> Jesus said,
>> 'If they say to you:
>> "Where are you from?"
>> say to them:
>> "We came from the Light
>> there, where the Light was
>> by itself.
>> It stood boldly
>> and manifested itself in their image."
>>
>> If they say to you:
>> "Who are you?"
>> say: "we are his sons
>> and we are the chosen of the living father."'

The Chosen Ones are learning how to be God, so that they can encourage the others to let go and learn how to be the same. Thus, we will all once more return to the unity of consciousness, which is what we refer to as God.

Summary

We are learning to understand about Accelerated Masters and Chosen Ones.

If you resonate with the descriptions, then you will know who you are and why you are here. Therefore, you cannot deny your mission to help uplift humanity, for to deny it is to break your agreement with God.

We are understanding that The Chosen Ones are those in whom the Christ Consciousness is awakening very quickly.

We are understanding that the same opportunities will be levied upon both the Accelerated Masters and The Chosen Ones in order to raise an army of light to assist the millions who will begin to awaken in the coming years of the new age.

Both groups are here to unfold their consciousness as quickly as possible so that they can don the mantle of Teachers, Guides and Facilitators, to those who are awakening and searching for their own answers to evolution of consciousness.

Their teaching, for the most part, will be given from within, through remembrance, guidance and illumination to truth from the emerging inner light. Their teaching will come from insight, but then confirmed by some method so that they can learn to trust what comes from within. Those who have been chosen for this mission will be pushed through many trials and tribulations, for to have such a light begin to emerge within you is a very difficult journey indeed. Many would consider that to have the Christ Light unfold within the heart would bring peace and love into your life. On the contrary, the light reveals truth and exposes the darkness, which lies beyond your awareness within and that is a most difficult and painful process to experience, although the unfolding rewards in terms of ascending are limitless.

Jesus said,
'I could transform the whole world in 3 days,
but few would survive it.'

Revelation III – The Third Book of the Apocalypse

7. "And the sky was filled with a great light and out of the light came forth many beings known and unknown. And they marvelled and asked, "What is this that fills our eyes?".

8. "And the angel Michael said, "These are they who have walked with the Father and are ascended, even to the throne".

9. "They are of the 144,000 children of the first born and are of every tongue and of every nation. For the risen Christ is in their heart, that the word may be fulfilled".

10. "And they carry the sign of the second coming of the Lamb, which is the prophesy of the resurrection. And all will be gathered unto the sacred city, being of one consciousness and of one family".

11. "And you will know the Christ, which is descended and made one with all who are of the sign."

12. "And they will make the sign to one another and they will know themselves pure in the Blood of the Lamb."

13. "And they will rejoice, for the Christ is descended from the Higher planes even to the darkest corner of the earth. For none will know fear, for the Christ is within."

14. "And the Cherubim will stand guard no more. And the gates of paradise will be opened and all will dwell there in the purity of Love."

15. "And the boundary of paradise will be the boundary of the City, which is of gold. Thus will end the cycle at the very instant of the second coming of the Christ consciousness."

Extract of *Revelation III, The Third Book of the Apocalypse.*
Courtesy of: www.wholisticworldvision.org

17

The Message

Jesus said,
'When you make the two One,
you will become Sons of man
and if you say:
Mountain move away,
it shall move.'

The Gospel of Thomas

You have already responded to the call, probably in many ways, if you have got this far in the book, but you probably have little idea how high is the purpose to which you are being called. The call is your wake-up call, but how much are you going to wake up? You have been allowed to sleep for perhaps many hundreds of lifetimes as you have drifted slowly into and through your evolution as a soul. In more recent lifetimes there will have been a little more activity, perhaps, but now is the time to really wake up. This is the big one, the final lifetime before the year 2012 when the period of Ascension accelerates towards its zenith. In many other lifetimes you will have had more choice than now. Choice is now extremely limited. Now is the time of no excuses, for when you make an excuse as a Chosen One or an Accelerated Master, you are making it directly to God — and, it just doesn't work anymore. Because there is no time now, God throws it straight back at you, always in a way, which causes difficulty or pain, because it is through adversity that we learn and grow. If we are not challenged, we do not progress. Now is the time for action, not excuses.

'But', I hear you say, 'God is a benevolent God.' Yes, you are right. His benevolence with those of you who have been called is all about waking you up so that you can find your way to his side more quickly than the rest. Any pain or suffering you receive is created by yourself as a direct reflection of your own denial of the inner calling. You only receive the reflected difficulty and pain in direct proportion to your denial of the light being offered to you. They are merely a reflection of what you are ignoring. It is the difficulty and pain of your separation from the God within you that is trying to emerge in this Ascension Period. If you attempt to prevent that emergence, through the denial of what is really happening, then the reflection always appears to be adversity.

The Message
The Call is about walking the path into the evolution of your consciousness. The Message is that you must now take responsibility to be all that you can be. Allow the light to emerge within you. Stop resisting the light and allow it to come forth from within. The seed of light was sown 2,000 years ago, in the Age of Pisces and is now bursting forth and emerging within you. Do not hinder its emergence.

> The Message is:
> It is time to take Responsibility.
> Take Responsibility for your Life.
> Take Responsibility and be Guided.
> Take Responsibility and take Action.
> Take Action to be all that you can be.
> Your Evolution is Your Responsibility.

Take Responsibility to be All That You Can Be
What do we really mean when we talk about the fast changing energies of these times? Well, the higher your vibration, the more easily the new and challenging energies of every day will transform your consciousness. Some are saying that each new year we enter as we close upon 2012 will bring a doubling of intensity of the unfolding energies. But the way the energy affects you depends on your vibration. Those with a low vibration will only be touched a little, because of the density within their own energy systems. Those with a higher vibration will respond more readily in the way they perceive reality. The higher the vibration, the less the resistance to light. This is why we encourage you to take action now. The more you can raise your vibration the more you will attain in terms of conscious shift in this period and the easier you will align with the changes that are coming for humanity. In turn, the more you can align, the more you will perceive the truth behind these world changes. The signs of change are everywhere, but the perception of what they truly mean can be difficult to understand until your vibration

reaches a point where you can see above the collective consciousness level of current world interpretation of the events. In order to perceive, you have to remove yourself as much as possible from the collective consciousness and this allows your perception to raise. If you can drive your vibration upwards at the same time, then you will begin to perceive the new reality as it is dawning and this will allow you time to adapt to the changes, rather than be plunged into the fear of change as it happens around you.

Do not worry, but learn how to go with the flow and adapt to the change. It is true, there will be much fear, but at the same time the fear will be caused because the people do not trust that they will be guided.

Imagination, a Key to Evolution

How can people be guided if they have never learned these gifts? Therein lies our limitation. If we don't use imagination, then we are lost. Imagination is one of the keys to evolution. Almost every day that goes by could bring a new insight or vision of reality, which knocks yesterday's understanding out of the window. If your consciousness is free to experience change, then change can be served upon you.

As we speed towards 2012, every tomorrow will offer limitless opportunities to experience reality differently. Dare you take a ride into the unknown? That is what is being placed before you. If you can let go of the security blankets you keep around your life, if you can detach, totally, from everything that you do and everything that you are, especially the way you create your own identity and how you attach that identity to the life, which surrounds you, then it is possible to become what the universe wishes to offer you. However, you do not know what that is, because it has probably not been created into our experience of reality yet. For every ounce of attachment you let go of, the light stimulates your imagination in individual ways that allow you to create your own future. Guidance has given me many, many world firsts to help ordinary people empower themselves and unlock their evolutionary potential and I can tell you, I could not have imagined any of them only a few years ago. Some of the techniques behind the way evolutionary light is brought into play for humanity are so bizarre, that if I told you how it worked you would think I was mad. In order to work with light at a high level, you need to be brought into it one step at a time in order to learn how to trust at a higher level. To merely step in is almost an impossibility as the concepts challenge too much. People who have done much spiritual work naturally think, 'how hard can it be?', but when the Universal Consciousness begins to play with you, that is when you realise you cannot walk the path alone.

The pathway is one which continually unfolds as the emerging light illuminates you. That light stimulates and then illuminates tiny seeds of possibility and if your mind is sharp enough to grasp them and your courage strong enough to act upon what is being offered from inside, then you will experience the creation of things that you could not have imagined only a short time before. But once the seed becomes illuminated, then you may become the creator and breathe life into it, guiding that seed into whatever the God consciousness is revealing to you. We are all surfing the wave of the future and nobody knows what that will be, but you can bet your money on two strong possibilities: it will be exciting and it will constantly challenge you to change.

Opening to Evolution

As you begin to work with healing energy, whether you know it or not, you are beginning to open the doors to *your* evolution, to *your* future, and to play *your* part in the Divine Plan, which you agreed to before you incarnated this time. Not only are you opening the doors to your evolution, but you are being asked to accelerate it in return for the gifts, which you are given. Your attunement or training in the various healing practises are merely the beginning, the first step into light. When you take that first step, that is when you say to your deeper self that you are ready. Everything, which comes after that first step is served upon you so that you can move more dynamically and energetically in opening your Self to Light.

Accelerate Your Evolution

Just as a flower senses the time to begin to emerge from the earth in spring as it responds to the changing energy of the earth cycles, those of us who have already been walking the path of light for some time sense the changes in every single day. Some days the energy is so high that it almost lifts you out of your physical consciousness and the next day everything can be extremely heavy. These are the contractions, the birth pangs of a new age. The sensitives among us feel the elation; the depression and the urgency swinging and varying on a daily basis. It affects us deeply, sometimes to the point where we feel we cannot go on, but we must.

A call to healing or to work with other humans is never anything less than a call to learn about your Self and that is the first place you begin on your journey. It is your time to blossom in this lifetime and take your place in the march into the light of Higher Consciousness. It is your time to be taught how to ascend and for some of you, much of this path will unfold quickly as you remember what you already know from previous lives. Coupled with this remembering of old, you will begin to learn about your Self at a deeper level in this life and as the two aspects of you merge you will eventually develop a great understanding of why you are here. At that point, you won't need me to tell you, but right now, maybe you do.

Opening the Doors

This is where healing energies such as the Reiki Light are so important in the grand scheme of things. As I have said previously, Reiki is a door opener for thousands of people. Reiki is the energy, which is calling to so many at this time, and has been since the 1980s. It is the perfect frequency to attract you. Just as moths are attracted to the light of a bulb in the darkness, so those who are awakening will often be called to Reiki as the first step towards the light of truth. When you understand how the Secret Agenda, or the Awakening Call works, you begin to discover that you don't accidentally find such things as Reiki, they are put in your path so that you fall over them, surprise, surprise. You then say to yourself, look what I have discovered. Once Reiki or any one of dozens of similar modalities of healing or energy work have opened the doors within you, the Universe can then guide you to the next thing that it wants you to experience and learn from. Look at the massive world-wide awakening we have experienced since the mid 1980s. There has never been a period of awakening like it. Day by day, it is picking up momentum. People move from that initial step, such as Reiki, to experience many aspects of energy or lightwork. It is all planned this way by the God-consciousness and Higher Guidance within you. Some of you may think that you have not found what you are looking for yet and you would be right if that is how you feel. If that inner guidance is still pushing you to seek, then you have not yet acquired all the tools or experiences you need in order to enter the next part of your Ascension.

More Illusion

You can't attune 20 people to Reiki and expect them all to have the same experience, for the God-consciousness within them is attempting to guide them to experience their own uniqueness by opening them to their own individual journeys.

When you have worked with light for a while, this, believe it or not, is the point at which so many people lose their way. They open themselves to the light and the light then begins to show them their limitations. This is where the big evolutionary problems begin to occur. Rather than going beyond their limitations, most people succumb to them and allow them to govern their lives, rather than digging deep to find the courage to overcome them. They become prisoners of themselves and continue to limit themselves by failing to see the potential, which lies untapped within them. In reality, most people become completely locked at a certain vibrational and thus, evolutionary level, by the issues, which have come up and begun to dominate their lives. They go into complete denial, pretending that the issue will go away, which it doesn't, for it is there to be overcome. Different people have different issues—hundreds of them—and what tends to happen is that life starts to go wrong when you are not facing these challenges. It not only goes wrong once, but it continues to go wrong until you face the issue. I have seen many, many people lose everything before facing the issue. The Guidance calls it hitting the wall. When you hit the wall, then you have no choice other than to look inwards to overcome the current limitation. I must be a slow learner, because I hit it twice, once in my late twenties and then again in my late thirties. Both times I lost everything, except the rented van that I slept in on the motorway service area, that first night of the second event. Shortly afterwards, my awakening began to accelerate very quickly. If you can't, or don't listen, then God just keeps taking it all away until you learn how to pay attention. It's very effective, I assure you, but the choice is yours. Listen up or hit the wall.

What You Resist Will Persist

Another problem is that once you have been called and the doors into light have been opened, you can't close those doors again. You reach a point where you begin to understand that there is no longer any choice. When you made that original step into healing light, you triggered what is called The Evolutionary Cycle, which determines that there is no going back. We'll talk more about this later.

Before incarnation you choose whether you are going to enter awakening in this life, therefore, at a higher conscious level, you know there is no going back. Also, now that I've told you about the Calling, you also know how this works. So, although we think we have free will and in a certain context we do, in reality we don't because that light will continually push us to evolve. Remember we are offered the choice to step forward before we are chosen, we were not forced to take this path. We are only chosen if God knows that we are truly ready. If we then exercise our free will and ignore what the light is asking us to look at, then it will persist in bringing the lesson until we have learned it. You can walk away any time you want, but you need to remember that whatever you resist will persist. Once the doors of light have been opened you will be pursued by light until you take responsibility and learn ever more about how the great illusion works. This is your path to freedom and enlightenment and that is why God makes it very difficult for you to sabotage it, though people do try very hard.

Jesus said,
'Happy are they who have been pursued in the heart.
It is they who have Known the Father in Truth.'

The Gospel of Thomas

Now I can hear you saying, as you try to figure out the chaos at present in your life, 'But, I can't possibly have agreed to this.' I often consider that preparing for incarnation must be a time of some excitement and euphoria, perhaps a little akin to getting ready to parachute out of a plane (not that I have ever done that). You can imagine girding up your loins to step out into that free-fall space of exhilaration. It is perhaps also like being with your friends in the pub after a few drinks and agreeing to meet up the following day to tackle something quite extreme, like a good ramble up a 4,000 ft mountain. The following morning of sobriety arrives, you feel the weight of toxins in your system, you consider what you have agreed to and you think you must have been mad. Of course, you weren't, you were only slightly out of your mind with intoxication or euphoria, a place where reality seems so much simpler than it is.

You need to understand that it was not you who chose this time to accelerate your evolution. You may have agreed to it and said to yourself that you were ready for it, but it is God who chose this time for you. It is God who pursued you in the heart and drew you to something, which excited you. He chose the moment that you would find your teacher and find the light. Once this process has begun, God will be working with you every single moment of the rest of this lifetime to help you unlock who you really are and why you are here now. If you don't hear the messages or you ignore the signs and signals being placed before you, then you could be in for a very rough ride.

Take Action

Once you step onto the path, there is no going back, so get used to that right now. You now have to take responsibility for driving your life forward. You need to be proactive, always looking at what is happing in your life, always evaluating every situation. If difficult situations come your way, then that is

God trying to teach you. If you are not achieving what you need to, at the speed which was agreed prior to incarnation, then more lessons will be brought in quick succession. Difficulty in life is always about God trying to awaken you to what you are ready to learn.

We are within the End Time Period and approaching the End Time very quickly. Everything will speed up year on year. Just look back for a moment at how much has changed since the 1980s. We didn't have personal computers or mobile cell phones, which can connect you via satellites to almost anywhere in the world; we didn't have DVDs or plasma TVs. We didn't have internet, let alone broadband, which again can connect anyone anywhere and also access information like never before. They are all part of the acceleration into the next phase of consciousness. We need answers quicker than ever. Look how fast the technology is moving. The technology can only move this fast if man's imagination is speeding up. You need to work extremely hard upon yourself in order to attain the crest of the wave of these accelerating times, but the rewards are incalculable.

One Step at a Time
So, you think that this is a tall order, do you? You think that the demands that the Universe will place on you in these coming years is perhaps a little unreal, or at least beyond any realistic level of expectation? If I said to you, God expects you to learn how to become God, you probably would think that impossible, but it isn't and it really isn't a tall order. It is the truth of what is coming, especially for The Chosen Ones. The reason it is not impossible is that it is a one-step-at-a-time process. The journey begins by looking inwards and finding out who you are, by learning to listen to your heart. In no time at all you will be moving forward on your path. But you will find it very difficult without someone to guide and teach you from time to time. Let's remind ourselves of the Mystic, Rumi's words, 'Whoever enters the way without a guide will take a hundred years to travel a 2 day journey!' Why do you think this is so? The answer is that in order to enter the way, or walk the path entails a completely different way of thinking than is programmed into the minds of humanity. We are programmed as people, not as Gods and so we need to not only learn how to think, do, be and perceive differently in order to see through the illusion and perceive truth, but we need to begin to lose our minds that are programmed that way. Losing your mind is a very scary process, but again, it comes one step at a time and when you touch into that 'Fear of Losing My Mind', you will know what I mean.

First step into healing and learn how to do it. As you work with the healing rays they will begin to transform you. You will begin to see, know and do things that you haven't experienced before and you will begin to open up as your intuition is fired by the healing light as it pursues you in the heart.

Your Mission

At this point, these words are specifically for you, the reader. Make no mistake, this message is for you. If it was not meant for you, you would not be here right now, reading it.

Your mission in this life is that you have been chosen as one of a group of individuals to lead humanity into the higher realms of consciousness as they unfold for us during this next few years. You have a very definite and important role to play in the Ascension of Man.

You are here to help people. You are here first of all as a healer. There are many paths of healing. Merely talking to someone is healing work. You are here to uplift others. You have been given certain gifts and talents, which will help you do this. The knowledge of these gifts is within your heart. The more you listen to your heart, the more you will hear it saying things like, 'You can do this.' Your heart will constantly be telling you what it is you came here to do. It is the God-consciousness within the heart, which is pursuing you to hear the message from within your Self. The only thing that prevents you from doing what your heart tells you is possible, is your own inaction, which is always deliberate self-sabotage. There is no more time for inaction. You have been called because you *can* do it. You *can* uplift others in some way.

At this point you will be thinking either that the writer is completely mad and you will put the book down, or you will be intrigued to know more and will continue. It doesn't matter, which of these you do right now, but, if you put the book down you will be sabotaging your future. That doesn't mean that you won't be able to catch up later, but it does mean that you are going to make a lot more work for yourself in the interim period. And, as for the writer, his ideas may just seem a little, 'off the wall' to some, but the application of his particular brand of magic is extremely powerful and very successful. His imagination is constantly learning how to dissolve the artificial boundaries of the illusion of our perceived reality and thus go beyond this limitation. His life is constantly letting go of the moorings and sailing on a new voyage of discovery. Unlike Cortez and Columbus, this is a voyage, which helps people to find their own treasure within and it sets them free to live within the beauty of it.

If you continue to read this book, then I am absolutely certain that you *will* discover who you are and why you are here; I am certain that you *will* become empowered. You *will* discover the pathway to your true mission and you *will* begin to understand how successful you can be. Please take note, that success is programmed into your heart, especially so if you have been called. If you have been called, then you cannot fail. Failure is not an option. There is no such thing.

Eventually, you will begin to understand and feel the Christ Light emerging within you. You will begin to understand about the End Time and what it means for the Ascension of human consciousness. You will begin to understand all the far-out ideas in this book and how it all applies to you and your life. You will come to know all these things because they will be revealed to you through your own pathway of revelation and when it comes from within, then you absolutely know that it is the truth. And, as that inner knowing burns within you, then you will move mountains.

Summary:
The message for you at this very moment in time goes something like this:

It is now your time to awaken.
It is now your time to evolve.

You are expected to learn detachment.
You are expected to continually transform into higher states of perfection.

Becoming detached allows your transformation.
If you hold on to things, you won't transform.
Learn to let go and become free.

You are here to raise your vibration.
You are here to carry increasing amounts of light.

As your light increases you will continually transform.
As you continually transform your hidden gifts and talents will emerge.

You have been given your Gifts and Talents to help you through life.
You are expected to earn your living through your God-given Gifts and Talents.

You are here to uplift and empower others.
You are here to help others discover themselves.

You are here to become a teacher and a leader.
You are here to lead humanity into higher consciousness.

You are here to play your part in the great Ascension into Light.
You have been called to assist all seekers to find the God
within themselves.

But first, you have to seek the God within your own Self.

You are here to learn how to go beyond captivity.
You are here to learn how to become free of mind.

You are here to allow the light to emerge within you.
The light is within the deepest part of your heart.

The light is the God-consciousness.
The light is the Light of Creation.

You are here to learn how to Create with Light.
You are here to learn how to Create with God.

Allow the Light of God within you to begin to Create Your Life.

Take responsibility for your life.
Take responsibility for your journey.

Learn how to become God.

And then move a mountain – just because you can.

18

The Laws of Evolution

Whoever enters the way without a guide will take
a hundred years to travel a two day journey

Rumi

Before you even begin to 'enter the way,' as Rumi terms it, or walk the path of evolution as we say today, it is imperative that you understand The Laws of Evolution, which we touched upon at the end of Part One. These are so fundamental and important that if you don't know and understand them, you will continually struggle to find your direction.

The overall keys to success are how to understand and achieve evolution in the least difficult or stressful way. Evolution is a big subject and there are, no doubt, thousands of books, which will give you instruction on what it's all about and how to achieve it through various practices. What you really need, though, is a practical understanding of how to keep things simple. For example, I have never seen a book, which tells you what to expect or exactly what happens as Spiritual Light begins to touch your life. We will be looking at this later.

Historically, people sought out the Guru and sat with them for years, learning the practices and obtaining the wisdom a little at a time. However, in the predicament we are in now, there is no time for this 'life-mission' approach. That does not mean this approach is not valuable and certainly, many are drawn to this path. But with the redistribution of the centres of light around the planet, with a more uplifting spiritual light now focussed on the west, whilst the left-brained industrial energy is focusing on the east, you will find growing centres of spiritual learning on your doorstep, so you don't have to trek half way round the world, unless of course, you want to.

Because of the acceleration of Universal Consciousness the spiritual seeker doesn't have to sit in a cave for thirty years any more. You can do it 'now,' and instead of using the Guru as a sounding board to see how you are progressing, you use your own heart. The heart will tell you everything you need to know. Just learn to listen to it. You are the *new* Guru.

The God-consciousness is trying to guide you into evolution and the God-consciousness is within the core of the heart, so your heart will not guide you in the wrong direction if it wants you to succeed. Only *you* will guide you in the wrong direction, if you don't learn to listen to your heart. A good spiritual teacher will teach you this as one of the first lessons. However, lessons and Laws are two different things. Although, there is no doubt that learning the lessons can be difficult at times, at least walking the path in the right direction should be relatively easy with the right guidance.

The Laws of Evolution

Before even setting out, it would be wise to understand The Laws of Evolution. However, as with many other things, both practical and spiritual, they don't seem to be written down anywhere! Try finding them. The whereabouts of The Laws of Evolution are as mysterious as the great mystery of life itself, it would seem. Before we look at The Laws, let's just revisit that saying of Chuang Tzu:

> Easy is right,
> Begin right and you are easy,
> Continue easy and you are right,
> The right way to go easy,
> Is to forget the right way,
> And forget that the going is easy.

The message in this poem is, 'Just do it, and trust that you can'. It is all about simplicity. For example, manuals and rule books are good to help you get started and understand the basic principles of what you are trying to learn, especially if you are learning a particular modality of healing work, but after that they become a limitation. As intuitive healers, you cannot use anything, which causes you limitation, otherwise you will not unfold your gifts. If something is difficult in the manual, then find a way to simplify it. The right way to go is easy. Easy is always right.

THE LAWS OF EVOLUTION

1. **The First Law of Evolution:**
   You cannot Walk the Path Alone.

2. **The Second Law of Evolution:**
   You need to Learn to Reach Out for Help.

3. **The Third Law of Evolution:**
   Act Immediately upon any impulse from the Heart,
   and the Universe responds immediately.

4. **The Fourth Law of Evolution:**
   Through Uplifting Others, So You Become Uplifted Yourself.

5. **The Fifth Law of Evolution:**
   The Power is Never Yours to Own

Did anybody ever teach you these Laws? No, that's right, they didn't. Why not? Because, nobody seems to know or understand them and they don't seem to exist in books! Or at least, I've not been able to find them.

Where did I get them from then and how do I know that these are indeed The Laws of Evolution? I gained the knowledge of them and how they work, through experience as many lessons and trials were sent to me in order that I might work them out for myself. I was not aware at the time that the lessons were of the nature of the evolution of human consciousness, but that is what they proved to be. The Universe continued to hit me with difficulty after difficulty until I learned. It was a non-stop bombardment. Eventually, through trial and error, I was guided to understand and ascend the difficulties. I might say that there were many patterns within patterns and many dozens of experiences, which led to the understanding of The Laws, but when you Know them and you put them into practice and help others to put them into practice, they become self-evident. I might say that in retrospect, I was guided to discover The Laws of the Evolution of Human Consciousness. But why should that fall to me? Why should I be chosen to reveal them for what they are? The answer is, why not?

Why did Sir Isaac Newton discover the Laws of Motion and the Universal Law of Gravitation? Why did Einstein discover the Theories of Relativity? Why did Ernest Rutherford discover that he could change one element to another by an artificial nuclear reaction? It was not because they were famous scientists that these Laws and Theories were bestowed upon them. It was because they were ordinary people seeking the answers to questions, which their imagination was fertile enough to present to them. Through constant seeking and probing, these ordinary men became extraordinary men, bringing to the world new things to challenge and push the minds of their contemporaries.

> Few are those who see with their own eyes
> and feel with their own hearts.
>
> Albert Einstein

Einstein was a profoundly spiritually-connected man as can be deduced from his writings. Newton was also interested in the esoteric, using astrology amongst other tools, which can be seen within his research work. So, why should an ordinary person labouring in the spiritual field not discover or be given an opportunity to learn how The Universal Laws work, especially if Universal Consciousness knows that they would share them immediately with anyone who had a desire to use them for Ascension? What is common to these scientists was that they were 'open' to experiment and discovery. They would act upon their inner impulses and drives. They had great imaginations and imagination is the key to the door of reality. Someone had to reveal the simplicity of evolutionary processes to help all those who are ready for Ascension at this time of Ascension. There would not be much point bringing these Laws to Earth in another two hundred years time. We need the knowledge now and we need it in a simplistic form. When you can unburden your Self from limitation you will see what is being offered to you.

> The true value of a human being is determined primarily
> by the measure and the sense in which he has attained
> to liberation from the self.
>
> Albert Einstein

The First Law of Evolution:
You cannot Walk the Path Alone.

Why can you not walk the path alone? There are many, many reasons, but essentially, because at a higher level of consciousness we are all one. How can you be alone if we are all one? You can't. As you begin to rise up the evolutionary ladder as your vibration rises, although you remain separate as in your physical body, you become more connected to the oneness of every-thing at a spiritual level, or what we might call, 'entering the conscious state of unity.' Therefore, the higher you ascend up the ladder, the less you func-tion separately in terms of your conscious performance. So, you cannot walk the path to the ultimate destination and remain separate, or alone. The sooner you understand this Law and begin to apply it to your own seeking venture, the sooner you will attain ascendancy into higher spiritual light.

The second reason this Law applies is that many people over many cen-turies have attained a high status in spiritual terms. This has often been achieved through serious and somewhat rigid privations.

A true spiritual teacher is one who has already walked the path; already learned how the Laws function through experience. What is the point in trying to walk it alone if someone else has all the answers you seek? Keep it simple; go easy. This would be like setting off on an expedition to find the North Pole without reading all the history and directions how to get there. Nothing short of Madness! Again, we are in different times right now and so the old ways are being superseded by the acceleration of consciousness and new ideas. The old ways are there if you want them, but we don't have time. We need to unlock our consciousness very quickly and this is why so many new teachers will develop in these times. Keep it simple, use the new tech-nologies.

Thirdly, the Light within the consciousness of a Spiritual Teacher is a great tool to align yourself with at certain times on your journey. That Light will penetrate your own consciousness and bring illumination to the problems and difficulties you may face, the limitation that you struggle to go beyond. A Spiritual Teacher has the power to open what needs to be opened within you. One step at a time, the Teacher can see what is the next blockage to overcome on your path. Your consciousness always presents the difficulties in a specific order. The teacher can see that order when they look deep within you. If you know what the issue or blockage is as a result of consulting with the Teacher, then you can accelerate your learning process. Also, it is worth considering that when you are drawn to a certain teacher or practice, it is often your inner guidance asking you merely to touch into the light of that person or thing. Merely being in the presence of a person who radiates light can trigger a powerful shift in your consciousness.

The Second Law of Evolution:
You need to Learn to Reach Out for Help.

The key word in this Law is *Learn*. Do you know that humans can be the dumbest of the dumb when life gets difficult. They doggedly continue to walk the path of disaster rather than ask someone for help. I bet you've seen this in action when you are lost in a car with someone. Will the driver ask for help? No. They just keep going, saying, they will find the way in a minute.

The trick with this Law is learning *when* you need that help. For most of the time you might be cruising along through life just fine, then one day you find that life is taking a bit of a downturn. Things are going wrong. Clients maybe dropping off. There is disharmony or disaster at every turn. This is the time you need the help of someone who has walked the path. You can guarantee that if there are a series of things going wrong in life then it is God trying to bring your attention to something that you are not getting right. That is the time to seek help and guidance, so that you can discover what it is that you are not hearing or learning.

At some level, you may know what the lesson is, but it is often clarity and confirmation you need in order to understand it. At first, it might not be obvious that a certain thing you are doing or not doing is the cause of the problem, but when guidance is sought, then the answers will be there for you to work with. Again, what is the point in struggling when somebody has the answer you are looking for. Keep it simple.

Bringing Humanity Together
You cannot walk the path alone, so don't try, is really the message from the oneness of all that is, where this Law is concerned. What Rumi is saying at the head of this chapter is that once you 'enter the way,' the diversion into separation cannot continue as you walk a higher path. The light is withheld from you if you don't work with The Laws. The whole process of Ascension is about bringing humanity together at a conscious level; about bringing the consciousness of spiritual seekers into a state of single communion where the power of thought and desire is more focused on a common vision, but expressed in a unique way through the individual. The vision is as yet unseen, as most people have not raised their vibration and consciousness high enough to perceive it. Although thousands have moved upwards in this recent period of awakening, the mass of the old consciousness is still on the other end of the seesaw, weighing it down. The awakened ones do not yet have enough weight to tip the seesaw into the new direction of the new vision, but it is coming.

Approaching Unity

To some degree, you are awaiting the incoming energies, which will show you the new vision; show you, in fact, how to create the new vision from within your own consciousness. As well as coming together at a higher spiritual level, consider telepathy, for example, which may unfold in these next few years. It is also the desire of the Plan of Creation to come together as physical beings in uplifting each other into the oneness of a perfect world. The key word then is Unity. We are all headed towards Unity both spiritually, in terms of consciousness and physically, in terms of collaboration towards the vision of a more perfect world.

Some Spiritual Teachers will have already seen aspects of this vision and even live it in part. I, for one, have not only seen the vision, but been given some fantastic tools, the like of which the world has never seen, which will help to unlock human consciousness and help carry us forward in pursuit of the skills to create the new vision. I am creating it daily with these tools, and also empowering others to do the same. The new tools and spiritual structures are being put in place, which will uplift thousands in the first instance and then millions. People will be able to step forth into their evolution *en masse*. I know that many new things are being prepared for us as we enter the new age, but the time is not quite right yet for the majority to avail themselves of these new tools; but you, the reader of this book are ready and the tools are at your disposal. All you have to do is find the courage within to try things out and then you will discover the magic, which awaits you as the Universe pours light into your being and begins to accelerate your consciousness.

I have tried and tested these powerful spiritual tools for mass awakening over a number of years to great effect and with tremendous success. The knowledge is with us now, but the consciousness of humanity at large is not ready to see the beauty and simplicity of it. To most people, the concepts of how I work in unlocking the evolutionary potential within people is too bizarre to contemplate, too far-fetched to imagine. But, I have used these tools and technologies with thousands of spiritual seekers and the results are always one hundred percent effective. In fact, The Guidance guarantees the success.

Individuals who seek enlightenment are one thing, they are ready and being driven, or pursued in the heart, from within. They know they are on a mission and when they find the answer that the inner guidance is trying to bring to them, they recognise it immediately through their inner knowing. The heart speaks to them. But the collective consciousness of humanity is truly not ready yet. This period of acceleration is bringing changes daily, though and I can see things moving in the right direction very quickly. As I write, in July 2008, I have witnessed an incredible acceleration since the beginning of 2007 and I consider that by 2009 we could see the mass awakening speeding up dramatically. The first of many could be taking advantage of some of these existing processes for the evolution of consciousness and of other new things that might have been given to us by that time. Many opportunities are still undreamt of at this time. All you need in order to overcome disbelief is an open mind. If something works for you, then it works, if it doesn't, then move on, but if you are not open to possibility in the first place, then how are you ever going to experience change or evolution?

Never say Never
We can never say never where the Universe or The Laws are concerned. Certainly, these Laws seem to be absolute in the way they function. If you seek help, then it is always delivered in some way or other. The Laws operate very strongly in your life when you apply them and it takes time for your consciousness to rise to a point where you truly *feel* them working. For the most part they will apply to most people in most circumstances, but we have to be open to the fact that sometimes, God wants to bring you a lesson that only you can learn, because nobody else knows it and you have been the one chosen to bring it into reality. That is when you are ready to become a serious co-creator with God. And, when you are ready, then God expects that you get on with the job as quickly, efficiently and effectively as possible. If that means that He has to step to the side of one of The Laws, then so be it. We mere humans would have great difficulty in stepping to the side of a Law. The Laws seem absolute for us, but flexible for God.

This brings us to the Third Law of Evolution, which tends to align itself in importance with a number of others Laws that will unfold for our understanding as we work together.

The Third Law of Evolution
Act Immediately upon any impulse from the Heart,
and the Universe responds immediately.

This Law is all about learning to feel the heart more effectively and then acting upon what you feel. The seed of the God-consciousness is at the core of the heart chakra. It constantly communicates with you through the heart and subsequently through the feelings. So, the way to hear God is to listen to your feelings. In our modern world where there is distraction at every level, it can be very difficult to hear the heart or feel the feelings. We have to awaken ourselves and try a little harder than perhaps we did in our tribal times when we were more connected with Great Spirit, or Mother Earth and at a community level with those around us, without the noise and distraction of the modern world.

As you learn how to hear what your feelings are saying, you begin to determine the guidance that comes through them. The more you can attune to the feelings and the heart, then the more you will receive your own guidance from within. The next lesson is then to begin to trust that guidance. When you hear and feel guidance prompting you to take action, it then takes courage to trust the guidance, but as you learn to do this, you will find that the Universe responds immediately. The Universe works like a reward system. As soon as you act, the Universe responds in a way, which confirms your action or your trust in the guidance.

The Pathway is:
Listen to your heart, learn how to trust, find courage and then act.

You will make the odd mistake and act when it is inappropriate, but don't worry about that. The guidance will throw you a curved ball from time to time as a tester so that you can perceive the truth of the guidance from thought or imagination. This is the process of learning how to discern between heart and mind. It is through making the odd mistake that we truly learn to feel the subtle differences of which part of our consciousness is speaking to us. It is wise to consider that the person who never made a mistake never made anything. Mistakes or errors are our learning experiences and when we are walking the spiritual path, then we need as many learning experiences as we can get.

The Fourth Law of Evolution
Through Uplifting Others,
So You Become Uplifted Yourself.

You could call this Law the Law of Sharing and Growth. It is about sharing *the* knowledge. Through sharing it people have the opportunity to experience something new, by putting the knowledge into practice. Whenever you put knowledge into practice, the result is experience and the result of experience is growth, which then eventually leads to wisdom. This is the pathway of this Law.

The Pathway is:
Experience, Knowledge, Growth, Wisdom.

Un-evolved humans acquire knowledge and keep it to themselves in the false belief that it gives them power. We might say on a certain human level it does. If you know something that your neighbour doesn't know, then you might consider that you have more power than them. But, this kind of power limits your potential for growth. It locks you into what we might call 'the selfish, or self-vibration'. The self-vibration is one of separation and limitation and until you can find a way to break out of this level of vibration it will seriously limit your evolution. In fact, it is impossible to evolve until you do break this pattern, for the simple reason that the Divine Law decrees that you shall not receive any Divine power until you pass on what has already been given to you. God does not give you power for yourself. It is given to share.

How this works is that at a certain point in your evolution, usually around the time of The Calling, you will be endowed with energy and light, which then begin to open certain gifts or abilities. Let's call these healing gifts, for want of a better description. When healing gifts are given, you begin to taste real power: the power to change reality; the power to create; the power to change energy from one state to another through transforming a negative state in a person to a positive state. This is what we Guides might call the 'first taste' of power. But, what happens then is that people covet that power, they don't share it through teaching others how to do what they have learned as they perceive that this would weaken their position.

The perception is that if everyone knows how to do this, then I would not have this special power and, therefore, would not be recognised for what I can do. Simply, it is an ego issue and the granting of this 'first taste' of power is designed to illuminate the inadequacies of the ego in this way. If the ego were not illuminated you would not have an opportunity to see into yourself and heal yourself of these inadequacies. If you could not heal yourself or move on from this level of heightened ego-association and attachment, then your vibration would not change and you would become locked in time and space in terms of your evolution until a time when you are ready to let go of that patterning. The inner illumination helps you to see the problem, but the hard work comes when you have to acknowledge to yourself that you are exhibiting these qualities. The next hardest part is allowing them to leave your life by adjusting your behaviour.

So, once the 'first taste' has been granted, then you are on your own to experience what you can do with it, both for yourself and for others. But, as soon as you begin to share the knowledge of your gifts in truth, not by pretending to share them in fear, which is also a little trick that the ego will play on you, then you will be endowed with the 'second taste' of power.

Each level of power that is given, brings with it the great opportunities to heal oneself of the next lessons of evolution that you are trying to learn. Each person will have their own individual lessons, but there are also some common lessons, too. The level of illumination, which is given is perfectly controlled by the Divine Source, which watches you every moment. Through each moment of this Divine Guidance the power is used to bring illumination at exactly the right level to help you learn. What we might say about this level of illumination is that it is not so strong as to 'give' you the answers without working for them, for anything, which is given has little value. You must yearn and learn. You must apply yourself with great effort and inventive thinking to the path. In fact you must learn to think both laterally and in reverse in order to help yourself to see into other realities. At the same time, you must consider not thinking at all, but feeling what is happening, feeling the answers that you seek and a combination of all these approaches will bring success to the spiritual aspirant. The gifts that will be given are priceless and the effort needed to attain them relatively little in terms of exchange, but for certain, if you do not work hard, then you will not see perceive or understand the lesson and then you will become stuck for some period of time until something in your reality changes to allow you to ascend. However, the tools and guidance to help you are always there. You just have to reach out and find them.

This Law, then, is about giving it all away, so more is given. It is a huge, trusting step as you learn to move into allowing the Divine to bestow upon you exactly what you need in order to learn. It is through the sharing that you uplift and empower others. You cannot possibly attain evolution without sharing what is given to you. As you step ever higher into light, then ever more gifts, abilities and talents are poured down on your life, allowing for greater experience, knowledge and wisdom to be obtained. This is one of the most powerful Laws to observe and practise. Learn how you hold on to your own power through fear and then you will understand. When you begin to understand and learn to let go, usually a little at a time, you will see the Universe bring the instant reward of an ever greater power.

As you begin to connect with this Law, you will find that it shows itself to you on an almost daily basis, reflecting back to you all the aspects of your ego-self that need slight adjustment. It will reflect your fears of letting go and sharing. It is a natural part of the growth process to learn how you covet power. It is natural for the ego-self, to hold on to power for security, but as you begin to go beyond the ego-self, so you begin to see the beauty and truth of sharing everything you have as the act of sharing brings new rewards.

The Fifth Law of Evolution
The Power is Never Yours to Own

When starting out in healing we are often introduced to the attunement process, which opens up the healing channels quickly. Once attuned the energy is there for us permanently. Any time we desire to use it, it switches on and it is ours to use as we wish. As we work with it, so it expands our healing channels and unfolds us generally.

When you begin to move to a higher vibration, then power is given to you at a completely different level. It is given so that you can learn how to use real power as opposed to healing energy. As you play with a higher level of power, so it begins to bring up your issues in a more dramatic form so that you can learn about the hidden or dark side of your being. As you learn to dissolve and transcend your darker aspects, even more power is given.

However, the power is only granted based on your ability to use it appropriately. Also, you will find that you have to learn new levels of trust in order to access the higher levels of power. You will also find that the power can also be taken away in an instant and this is done when we are not quite walking the path accurately enough based on your guidance. The higher levels of power are granted to fine-tune your ability to find the exact path that you should be on and you will find that the power is used to steer you in the right direction. If you are off course, then you will feel the power being withdrawn.

This is just a learning process and what you are trying to learn at this higher level is that everything that you know has virtually no value any longer. We often think that we don't know enough and we study and attend courses and try to retain masses of knowledge. When you are ready to work at this level, you will discover that you don't need to know anything, that your guidance will bring you all the answers you need and you should learn to trust that you can deal effectively with anything that comes your way through guidance and not through learned knowledge. As you become totally detached from the healing process then all manner of things can happen for others, merely by your presence radiating the light in an unconscious way.

The Pathway is:
Total detachment, total trust, being present in the moment, being absent from the event. Just being the bystander and allowing the power to work through you. Acknowledge the power, give thanks and remain detached.

The Law of Reflection

All the above Laws are merely aspects of a greater Law, The Law of Reflection. As you step into higher light and power is bestowed upon you, a learning process begins where you experience how you create your own reality and how you draw situations towards you in order to learn how to transcend from the level of the collective consciousness of humanity. The lessons get bigger and harder each step of the way on the path and the lessons are often brought to you in the most unbelievable and bizarre ways. In the beginning you won't be able to figure this out, or get your head around it as the issues, which come towards you will make no sense, and that is because we don't have a vibration high enough to perceive the truth of the lesson.

For example, say somebody you know who is fit and young dies suddenly. There is always a reason and often it is concerned with the lessons that the person has chosen to experience in this lifetime. The death, or passing, might not make any sense to those of us at a human collective consciousness level, but if you can attain an insight from a higher level, then all is explained. But, you might then say, 'What about the emotional pain of those left behind?' When you can perceive the picture at a higher level, then you can see how each person chose to experience that loss as part of their journey of learning.

If you consider a situation where two people are involved, like, for example, a rape victim and a perpetrator. There is already a pre-existing agreement prior to life between these two people, that one will subject the other to what seems to us like a terrible experience, but the victim might have chosen to experience that so that they can learn how to pass through huge trauma, let go, rise above it and be free. We are not allowed to judge, because unless we can see the chosen life plan, we can't possibly understand.

There is no such thing as a negative experience in the Earth realm. Everything is completely positive and is served as a lesson that has been chosen and agreed to prior to incarnation. When you can connect into the eternal flow and see how short and simple lives are on earth, then you will have a completely different perspective. That does not mean that we don't feel the pain when we are on the path and learning, but eventually we go beyond that pain, because we touch into universal understanding and that dissolves the emotional attachment, which causes the pain. If a difficult situation occurs in life, merely ask yourself these questions and you will begin to discern the answers you need.

How did I attract this?
Why did I attract this?
What am I trying to learn?

As you begin to discern how The Law of Reflection works and what it brings to your life, then you are truly beginning to enter fifth dimensional consciousness, whilst still inhabiting third dimensional reality. You are stepping onto the bridge between the two realities with just a foot in the next level of higher consciousness.

Laws are Given

I wasn't given The Law of Reflection in one go, it probably took me about four or five years to figure out the whole picture through trial and error, which included figuring out how the other Laws above functioned, all of which form aspects to the greater Law of Reflection. I was being guided and taught in how to open the doors into the Universal Flow in order to allow Light to stream forth into Earth in unlimited measure. The Guides were trying to give me a Working Structure, something that humans could easily understand and apply to their lives in order to transcend. What would eventually reveal itself though was that this Law allowed people to learn how to conduct the Universe as a conductor conducts an orchestra. The only way these Laws could be given was through my own ability to learn how they worked. I was being driven to teach others how to access this level of reality, but I needed to understand how I had managed to access this level of Light in order to share the knowledge with others. It was not an attunement process. The Light had been bestowed on me. But what had I learned and what did I know in order that this could have happened?

I reached a point where there was some urgency and I was being pushed every single day to write out the 'rules' or 'guideline' which governed this Working Structure that would allow others to learn how to access the Universe at this level. No matter how I fine-tuned these rules, Guidance kept letting me know that I didn't quite have it right and so I continued amending the text a little at a time looking for that feeling which tells you, you've got it. Then one day, as I was working at my desk, I sat back and my eye fell on a book by Yogananda lying beneath the desk. It was entitled *The Laws of Success*. As I saw the word Laws, something lit up within me and I knew instantly that it wasn't the 'rules' or 'guidelines' I was trying to craft, it was 'The Laws'. The very moment I had seen the truth of what The Guides were encouraging me to find, The individual aspects which make up The Law of Reflection were then given in an unbroken stream as I typed them. They were perfect as they unfolded from my keyboard in less than two minutes, in their entirety. My battle of trying to write this for some 3 or 4 months was over and the lesson I was trying to learn was this:

Rules are made by man. Laws are Given.

When you've done the work and when you are truly ready at a vibrational level, then you will be given what you need. Even though The Laws had now been given, it would take me another two to three years before I fully understood the implications, when again, I would be given some new teachings which would simplify and revolutionize the way I could help people to avail themselves of the transformational power of these Laws. Each time a deeper level of truth is revealed, huge shifts are attained and this is all in line with the greater shift into 5th dimensional consciousness as the accelerations increase, pushing all those who are ready to do the necessary work to pass through the doors into the Aquarian Age.

We will explore all the aspects of The Law of Reflection in detail in the next book, but the above Laws will take you a long way to being ready to work with this higher Law by the time it comes to you.

Summary

Understand the Laws of Evolution. Try to see the bigger picture.

You can't do it alone because it is not part of the Universal Plan for humanity to be separate.

You can't do it alone because we are all on the same journey to the same destination.

You can't do it alone because you have to share the secrets of the pathway as you discover them.

And, that is how we will all find our way home.

Then we will become one again.

PART THREE

The Ladder of
Ascending Possibility

19

The Keys of Evolution

The Keys of Evolution are a guide to the right direction in which to attain the path of Evolution of your Consciousness. Evolution and Ascension are a one-step-at-a-time process, as you learn how to raise your vibration and feel what that is like. Knowing, which steps to take and in what order will greatly enhance your success and take you to each succeeding level in the shortest possible time. This does not mean that I am devaluing the journey in any way. It is a serious journey and cannot be approached with flippancy or lack of respect. You are treading a path into higher consciousness, to the level when you begin to expose the God-consciousness within yourself. You will not be allowed to pass any particular level until you are truly ready. You will need to have understanding and knowing at the deepest level within, to have a sense of the responsibilities, which rest upon your shoulders for the journey. The Journey is both for your Self and for mankind. Take this one step further and look at it like this.

Mankind is only the vehicle for conscious awareness to learn and grow. As you evolve, you will not need the physical body. Your consciousness will eventually evolve to reach a point where you go beyond the need to be here in human form. So we might say that you are not here to save humanity, you are here to save your Self, or to save your consciousness and you save it by learning to evolve it. As consciousness evolves, then you will be able to share what you have learned and others will be able to follow. Therefore, by saving oneself, one saves consciousness and somewhere on the journey, consciousness will have no further need of the vehicle of a physcial body. Humans will leave the earth and it will be allowed to return to paradise. So, what we might add to this is that humanity will save itself as a by-product of each person taking responsibility to work on their own evolution. It is nobody's responsibility to save humanity, but everybody's responsibility to save themselves and through this process, humanity is saved.

Use these Keys as a guide only. Nothing is set in stone. Nothing is absolute. But, from experience, I know that they will help you. Most of the path is just common sense. Find what works for you and what doesn't, then leave behind the things that don't. It is that simple.

These are not mutually exclusive keys, there are many ways to access energy and light, but they are most certainly keys, which had a powerful effect on my own unfolding process.

The 1st Key: Working with The Laws of Evolution

The First Key is to pay a great deal of attention to The Laws of Evolution. Work with them constantly. Firstly, understand that you cannot walk the path alone; secondly spend time learning to understand when you need help and when you are in the flow of life. Sometimes things can be difficult, but you can still be in the flow, as it were. The way to try to judge it is like this:

If you are on the path, then for sure, lessons are coming for you all the time. The higher up the ladder the more lessons and the greater the intensity. But, by the same token, when you find yourself higher up the ladder, you've learned an awful lot about how to solve your own difficulties. It is nearer the beginning of the path that you need the most help. The same lessons will come to you over and over again until you learn them. A little at a time you will begin to discern the patterns and as you do this, so you will have success. Therefore, sometimes the lessons will be coming thick and fast, but you are actually flowing through them and learning, so what you are looking for is the 'feeling,' or 'inner knowing' of whether you are in the flow or stuck.

If you are in the flow, then the difficulties are usually surmounted within a few days. Typically, you go down into a deep place, or everything is going wrong, then you seem to turn a corner and you 'feel' that you are coming out of those difficulties and that issues are being resolved. If you are stuck, then you will find that difficulties just keep mounting up, one after the other, and nothing seems to get resolved.

Look for signs in the physical world too. For example, at one time our garden drains became blocked and every time the drain man came to clear them, they blocked up again and he could not find a cause. This was God's way of showing us that something wasn't flowing. Sure enough, with a bit of application to life and business in the right areas, the drains were fine again.

The 2nd Key: Learn to Dowse

Dowsing is the key to perceiving and understanding that which you cannot see in the physical world. Dowsing taps into your deeper consciousness and inner knowing. It opens them to you as tools with which to perceive. You can use dowsing for all manner of things—to determine the right course of action to take to resolve a difficulty, for example. It is a tool, which I use every day in my work. My own vision and perception operate on a level where I can see into very deep consciousness without any additional aids to help me, but when I am on unfamiliar ground, perhaps dealing with something that I've not encountered previously, then dowsing is a good method of double checking. Practice enables this skill to be honed to perfection and you will find that it is a tool upon which you can totally rely. Using dowsing opens the inner being in a way which helps your overall journey. By using dowsing you are using the intent to find out. It is a tool for seeking and when you seek with Truth in your Heart, then you will find. When you seek in truth, you activate the Universal Consciousness to bring you the answers. Work with it and learn how to trust it.

The 3rd Key: Learn to Heal

The Third Key is to learn some form of healing. Open your heart and your mind to any and every possibility that will bring you into contact with the healing world. This is very much the first step in 'Healer Heal Thyself.' Ask for guidance constantly and learn to hear and feel it. As you learn, follow what your heart is telling you and learn as many aspects of healing as are presented to you. The key point in learning to heal is that it opens your subtle energy system to Energy and Light. Working with Energy and Light then gives you the opportunity to develop your sensitivities. As you become sensitive to electro-magnetic energy, you will be able to sense and then see the aura and then the chakras and maybe, the energies in nature too. As your sensitivities open, your whole life will begin its transformation stage, for as you become more sensitive, so you begin to see into things that many, because of their ignorance, fear, lack of effort and pioneering spirit, say is not possible. Life, in all its forms, seen and unseen is there to be discovered and marvelled at.

Learn everything you can about subtle energy, the chakras and the aura. Read books and then see if you can find what the authors speak about in these invisible worlds. As you discover subtle energy, you discover new dimensions to life. As you learn to heal, you will discover the very energies of life itself. You will discover the force of creation.

The 4th Key: Keeping Your Energy System in First Class Order

Ensure that your energy system is in first class order at all times, for if it is not, then you will not be moving forward as you should. The result will be that instead of the Universe bringing you opportunities for growth and success, it will be bringing you messages that something is wrong. Instead of moving forward, you will either be running slow, treading water or gradually approaching the sticking point.

Vibration is everything. Every chakra should be running at its maximum capacity at all times, processing Energy and Light. The aura must be as clean as it can be, illuminated, positive, vibrant. In reality, when you are first starting out, it takes time to tune your energy system to a point where it will stay in tune. The body's natural balance is usually one of being out of balance until you train it otherwise. This is because we incarnate, particularly we in the west, into cultures that have lost the arts associated with the inner being. Therefore, like a motor car that is never serviced, we enter the world with an incomplete cultural view and nobody takes a look to see how the motor — the subtle energy system — is working

Something I learned, which was invaluable in teaching me about a balanced energy system was Health Kinesiolgy. Working regularly with a group of like-minded people, I developed my sensitivity to the energy in the meridians and chakras and began to continually bring my subtle energy system into balance. We worked together one evening a week most weeks and after a couple of years, the latent intelligence in the body had learned what balance was all about. From that time on, the subtle energy system learned to balance itself whenever it went out of balance. That was a major step forward for me on my path and shows how long it can take to train your body consciousness into stepping up to a new level as its natural propensity is to fall rather than rise. You never hear of anyone having trouble lowering their vibration, do you? No, that's easy. All you need to do is get drunk every night for a month and take up smoking. Your vibration will soon begin to seek out a different level of reality, a little lower than your present one, unless of course you smoke and drink every night already. But one assumes that if you are on the path, then you are at least beginning to move your vibration upwards, in which case, you won't be smoking and drinking, will you?

Each level of energy throughout the whole of the subtle system is trying to communicate with the system below it. Higher Light enters at the crown chakra and tries to flood the Lower Mental Body. Perceive the Lower Mental Body as the reservoir of highest light within you. The more clarity you have in it, the higher the vibration you can hold and by reflection, the higher the vibration you can hold, the more clarity you have. Imagine a bridge stepping downwards to every other level, through Emotional Body, Etheric Body, into the Meridian System and finally the cells and organs of the physical body. All these bridges are the communication channels for light as it filters down through each vibratory level. If those bridges are open and each level of energy can flow downwards with ease from the highest of the subtle bodies to the lowest of your vibrational world, then the whole system is being fed in a balanced way with energy and light. Imagine a cascading mountain stream: that is how light should flow through the different levels of the subtle energy system.

As you move to higher states, if you have a powerful, finely-tuned system, you will find that it needs maintenance to keep it that way. The reasons will become obvious later. Eventually, you do reach a point where things seem to come together for you and you don't need to be as vigilant. Your innate consciousness learns to understand what you are trying to achieve. This is when your vibration is extremely high. At this point, we might say that certain aspects of your consciousness know how to keep you in tune, because they have learned what a balanced state is and what a balanced state is not. So, what you find is that the energy system becomes self-maintaining. However, this is not until you have spent much time learning to attune to the subtle world.

Light entering your life can have the most bizarre effects. Just because light is coming to you does not mean that this is going to be a straightforward and uplifting journey. On the contrary, light can, and usually does, cause a lot of trouble for you. However, there is always a reason why this is so.

> The Spiritual Path wrecks the body
> And after, restores it to health.
> It destroys the house to unearth the treasure,
> And with that treasure builds it better than before!
>
> Jalal ad-Din Rumi
> Persian Mystic, 1207–1273

This saying from Rumi sums it all up. At one point on my own path, I touched a place in time and space, which my system was not strong enough to witness. I didn't seek to be there, it just happened as I was following guidance. As I touched the energy of many thousands of years ago in this earth realm, I became so ill I had to lie down immediately. It took me three days to recover. However, at the moment I touched it and it only lasted a few seconds, I was given the message, *Everything will be renewed*. This is the same message that Rumi speaks of above. I was given to understand that this meant absolutely every aspect of the subtle and the physical.

Learning how to feel what is happening within you in terms of your subtle energy is one of the most important things you should work towards as you begin to understand healing and evolutionary light. Ultimately, this ability will enable you to maximise your vibration and when your system is running in a maximised state, then the Universe can bring you what is rightfully yours. You will stand in preparation to receive.

The 5th Key: Keeping on the Path

Keeping on the Path might not be as easy as you think, because what the God-consciousness wants is that you learn many and varied things, for it is through your own experiences that you grow into a valuable Spiritual Teacher with practical knowledge to impart. The very best form of all knowledge is that born of experience. Use books and DVDs for inspiration and to fire the imagination, by all means, but note that the only real way to learn is by doing, by experiencing energy first hand. Often, the very best Healers and Spiritual Teachers are those who have walked a many and varied path. Don't be afraid to branch out and experiment.

You may be quite content following a particular path in the beginning, learning and enjoying your work. However, at any time, God might be trying to influence you to a new direction. Don't forget, everything is changing all the time and new things are coming to the world, constantly in these accelerating times. You may already be a powerful healer and very effective, perhaps with a successful practice and a long track record, but if God wants you to move in another direction then you need to be able to hear that call. If you are not changing, then you are not evolving. Gone are the days when we learned something and then practised it for the rest of our lives. If you are attached to what you are doing and you don't hear the call then things are going to get very difficult for you. This is a big problem for many healers who have walked the path for some time. All of a sudden they find that their work becomes difficult, their energy is not as it should be, perhaps they find themselves drained and with no strength. Client numbers may be dropping, with no new ones on the horizon. Everything seems to be closing down. The whole picture can be extremely alarming.

You end up asking yourself what healing is all about, because it doesn't make sense anymore. You've put all this time and money into your development, you know that you have had amazing results in the past, but suddenly nothing is working for you. You question everything and come up with no answers. 'If God gave me the gift of healing why does He not send me people to heal?' This is the question, which most often arises. When you can see deep enough to find the answers, they are always there.

There may be many paths for you to walk on your evolutionary journey and just because you have become very proficient and comfortable on one doesn't mean that you are going to continue with that path forever. So, keeping on the path means following the 'right path' as guided by the God-consciousness within you. If you are being called in a different direction and are not hearing what is going on, or there is some lesson that you are not seeing, then many things might start to go wrong for you. You will be stopped in your tracks, either a little at a time, or very quickly, dependent upon what the Universe wants you to do next in order to serve yourself better.

In the case of students who have entered into training with us, many of whom have had long and broad careers in many aspects of healing, often practising a whole raft of methodologies, as they step up into this light, it often crushes them to the point where they eventually realise that they have to drop everything they have been working with and take on the new mantle that is being offered to them. It is not me that is offering it, I am merely the vehicle that the light is presented through. When God-consciousness attracts you to a new light, it doesn't expect you to hang on to working at the old level. The ones who persist in clinging become troubled until they let go and awaken and for my part I allow them to learn that for themselves. It is not for me to tell them what to do, it is for them to experience the light and learn what it is trying to show them. However, I am there to answer their questions when they are ready to ask them. To give them all the answers is to disempower them and the nature of the spiritual path is to constantly become ever more empowered. It is the duty of the guide or teacher to assist the student by pointing them in the right direction to learn the lesson for themselves and so gain the maximum empowerment from the experience. Letting go of something that you might be brilliant at can be a daunting process and many cannot see that what is being offered will always take them higher than their present state of expression.

The Path Through the Forest

For a moment, visualise a path through a forest. As you walk along it you come upon many turnings, many paths leading from the main path. At times, it might seem that some of these other paths are in fact the main path themselves and it becomes difficult to determine, which path to follow. The darkness of night might even fall and, rather than risk taking the wrong path, you might consider resting for the night and then trying to discern the right path when daylight comes again. Eventually, you might even consider that you are stuck and just don't know, which way to go. This is the time you need to *reach out* and ask someone for guidance, for if you go down the wrong path you could end up losing a lot of time and experiencing things, which are not important for your particular pre-destined journey of evolution.

However, you might actually need to experience what is down some of these other paths before returning to the main one. Alternatively, you might take one of these side routes and it suddenly becomes your new main path for some considerable time. By the same token, you must trust that everything is unfolding exactly as it should. It is impossible to go too fast, but it is possible to sabotage yourself and not attain evolution in a time cycle that is appropriate. What prevents you attaining the maximum speed is always your own limitation in the way you apply yourself to the tasks that face you. Sometimes those tasks seem insurmountable, but when looked at and broken down, they never are.

Sometimes we have to experience odd little detours from the main path through the forest merely because we need to touch an energy, whether it be of place or person, that is needed to connect us with a memory of who we were, or what we have already achieved in previous lives, so that we might awaken that aspect of ourselves in this life. We might just need to touch an energy, which will catapult us into our new future. We can say that there is never a wrong path. We are always going down some path because we need to experience something there.

I once had a reading in my early days of seeking and I was told that I went down many dead ends. That might have been so at that time. I was certainly trying everything that I could find, but perhaps that was my process of elimination that allowed me to be absolutely certain when I found out who I was and why I was here.

Clarity

As you can see, at certain times on your journey through the forest, it is easy to become confused, lost or even stuck and unable to make a decision. At this point, the name of the game is clarity. The way to obtain clarity is to reach out and get some guidance. If you do not have clarity, there will be a reason for it and the answer to that reason is always visible in the energy system at some level.

Everything in Balance

Don't make a habit of obtaining guidance too often though, because the God-consciousness within you will see this as trying to abdicate responsibility for your own decisions. You must take responsibility for your own life. Subsequently, lessons will be brought to you about this as part of your growth. However, good guidance at the right time is a very necessary part of walking the path as you learn to evaluate the right teachers for you at any particular time. The process is really one of learning how to trust in association with being in the flow, which we discussed earlier. A little guidance at the right time to help bring clarity is not abdication of responsibility, rather it is the process of seeking the answers until you find them. If there is lack of clarity there is almost certainly darkness in the aura or crown chakra, therefore, the guidance and a little energetic intervention will put you back on the path.

Reaching out at the right time is part of humanity coming together as one, which of course is the First Law of Evolution and in turn, part of the Universal Plan. Ultimately, good guidance at the right time will bring you clarity, which then helps you to determine your path. It will reinforce your own judgement and bring confidence and in turn, empowerment. It will sometimes give you the signs you are looking for, but more often than not, it will confirm what you already know at a deeper level. When the guidance comes forth, you will recognise it for what it is and it will *feel* exactly right.

Guidance is not provided to give you all the answers at every turn, it is to help you find your own answers from illuminating your own Truth within your core. Do not abandon yourself to a Teacher, Psychic or Guru. Become your own Guru, but allow others to guide you through the forest when you feel a need to ask some directions.

The 6th Key: Becoming Empowered

A good spiritual teacher will always push you away. They will *never* pull you in. They will look at your situation and help you to see what is going on in your life, bringing clarity to help you to make your own decisions. Not doing the work for you, but illuminating what needs to be done with guidance and help in how to go about it, they will help you to understand what is the right way for you. Although, the destination is the same for all of us, each person's path is an individual one. Although, we will all have to learn the same major lessons, the order in which we learn the minor ones on the way is different for each person. Through reaching a certain level on the path, the Teacher or Guide is given the power to see how to help you, how to locate the issues and challenges within your consciousness that need to be overcome and in the order in which they can, indeed, be overcome.

As they look within you, it involves opening your consciousness in order to see. To open the consciousness, light is used to illuminate the darkness within. The process of working with a teacher in this way automatically stimulates an evolutionary event without you even doing any work. This is what happens:

When you seek out the teacher, the God-consciousness is already looking at how to reward you for your effort. As the teacher uses their light to see what limitation is within you, the light that is used falls into you in order to open the truth within. Merely looking in brings enough light into you to begin an illumination process, which will help you to find your own answers. If you then go on to do some work with the teacher, this takes things to a second level.

Empowerment is about the teacher bringing forth guidance, but also bringing their light to you to help you to transform. The teacher is merely a guide and facilitator. The teacher does not fix things for you or heal you. In fact, the only person who ever does the healing is you. You bring about your own healing when you are truly ready to let go of the issues, which compromise you. However, merely entering into a deep consultation with a teacher will begin the healing process.

A good teacher will empower you by teaching you how to understand what is happening in your life as a result of what is happening within the deep consciousness. For example, when I work with someone for the first time, I don't then tell them they need to come back next month and we'll do some more, because that is disempowering them. I don't make a future appointment for them either as that is also taking power out of their hands. Rather, I tell them what to expect as a result of the work being done and then I teach them how to know *if* and *when* they might need to do some more.

I also teach them how to know who is the right teacher for them at any one particular time. They might need to work with a number of different people at different times to obtain different experiences. However, it is important that you try to limit your work to one teacher at one time, so that you can gain a full appreciation of the benefits you are gaining from any association. If you work with more than one person at one time, you can *never* know who helped bring about change for you.

The development of your own Inner Knowing is the key component, which you need to learn as soon as you can. Think, 'independent.' That is what you are, an independent person. Learn how to judge for yourself where you are on your path and whether you need help or guidance at any time, but focus on the fact that you are independent and this is your independent journey. Stand in your own light and power, but don't be afraid to ask for assistance when you need it. You will soon find the teachers who are on your wavelength. Step into their light, see how it feels. If it feels OK, then continue. If their light does not resonate, then step out again. Sometimes you will touch in to the light of a teacher for a single experience. Sometimes you will return many times. Each new day is moving you forward into new experiences. We learn to feel and judge what we need each new day. Because a certain person helped us fix ourselves one time does not automatically mean that the same person is right for us at another. Constantly review how you feel as your inner radar scans the horizon of spiritual and evolutionary light in its search for assistance.

When you are truly ready to let go of old patterns you will find the teacher or guide that you need. The Universal Consciousness is watching you, every moment of your life, from within you. That Higher Consciousness always knows where you are on your journey and when you need help. It will always try to guide you into self-empowerment, but if you need to learn the lessons of giving your power away first, then that is where it will lead you.

The 7th Key: Do not Cease from Seeking the Answers

As you know, once you are called, there is no going back, so you may as well step up and take your place in the unfolding universal plan.

The Seventh Key is, 'Don't ever cease from seeking the answers'. Once you have been called to evolution there is only one end game and that is attaining oneness with God. Until then you haven't finished your journey. If you are still having incarnations on earth then you haven't finished your journey. If you are here at the birth of the Age of Aquarius, the chances are that you have an immense journey ahead of you, because you will have chosen this time to incarnate specifically to take advantage of the powerful, uplifting, accelerating energies of this time now available. Forget the destination for now. If you are going to attain it, allow it to creep up on you unawares. Just learn how to walk the path with clarity and precision, one day at a time and one step at a time and allow God to do the rest. The destination will then reveal itself when the time becomes appropriate.

Oh, and by the way. You will hear many people say that they have learned everything that they came to earth for, that this is their last incarnation as they don't need to come back any more. These people are so disconnected from reality that they will be in for a shock when they return to base for the debriefing. This level of arrogance is astounding. It is like saying, I'm God now, so I don't need to do this any more. Human perception is so limited, it is impossible to even grasp a fraction of what reality is all about. The picture is so big that a mere glimpse of the smallest part of the light, which is God would kill you instantly. The human condition is so small that it is impossible for me to find words to describe it, without going to the Thesaurus, and I'm not doing that right now.

The destination of human consciousness is the full realisation of the Christ consciousness within us. It is becoming one with God, a dissolution of all aspects of the ego-self as the last drop of the darkness of separation is burned up. If anyone tells you that they, or you, have completed all the human incarnations that are necessary, ask them how they turn water into wine. No, hang on a minute, that's a bit too easy. Ask them to show you how to walk on water. If they can't walk on water, then they have a lot more work to do down here.

The 8th Key: Riding the Wave of Time

The Wave of Time is a location in time and space. It is also an energy, which can uplift you and accelerate you to an extremely high vibration. Riding the Wave of Time is about always being in the right place at the right time; always as regards your spiritual journey. When you have learned how to Ride the Wave of Time, you are constantly becoming something else by the second. You are constantly becoming all that you can be in every moment of life. We will look at The Wave of Time in detail later in the book.

The 9th Key: Attaining the Universal Flow

The Universal Flow is a stream of pure consciousness on many levels. It is moving forward eternally, regardless of whether you are in it or not. Some might call this flow The Law of Attraction, but it is much more than this. The Law of Attraction is the way you can draw things into your own conscious flow, or manifest in the way you adapt your creative thinking, but this is very different from attaining the Universal Flow. The Universal Flow functions at a much higher level. When you can attain this flow, you become a part of the creation process itself and the flow allows you to perform all manner of functions at a higher level without actually doing the work. Literally, imagine it and it is done. But there is a period of apprenticeship to enter into in order to do this. However, each step you take reveals more of what you can do as you are ready to learn how to do such things as may be presented to you.

The Universal Flow is a stream of energy and consciousness, which is continually moving and flowing in the direction of eternity and if you can get yourself into this flow, then it will uplift you and carry you forward with it. The only way you can attain this is through a high vibration where your vision, perception and intuition are running at the highest level possible and synchronised with the speed of universal consciousness as it unfolds. The Universal Flow is attained after you have learned how to Ride the Wave of Time.

The 10th Key: Arrogance and Humility

Don't ever think that you know all the answers. None of us does and most of us never will, because as humans it is impossible to touch and hold consciousness, which is so illuminating that you can see and understand the bigger picture. You might have some of the answers for a time, but then when your vibration moves to a new level you find that everything you thought you knew does not apply further up the evolutionary ladder. The illusion folds back and a new view of reality reveals itself. When you experience this, it is always amazing.

We are chasers of Truth and the funny thing about Truth is that it constantly changes as your vibration changes. The only Truth you can ever stand in, is your own Truth. Therefore, you work with what is True for you right now, but you remain ever open-minded that the Truth you have is only temporary. When you have learned what you need from that level of Truth and you are ready to let go of it, you will move up the ladder. When you move up the ladder, many aspects of your Truth will begin to change to reveal a higher Truth, a kind of peeling back of the image of your reality to reveal another layer beneath. Eventually, you come to know that everything within your life is illusion, but that you haven't transcended enough of those layers yet to see the perfect truth. So, you merely continue on the journey, marvelling at every new level that is revealed.

As we have said, a common problem early on the path is that the power of the light activates the ego and the result can be arrogance. Don't worry about it if it comes up. Just acknowledge it and learn how it works. Don't try to subdue it, but allow it to dissolve over time. Just see it as one of the negative expressions, which is showing itself for you to learn from.

The power of the light also activates many fears, one of the first is the Fear of Letting Go. When this is activated, what you find as you are reaching the first levels of being a teacher is that you capture your students. You begin to try to control them. You create your own tribe as it were and you fear anyone stepping outside of the tribe and you try to manipulate and control them to remain under your command. In the early years of working with energy, almost everyone goes through this process. Many, many people have great difficulty moving beyond this level, because when they have tasted that power, they can't let go of it. They become prisoners of their own fear, the Fear of Letting Go. Another issue, which comes up is one of jealousy, if a student begins to accelerate beyond the capability of the teacher. This presents many lessons for the teacher to learn, the first one being that you are only a teacher at this present level until you learn how to let go and move on, then you will teach at another level and then another and so on.

To be successful, the path must always be one of humility. We are only humans and as such we have absolutely no idea what this game is all about. The picture is far too big for our meagre consciousness to comprehend. Our conscious capacity is virtually nil in comparison with that of the Universal Consciousness. Learn to walk the path in none judgement of others, understanding that wherever they are on their path, is merely where they are right now. Yes, they might be stuck, or processing some deep aspects of their own learning curve, but tomorrow, they might be way ahead of you or I. The Universe has a way of illuminating those it wants at the top and this illumination can happen at any time to any person. We are all exactly where we are and no further. And, if any of us had the big answers, then we wouldn't be here on earth. So, chill out, live each day as it comes, don't bother competing as that doesn't get you anywhere, work diligently at whatever the Universe is sending you today and don't worry.

The 11th Key: Learn to Laugh

Once you have been called and you have stepped onto the path, then there's no going back. Forget choice as it is a thing of the past, no longer available to your present level of being. The Universe will continue to pull you up the spiritual ladder. The more you resist, the more difficult life will become. This is the key where you have to learn how to begin to laugh at the absurdity of the whole game. Not only the game of life, but the game of many lives. The game of evolution as we work our way through one Great Cycle of Time after another on the Fundamental Plane of Eternity. When you touch into the nature of eternity, it truly brings up phenomenal fear within you, for at one level, it feels like you are on a treadmill that you can never get off, but on the other, you know that these feelings are just the limitations within you and at some point on this path, *you* will be creating Universes of your own some day, once the fears have all been dissolved.

Therefore, at times, as the Universe smacks you on the back of the head with the baseball bat of Wisdom, time after time after time, it is imperative that you develop a great sense of humour. If you can't laugh at the irony of the situations you *will* find yourself in, and knowing that it is your own inability to learn that put you there, then you will be in for a rough ride. As well as humour, a sharp sense of irony is also a must. Frequently, in a state of exasperation, you will find yourself asking:

'How am I creating this?'

or ...
'I could not possibly have agreed to this before I incarnated.'

or ...
'What is all this chaos trying to teach me?'

Despair is a good place to be sometimes, because it can only get better ... now that's irony.

Summary:

These keys are not definitive, but they have worked for me. We are all on our own journey and, therefore, we all have to find our own path. However, there are many common factors to be experienced as we ultimately arrive at the same destination.

I view it like this. I'm an ordinary guy, but through certain trials, I learned how to work with certain Universal Laws through the application of certain Keys.

The Keys may not be definitive, but I think that The Laws are.

You may well find some additional keys of your own. That will be good.

But, I think you will find that The Laws don't bend.

If these Keys and Laws work for me on a wet Monday morning in Manchester, then I'm pretty certain they will work for you, if you apply them the same way I do.

You have free will. I can only share with you what has worked for me and that is all I offer.

You must find your own path, that is your responsibility, but if the knowledge from my own journey can make it any easier for you, then please feel free to use and adopt whatever you need.

We are all here to help uplift each other. I hope this work uplifts you into your own empowerment.

20

Stepping onto the Path

There are those who have absolutely been chosen to walk a spiritual path in this lifetime — and they know it. It continually calls to them. Often, their gifts have blossomed early and with such consuming force that it is difficult to deny them. Although, my own gifts began to unfold later in life, I can identify with that all-consuming force, which cuts through you, like a Roman sword in a previous life. These awakening souls have often surged forward with a great level of confidence and knowing and many of them are earning their living by using their gifts. This is as it should be.

However, what is of great concern is that there are those who have the essence of the gifts and have always been afraid of them, have pushed them down, denied them and as a result are usually suffering in some way through their fears, which cause the denial.

A third group have been walking the path for a long time, whilst struggling to understand the bigger picture — who they are and how they fit into the world at large — because their inner nature is essentially spiritual. These people know to a large degree that they are gifted, but are completely lost. Finally, there are those who are only just awakening in the light of these changing times. If they can learn the lessons needed in the time available, they will all go a long way.

When I help people to understand where they are now and where they could be by unlocking their inner potential, it is common to find that they have always been drawn to spiritual matters, but have not really acted upon that inquisitive pull. They have been too caught up in life to hear their inner voice and the guidance it has been trying to bring forth. Often this situation has gone on for years. It is not difficult to find the issues in such people and they can always identify with them at some level when you lay them out for them. What they have always been missing was somebody to see the picture independently and explain their life and purpose to them, based on the issues revealed from within. The lack of determination to hear an inner message and act upon it is often due to a distinct lack of self-belief, based on an inability to trust what is within the Self.

Not having sufficient connection to or belief in what is calling you from within is essentially due to societal programming. Society dictates what it thinks we should be and do, but there is nobody available to nurture our inner being and help guide us onto the path. We can't change what has gone before, but we can change what is to come, when at last we accept that we are here on a spiritual mission, our own individual mission, rather than one which fits society's norms. Those who fail to learn how to think for themselves will not enter 5th dimensional consciousness. The present limited conventions of society do not allow the freedom of thought and being to promote transcendence.

Seek and You Shall Find

When working deeply with people, you find patterns emerging in all manner of different ways. One common pattern is of people arriving at my door who are between the ages of 38 and 42 years. It is so common as to be almost unbelievable. However, when you begin to understand a little more of the universal picture and natural cycles, you realise that this is the period of time when certain astrological phenomena are beginning to act upon your life. For example, Jupiter completes its cycle and returns to the position in your natal chart at around the age of 36. Uranus takes up a position *opposite* its natal position, or opposite where it was when you were born, around 40. Oppositions in astrological terms mean big energy and big energy means big change. Around age 50 Chiron, the wounded healer, returns to base. So, you can see that from around 36 years of age, some big planets and powerful energies are beginning to influence your life.

My Guiding Consciousness likes to make things as simple as possible and describes life periods like this:

Your first 20 years is about learning to be a child in the Earth Realm.

Your second 20 years is about learning to be an adult in the world.

As you enter your third period of 20 years, it is time to awaken to the reason you chose to be here. It is time to awaken to your life mission.

Perhaps the most profound significance is that 40 is the number of transformation as demonstrated when Jesus spent 40 days and nights in the desert in order to transform his consciousness. In awakening humans in general though, 40 days and nights is far too short a period to go through the type of transformation that Jesus did. Anyone who has touched into the deep and real nature of inner transformation knows that it is a tremendously difficult process and Jesus alludes to this when he says, 'I could transform the whole of humanity in three days, but few would survive it.'

The Spirit of Your Age

Another way of seeing how patterns influence your life is by looking how chakras respond to different time periods. For example, roughly speaking, you could say that each chakra begins to function at a deeper, more power-ful and more connected level at a particular age. From birth to around seven years is the time for the base chakra to be active. The Base Chakra is all about survival and physical functions, a period when we are trying to become established on earth, growing and grounding. It is a period when we are put-ting down roots, which will then serve us for the time we are here.

Herewith, with the kind permission of Anna Jeoffrey and Philip Salmon, is a short extract from a presentation given in March 2007. This gives an addi-tional view of how different periods in life develop in relation to chakra development. (*Anna and Philip teach The Bach Flower Remedies at Ainsworths in London. For more details see www.energyworks.co.uk*)

The Seven Ages

Baby to 7 years	Base Chakra	The Self
7 to 14 years	Sacral Chakra	One to one association
14 to 21 years	Solar Plexus	The Gang – belonging
21 to 28 years	Heart Chakra	Family
28 to 35 years	Throat Chakra	Songline – Country
35 to 42 years	Brow Chakra	Planet
42 to 49 years	Crown Chakra	Universe

Copyright of the above Anna Joeffrey

Spiritual awakening can occur at any time in your life, even though, until this present speeding-up of Universal Consciousness, the majority of people began to open more deeply to themselves at around 40 years of age. This period of awakening is also known as the mid-life crisis, the point where people suddenly realise that they are unhappy or unfulfilled, or have completely compromised everything that the inner voice has been telling them. As a result, they have ended up in a life that has no meaning, although, by society's standards they may have good jobs, a family, a place in the community and, to all intents and purposes, be seen as a perfect role model for someone to look up to. The outer view is that they have made it, the inner view is often something completely different, reflecting lost opportunities, complete self-denial, inability to get what they need, or want in order to nurture their selves.

As Universal Consciousness speeds up, many of the people being born into earth at this time are already programmed to awaken earlier. Many teenagers have fully functioning psychic ability and some are even drawn to healing at an early age.

Whatever forces begin to awaken you or, we might even say, disturb you into wakefulness, stimulating you to begin searching for answers, can assist you in finding what you need. If you don't make the effort to seek the answers, then the Universal Consciousness will not act to support you.

Many people hit that mid-life crisis point. Some even have breakdowns, but that's OK. A breakdown is a very positive thing. It is the God-consciousness within, telling you that you cannot go on like this any longer, that you are going in the wrong direction. It is a breakdown of rigid patterns as your consciousness forces you to clear out the old ways and step into your new identity. I've had two of them, one when I was 28 (the planet Saturn returns between ages 27 and 29 and hits you in a big way); the other began when I was 38. This latter event was also my healing awakening, a process, which took about three years to pass through. Breakdown or healing awakening is really one and the same thing, it is only the degree of intensity, which varies. Some higher conscious force is simply ensuring that you change your ways. If the inner upheaval is dramatic enough, then it is painful, often disturbing, but always successful. Mine was very painful emotionally and I went through some alarming physical events too. Talk about turning the heat up on you! But it had the desired effect. Breakdown is also breakthrough. Breakdown is about breaking down the barriers of resistance that prevent you becoming what you came here to be.

At around 40 years old then, people often find themselves seeking a new way. They discover that happiness is not down the road they thought it might be; that there is so much more to life than they have currently sampled. Often, people change course in life completely and as we have seen these past few years, many retrain in some kind of helping or caring role as they realise and connect with their inner voice, helping them to see that they are here to help humanity, or the planet in some way. In recent years, many colleges have been offering courses in Complementary Therapies, (to my mind they should be called Primary Therapies). Some people discover spiritual healing, or one of the many other forms of healing and energy work, such as Reiki, which in these past years has been a great and universal opener of the doors to subtle energy for millions of people. Some might hear the calling of homeopathy, crystals, nutrition, earth healing, geomancy, angels, working with and healing animals, etc. There is so much choice these days that there is absolutely something for everyone and, what is more, that consciousness, which is awakening at your centre is trying to guide you down the path that is right for you.

When you begin to awaken, you are usually drawn towards something of an energetic nature, towards working with energy on some level. This is because the spiritual light is delivered to guide you into some kind of work, which will speed up your evolution. In order to do this, you have to work with energy and light. As you do, you are then firmly placing your feet on your path of evolution.

As the Aquarian Light increases in intensity and speed, year on year, we find that many people are awakening much earlier than they might otherwise have done. This is partly, because as they enter this realm they are already awakened from previous lives to a degree. They are already prepared. And it is partly because they choose to be born to parents who are already changing and awakening and, therefore, find themselves in a home sphere influenced by the spiritual light in which their parents are already vibrating. They are choosing a high vibrational environment to incarnate into. A third reason is that many of the newborns of this time are more sensitive to the new light and it is, therefore, influencing them at a younger age. We also have very advanced children, such as the Indigo Children and the Crystal Children. All of these people will still be affected by the appropriate astrological energies at the appropriate times in their lives, but these energies will then serve to touch them at a deeper level, because they are already opening quickly. The speed of their vibration means there is a lack of energetic resistance in their subtle bodies and consciousness. It is energetic resistance to change that causes the breakdown scenario. So, as people surge forward into the new age with a high vibration, those astrological energies will serve to assist their development, rather than stopping them in their tracks to awaken them. Rather than a period of breakdown, realignment, awakening to change and the development of new vision as has been the pattern in the past we will see acceleration because of the lack of energetic resistance.

It is interesting to work with such advanced souls. I have worked with a number of younger people, helping unlock their lives and pointing them in the right direction. Although, they have amazing spiritual connections within the spiritual channel, some of their deeper knowledge and understanding is not yet ready to be tapped into. It is as if it is shielded and programmed to open in some kind of predetermined time-line. This makes life very difficult for them in many ways, particularly because they know that they are here to perform great things. They have the deeper knowing within them, but the universe is holding them back to some degree, until they are ready to step onto the world stage. As one teenage girl said to me, 'I just want to go out with my friends and be normal'. However, when you have powerful spiritual gifts and someone upstairs is trying to guide you in how to use them for the benefit of humanity as a whole, life can be very difficult.

Summary

As you are called to step onto the path, the journey can be exciting, exhilarating and awesome as your whole being begins to develop new abilities, especially intuitive abilities, but if things are not running quite as smoothly as you think they should be, then something needs to be looked at. If you can't quite figure out what it is yourself, then that is the time to reach out and get some help.

The Key is to constantly look within and be truthful with yourself.

The truth within is what is trying to emerge. Therefore, your truth is all that matters.

Do not try to follow society's line or anyone else's. You are on your own path.

Allow your life to open up by listening to what brings you happiness within.

Read anything you can that will help you to understand what you are going through.

Trust that you are being guided constantly, but that guidance can only bring you the answers when you actively seek them.

21

Now is the Time

As you first learn to work with energy and light, your abilities are still sleeping for the most part. The way things usually unfold is that first of all you begin to sense energy. The way it worked for me was that I began to sense entities, then feel and see tree auras and the energies in the earth, such as ley lines and earth flows, like rivers of energy feeding the landscape. Most people, though, begin to feel or sense the aura and chakras, or energies, around a person.

The next level of attainment is often a glimpse of colour as you begin to see the light of the chakras or aura. If you can bring the right levels of light into your client in a healing session, they will often experience vivid colours with their eyes closed as their higher senses become illuminated. The first colours perceived in this way are usually green or purple. As the healing light enters them it temporarily lifts their consciousness to a point where they can perceive slightly higher frequencies of light than normal. If you like, they are being held in a higher space, bathed in your higher light as you bring forth the frequencies that you are attuned to. If they see green, they are usually experiencing the opening of the heart and the light is then spilling out into the central channel, where it flows throughout the energy system. This can be described as, 'illumination' and happens in order to help them perceive that something is taking place within them. It is that, 'confirmation' process we have talked about, which is so important for the novice on the spiritual path, helping them to discern and understand subtle forces. Also, it is a kind of message, so that they know that the healing is working at some level. If they experience purple, this is the opening of their own spiritual channel, usually facilitated by their own Guiding Consciousness, allowing higher light to enter and mix with the healing light being channelled by the healer. Again, the main reason for this is to gain experience of an altered state of consciousness, thus giving them confidence in the healing experience.

Early Perceptions

As you work increasingly with channelling your healing energy to others, your gifts begin to unfold and your abilities develop. You may then start to see chakras in more detail and to sense and see the energy blockages. What comes next is that you can often relate these blockages to issues in the client's life. You then begin to learn how to link blockages with emotional energy. You will find that God keeps sending you the same type of problem in a number of different people, so that you can become proficient in understanding the patterns therein. Yes, that's how it works: your clients become your teachers through the issues they bring to you. It is a two-way exchange. You help them with energy and light and they help you to learn and understand. When you have learned the ins and outs of a particular problem or pattern and you have had some success at helping the client heal from it, you will then find that new lessons and challenges are brought forward for you.

However, the point I wish to make here is that more often than not you are dealing only with energy and energy blockages at this early stage. For example, when you learn to see into a chakra you will discover that there are thousands of different levels of both energy and consciousness. When you experience a blockage in a chakra, it is often only a very small area of the overall chakra that is compromised, but you will probably perceive that the whole chakra is blocked in the early days of your healing journey. This is because of the way your higher consciousness and the client's higher consciousness interact to present the issue to you. If the whole chakra was closed down, your client would probably be suffering in a very severe way on a physical level. However, when you are learning, you perceive the chakra as a whole energy structure and not through the detail of thousands of frequencies of energy and consciousness.

Getting Deeper into Life

With the levels of light presently available to healers on this planet, most people cannot get their consciousness much beyond the energy levels we have discussed. All the common forms of healing light can only take you to a certain level of development and then you have to seek something more powerful.

The first great wave of the healers of today have been walking a path of evolution with the first rays of healing energy since around 1988. Although, these are healing rays or frequencies of energy, their real intention is for you to learn how to use them for your own self-transformation. The fact that we can use them for the so called 'healing' of others is a bonus. But when we examine what we are doing with healing others, we are really only helping them on their own path of self-transformation. The whole game is about self-transformation, but in order to get the game to work properly for us, we have to do it through working with others.

As Universal Consciousness speeds up, some new rays of light have been emerging since about 1999. These new rays are absolutely phenomenal. Some of them are unlimited in what they can do for the transformation of human consciousness. We are seeing huge shifts in consciousness on many levels at present. People are waking up dramatically and just as there was great and sudden social change in the 60s you are going to see great change in the level of light work being done in this coming period. People are learning to fly with light. Light is opening them to new levels of under-standing and as it comes into their consciousness it illuminates the things, which need to change. This new light will challenge you like you have never been challenged before. It will challenge you to change, continually.

Your Challenge

Your challenge at this time is to go beyond your limitations. Those of you who do not face the challenge will be left wanting. The God-consciousness is pushing everyone to awaken and rise up, but it is pushing those who have already been walking the path much more than anyone else. It is pushing you to be the leaders of tomorrow, for you are already on the path.

As a healer, you are being pushed to go beyond what you can see and perceive in terms of energy blockages, to begin seeing into consciousness. The difference between being a healer and a lightworker is the difference between being able to see into energy and into consciousness. When you can see into consciousness you can begin to understand the reasons certain things happen, or why people suffer from certain illnesses.

For example, if a person came to you with a cancer, you can see how they are manifesting that level of dis-ease. You can see into their life lessons; you can see into their soul; you can see what God is trying to get them to hear. Also, you can then help them to learn those lessons. As the lessons are learned and the person begins to let go of the patterns that are causing the dis-ease, then the cancer may have a chance to recede.

We are not healers. None of us heals others. The only person who heals is the person who is suffering. They heal themselves. We are merely facilitators in the grand scheme of things. We facilitate the flow of energy and light, we bring light to illuminate the darkness within. When the darkness is illumi-nated, then we can see the pathway out of it, the pathway into the next phase of evolution. We can guide the person in the right direction, but we cannot take responsibility for them and Universal Consciousness will only allow us to do so much. Each person's path is their own responsibility and they must learn to take action for themselves. We can bring guidance and if the guidance feels right to them, they should follow the guidance.

We Have Already Run Out of Time

It is time for you to go beyond where you currently work. If you resist challenge and change, the Universe will be unmerciful in the lessons it brings you. You will be astonished at the patterns, which block a person's progress when you learn to work with light at a level that allows you to see into consciousness.

As Universal Consciousness continues to accelerate, there is no time left to pretend that things are OK. Things are not OK at any level on this planet. Just take a look around you. There are lies and deceit at every turn. The illusion is falling apart at the seams and those whose vibration is raised to a certain pitch can see through the illusion, which is presented to us every day by the collective consciousness of humanity. You have to learn to step away from the illusion, to step out of the pervasive waves of collective consciousness, to step into truth. As you take these steps in a determined fashion, you will be amazed at what is revealed to you.

We talked earlier about power. There is an endless supply of power, but the power is never yours to own. Power is granted to you as you learn to use it responsibly and appropriately. There is more power than you can ever use and God wants you to have it. It is being held out to you permanently. All you have to do is reach out and take it by learning how to use it to dissolve your own limitations first. As you work upon yourself, so the power will be given to you.

It is time for you to go beyond your present limitations. Time is moving faster than you can possibly imagine. It is not illusion when you say to yourself, 'where did the time go, or where did this year go.' It is really the Universal Consciousness that is speeding up and this presents the illusion that time is moving faster. Time is like an ocean wave carrying you towards salvation. As each successive wave lifts you and carries you forwards, the Christ Light within emerges a little bit more and as it does so, most people begin to resist it, becoming rigid in the denial of it. This is crazy, because if you speak to the spiritual people, they all want more, but when you look deep into their consciousness, you can see the fear of having more and the fear of allowing the light of God to emerge within them.

Each wave that comes forward is beckoning you to get on board. Each wave you miss leaves you thrashing around in the trough behind it. When you are in the trough you are going nowhere.

Now is the time!

Now is the time to learn!

Now is the time to learn how to Ride the Wave of Time!

VISION – A Gospel for Our Time

A wonderful piece of work is a book called VISION, which was originally presented to the world anonymously as a tribute to Universal Consciousness, which gave the text in an insight so that we might understand more about the journey into Ascension. The book is very short and simple and is presented as a Sacred Text to be read as a meditation. When you take your time with the words in this way, then light surges through the words and illuminates your heart. Like a number of things that are being given to us as tools to help unlock our consciousness in this time of Ascension, VISION brings light into the core of your being as you read it, helping you to find your way out of the darkness.

Quote from a Reader

'This book is amazing. Not many words, but those that are there take you on a phenomenal inner journey. It is like someone looks into your soul from the pages and unlocks something that you can't understand as you read it. You just end up having this inner knowing that something is unfolding both within you and upon Earth at this time and we don't fully understand what it is, but that we are a part of it. Each time you look into this book, it seems to look back at you in a different way — a guiding way — an illuminating way. It's not so much a book as a tool that allows you to feel God working within you, unlocking the deepest aspects of your being. Don't be fooled — this is not a book like you have ever seen before. It is something that communicates with you like a living Being!'

The Author

The anonymous author, Scorpio 851, was myself, but guidance later required me to acknowledge VISION as my work, even though I was given the original vision from which I created the text.

See www.visionbook.co.uk and www.thevisionjourney.co.uk

22

Reading the First Signs

Jesus said,
  'They know not how to probe this revelation.'

The Gospel of Thomas

Rarely do we find that our paths are similar to others', for we are all individuals and God expresses his consciousness through us in an individual manner. We all possess completely different abilities and talents, although, they are unformed or undeveloped in the early days. In the beginning we might well find that we work in groups with others, but eventually we will walk our own individual path. However, there is much to learn and experience before we get to that point in our lives. The key word here is 'experience', because you cannot possibly learn to be a powerful healer or lightworker from reading books. You have to walk the path in a practical way and experience many aspects of energy in order to understand how it affects you and how you can use it to help bring about change in others.

As soon as you step onto your path of working with energy, you can suddenly find things going wrong, or what you perceive to be wrong. Once you start working with energy, energy starts working with you and whilst the results can be brilliant and easy for the few, they can be brilliant and difficult for the many.

No Such Thing as Negativity
Learning to read the signs is about understanding what is going on at any one time in your life. Without doubt, the path of evolution is not all sweetness and light; there can be dark moments of doubt and despair too. However, you must understand that there is no such thing as a negative experience. It is only the way we view each experience and judge it that

gives it this label. Very often, people experience difficulty and then walk away from it rather than try to understand the lesson within. Amongst other things, this book of modest experiential wisdom is designed to help you discern what is happening at these apparently negative times, such as when you have that absolute knowing that something is wrong with you, but everyone tells you that nothing is wrong. Have you experienced this yet? This point is for everyone, teacher, student and spiritual seeker alike, or even those who are just meandering through a relatively ordinary life—not that I expect they will be looking in this book.

Whilst discovering your path as you work with energy, you may find that something goes wrong with your energy system. When you know that something is wrong, you *absolutely know it* at every level of your being. You might go back to your teacher with the problem, or even to other teachers and healers, who may all tell you there is nothing wrong, but *you* know that there is. At this point you will begin to question your sanity, to ask why they can't find the problem and that is a good place to start.

It is just the same when people go to the doctor. They don't go if they are feeling well, but when they feel that something is not right. On the spiritual path, even though we are empowering ourselves to find our own answers from the Truth within us, when we have exhausted the route of healers, therapists and spiritual teachers, in desperation we might then seek out the doctor. It is very common. The doctors do the tests and then tell you, 'There is nothing wrong'. What they really mean is that they can't understand or find what is wrong. If you have an energy system problem, they won't find it anyway, for this level of knowledge does not exist for them. The doctors then push it back onto you and the result is that you end up in confusion, because there are two conflicting opinions.

Your Inner Knowing telling you that something is wrong

versus

The opinion of those who cannot find the answer
and so say nothing is wrong

In this situation you absolutely need to trust your own feelings and Inner Knowing. Those of you who continue to seek the answer usually arrive at the door of someone who can perceive what is going on and help you to resolve it. Finding the right person can sometimes be somewhat of a journey in itself. However, what God is trying to do is connect you with the next person that you need to work with. Therefore, what He does, in His wisdom, is give you something that is difficult to solve. If it is difficult to solve, then the work you will have to do in order to solve it will be a huge learning curve. The more you learn, the more useful you are to God in this time of Ascension. Clever game, isn't it?

When I was a healer, people would often arrive at my door after a long experience of trying to find answers. They would already be thinking that I would tell them nothing was wrong. However, once the energy system and consciousness are fully investigated and the problem understood, then an explanation could be given as to how the issue had manifested, which often provided great relief to the person, if not elation. To discover that it was not their imagination after all, would begin the healing process. When you can also reveal to the client how the issue was blocking their progress and the lesson they were trying to learn from it, there is even more room for celebration. The healing begins just because of the knowledge gained and the vindication of their own Inner Knowing.

The fact that we might now be able to help fix the problem is for them secondary to discovering that their *inner knowing* was right after all. Once we can see how the problem works, we can then determine a plan to bring the life back on course and teach the person the lesson, which was being presented to them.

I always take the view that if someone says that something is not right in their life, then they must be correct. Everyone knows their own self and how they normally feel. If something suddenly changes in your life after working with energy and that change brings discomfort or disharmony on any level, you will know it. What you then need to do is work with whoever you are guided to until you find the answer. Obtain the best understanding you can of what is producing the effect and then you can figure out a way of correcting the problem. If something goes wrong with your energy system you most certainly *will* know it and if you can't find immediate answers from the people you are consulting then you need to widen your search.

Seeing is Believing

There are many healers and teachers in the world today, all progressing as the burgeoning light of the new age bathes their life-missions with opportunities. Each year that goes by will open them to greater depths of imagery and understanding with their clients and students. When searching for answers to your problems though, you may well encounter many who cannot yet see deep enough to resolve what is troubling you. That is OK, because you are being shown a pathway to the person at the right vibratory level to assist you. Don't take no for an answer, keep searching and you *will* find that assistance. If a person can't see deep enough to understand the problem, this is only due to their present level of development. Time, energy and light unfolds the abilities in all of us. If your client presents with a problem that you can't fathom, then help them to seek an answer elsewhere. If your client is complaining of a problem and you can't see it with your present level of vision and perception, then you can't fix it. Consult with others and you will both benefit.

Being able to see deep into the subtle energy system is only the beginning. When you have learned how to do this, you then begin to move deeper and learn to see into consciousness. When you do see into consciousness you can then learn to see into past lives and soul levels. There are never-ending depths that you can project your consciousness into, in order to find answers.

Don't Judge and Don't Criticise – Always Uplift

Why is it that so many healers and teachers cannot see into such great depth? Quite simply because they tend to lack the following:

Experience
Knowledge
Ability
Power

You might find yourself asking why, if such people are teachers, they do not have these attributes and abilities. The above is not a judgement or criticism. Think about what is happening on planet earth. We are all awakening, some more quickly than others, but for everyone, the awakening process involves a steep learning curve. We are all going to get to the point where we can see and perceive into the deepest consciousness, but one step at a time as we learn our own lessons as they are presented to us in our particular predestined time frame as agreed prior to incarnation.

As we have said, one of the problems involved in working with energy and light is that in the early days it constantly trips you up with ego-based scenarios. When you make a serious conscious shift, it takes you to a place so far ahead of where your vision and perception previously stood that the ego thinks it has all the answers, or at least a whole lot more than it had previously. The ego-self trips you up with its own enthusiasm and omnipotence. It becomes a greater part of you as it becomes illuminated and inflated by the light, rather than becoming a lesser part through the wisdom you might imagine would be imparted as your vibration increases. You will find it increasingly amusing as you learn how light often brings the opposite of what you expect. Do you remember me saying that you need to develop a keen sense of irony?

For a while after an evolutionary shift, the God-consciousness often sends you a whole rake of new and different cases, teaching you how to solve them all. Boy, this adds even more power to the ego-self. Then God sends you something you are not yet ready to see and that then challenges the ego into letting go of its exalted position. But, in reality, you and your ego can't let go because to do so is to abdicate your power, or what you believe to be *your* power. What most people don't understand is that the abdication of power is the next step on the ladder. The lesson is one of humility. Stand back, have the humility and courage to say you don't have the answer. When you adopt this position you will then be taken through the lessons, which will allow your vibration to rise to the next level. Then you will have the answers.

This is merely the Truth of the Path, the Truth of the situations, which we are all faced with at some time. We are all at the right place on our path of evolution. We are unfolding and evolving at the pace we are meant to. All teachers are teaching at their present level of knowledge and ability and by Universal Law, they will only attract students and clients who are ready to receive at this level. By the same token, students and clients will only be drawn to the teacher they are ready for. Everything within this cosy picture will be working exactly as it should, in terms of everyone's evolution, client, student and teacher alike.

Even though we can say that everything is unfolding exactly as it should be, what we often fail to see is that the Universe is really pushing us all very hard. There is no time to waste. We should all be working at the cutting edge all the time. When we are working at the cutting edge, we are almost out of our depth, so to speak. This is the place where we begin to understand the concept of lacking Experience, Knowledge, Ability and Power. At whatever point on the scale we might be, the ego-self seems to think it knows it all and that its host is the best in the world at this particular game. Mad and bizarre, but you need to experience this level of illumination to understand the issue. However, one step at a time, we learn how to use the ego at the appropriate level for our work and also how to dissolve it as we pass through the evolutionary lessons that demand that we do. Eventually ego will cease to exist, but don't kid yourself that you have dealt with it all, because the place you reach when it is ultimately dissolved is that same place when you learn to walk on water. Just imagine for a moment that ego is heavy. If you still sink when you try to walk on water then you've still got some ego within you. Easy, isn't it?

Those who are working at the cutting edge of their ability are always pushing the envelope, but that is where every healer, lightworker or spiritual teacher should be. Anything less is denial of the journey and the reason you are here. For my sins, I am always pushed by spiritual sources into an ever-changing landscape of new challenges and I know that I don't have a choice about facing them. As you unfold, you too will reach a point where you know you have no choice. The path is mapped out for you.

I began my journey with no psychic or spiritual gifts or abilities at all, but as I have continued to work diligently, there has been a constant reward from the Universe. In the face of things that are given, there is absolutely no problem in developing humility, but at the same time the humility can be a problem. Jesus said, *No one lights a lamp and puts it under a bowl.* What He means is that once the light has been lit within you, then you should not hide it, but place it where others may benefit. This can be very difficult sometimes without the message seeming to resound with ego. My particular gifts, for example, have allowed me to create a number of spiritual world firsts that help uplift and evolve others. Some of the insights that have been given to me were so powerful when they came through that the waves of energy, which accompanied the insight was enough to physically knock me off my feet. When you are given such amazing things, you know that you are merely being asked to present them to the world, or to put it another way, you know that you have been chosen to bring them to humanity and this is where the great difficulty lies. It is almost like the Universal Consciousness is saying, *so, how are you going to tell people that you can do that?* Finding the balance between humility and bringing the message of the age forward is incredibly hard, especially when your consciousness can perceive when people are not ready for the message, knowing they will judge you from their limited perspective.

The spiritual path is open all the way to the top for everyone and with dedication, a little application and guidance many of you will achieve great things. Jesus said, *You will do greater things than I;* this is alluding to the times ahead, where so many will begin to carry His Light. We are now unfolding into those times. I have been given the experiences that brought the knowledge and wisdom and then the power was laid upon me like a mantle. This is the power to help others unlock the same within themselves that has been unlocked within me. One step at a time, I am convinced that many can learn how to work and walk through life in this amazing way. The only thing preventing your evolution will be your Self.

We never stop learning. If you are not pushing and challenging yourself constantly, then you are denying that there is anything more to learn. As a facilitator for change, by whatever mode of work you practise in this time of Ascension, you will not be allowed to sit back on your laurels. Consciousness is changing so quickly and offering us unlimited opportunities to do things, which have never even been imagined before. This is a time to allow the illumination of your imagination to help create a new reality.

We are All Out of Our Depth

God is pouring light in faster than we can learn how to use it. This is because the Universal Plan is to evolve us quickly and if we turn away from challenge then we will not evolve. The Universe, by pouring in all this energy and light, is pushing us all beyond what we think our capabilities are and so forcing the issue of evolution upon us.

My own path has been meteoric in the way it has unfolded. My consciousness and ability never cease to bring new and deeper understanding of situations, affecting the whole of humanity as it heads towards great change. Today, I stand in a unique position and as you read through this book you will begin to understand that I have been placed at the cutting edge of human evolution. I have walked the path of learning very quickly, as a result of having thousands of clients literally thrust upon me over the years for this very necessary learning experience.

What 'being out of your depth' means for the majority who are in the midst of evolutionary transformation is that as they work with the light it keeps tripping them up. Sure, it trips me up too, it gives me challenges and when you work a little higher up the ladder, those challenges become bigger, sometimes, necessitating a lot of probing and searching to find the answer. The Universe has ways of guiding and showing me, but the answers can sometimes be difficult to see because they are always just a league away from my present vibrational level. It's a bit like the carrot and the stick.

Finding Courage and Facing Truth

What happens with the majority of apprentices to the path and we must not forget that we are all apprentices, is that when the light is poured into them initially, they fall at the first fence and the teacher then often can't discern why. Students say that they are having problems and the teacher doesn't have the answers. What is happening is that the Universe is deliberately creating these difficult situations for both parties, student and teacher alike, so that they can both discover their limitations. The next part of the game is to discover your courage to face the dilemma and stand up and say to yourself that you don't know what is going on. You are out of your depth.

As soon as you can bring yourself to Face the Truth and Verbalise the Truth, admitting that you don't have the answer, you are stepping into Courage and Truth. As soon as you can do this, then the Universe will take you to the next level. It will show you what you need to do or who you need to work with to find the answers you are looking for. It will find a new teacher for the student and it will find a teacher for the teacher. But, it won't do this until you are ready to face the Truth of the situation

A Scenario

In a student and teacher scenario, where a student develops some kind of energetic problem and goes to the teacher for help to solve it, the teacher will then use all the tools of their Experience, Knowledge, Ability and Power to help the student. However, if the problem is beyond the reach of the teacher's skills, vision and perception and they are thus challenged by it, what they often do is ignore the problem and hope it will go away. Worse than this, they will sometimes tell the student, 'this is your own stuff,' when in reality they don't understand the situation and they just push it away in a dishonest manner. It is OK to tell a person that, 'this is your own stuff,' as long as you can see that this is the Truth. But then, a good teacher will guide the student as to how to approach the issue, giving them something to work with to help them understand and overcome it.

What the teacher *should* do in this situation is work with the student to find someone who has the Experience, Knowledge, Ability and Power to help them. What they often then find is that whoever they are led to will have the answers that both of them seek. Illumination of the issue will bring teaching and knowledge to both parties. The result is an opportunity for the teacher to work with the third party as well, enabling themselves and thus, their work, to evolve to a higher level. This is a perfect example of a very common scenario. The moment the teacher enters humility and acknowledges that they don't have the answer, then God-consciousness will be working overtime to help them out.

As the teacher, *you* think it is all about the student having a problem. In reality, in most cases, it is about the Universe challenging you, the teacher, and trying to push you to a new level by showing you your limitations. As you attain the new level, so you will be able to see and solve these problems for your future students. Also, the Universe will then be able to bring you new students because it knows you have advanced in your Experience, Knowledge, Ability and Power to serve them well. If you can't serve your students with what they need, you will find yourself without students and clients for that matter. This whole process is about a permanent pathway of evolution. Once you begin to walk the path of light, then the God-consciousness within you expects you to continue walking it and that means continually facing the challenges, which come up for you, not pushing them back on others and not walking away from them.

Flaws and Weaknesses

The light is poured into our work at this high level in order to expose our flaws and weaknesses. We all have them and the light is used to illuminate them. When we have the courage to acknowledge them, then the light will begin to help us to overcome them. The way the Universe helps you out is usually by crossing your path with some information that leads you to someone new who has the Experience, Knowledge, Ability and Power that you need at that precise time to help guide you out of your present limitations and on to a higher path.

Some of us have to find those answers ourselves, from touching the light at our core, for others there are teachers who can help. On my own path, I have always been guided to find my own answers and that can be a lonely and difficult journey sometimes, but there are reasons for it. There is an old saying that, 'when the student is ready, the teacher will appear'. As I sat in the Beech Hill Stone Circle in the Sussex sunshine one afternoon with some friends, I was asked, 'Have you ever wondered where your teachers are?' 'All the time,' I replied. My friend continued, 'That's because all your teachers are in the astral realms '. I understood his point, of course. The God-consciousness walks this planet in many guises and it is the Christ Light at our core, which is the ultimate teacher for our spiritual journey. Whether the light is given directly from that ultimate source within, or comes via some form of message or messenger from without, be certain that it will be delivered. When you really need the lesson in order to transcend your present position, then it may come from what may seem the most improbable, incomprehensible or bizarre source in an equally incomprehensible form. This can seriously challenge your logic and your sanity to a point where it seems like you might lose your mind. You have no choice, but to continue to address what faces you, until you receive the clarity to understand the lesson.

Of course, something within us always knows the answers at some level, but it is still comforting to think that whenever you are in difficulty and fighting the darkness within you, someone might just enter your life with the answers that you seek, with a clarity of expression that you can understand. I have been challenged to find most of my own answers on this path, but there have been moments too, of lucid guidance placed before me to confirm that I was heading in the right direction.

Summary

Don't ever think that you know it all.

Be aware that the light illuminates the ego, sometimes dramatically. It does this so that you can appreciate how it fools you.

Learn humility and the God-consciousness will continually help you to transcend.

Difficult situations with students and clients are always opportunities to learn. If you can't solve the issue, help your student or client to find additional help. In that way, you will often discover that God is really trying to help you to a higher level, by showing you a limitation within yourself.

Learn to read the signs that are sent for you.

Learn to reach out at the first sign of difficulty.

23

The Ladder of Ascending Possibility

Jesus said,
>   'When you Know your Selves
>   then you will be Known,
>   and you will be aware that you are
>   the sons of the Living Father.
>
>   But, if you do not Know yourselves
>   then you are in poverty,
>   and you are the poverty.'

If you are entering the spiritual path, or the path of evolution as this is closer to the truth, it can be very difficult to estimate where you are on that path. As we have said; as light touches you, it illuminates and inflates the ego-self and, therefore, this aspect of you will always give a false perspective of where you really are. Therefore, we have produced for you this rough guide, so that you might estimate where you might be at any particular point on the path, in association with your abilities. Once we have a rough guide to work with, then we can move on to more practical aspects of helping you to walk the path through a deeper understanding of energy and light.

Holding and Channelling Light

One of the first major concepts to understand is the difference between being able to channel light and hold light. In short, anyone can channel light, but it takes a considerable degree of development in order to hold light.

For example, many people begin to channel light while still children and are consciously aware of it. One of the noticeable signs is that people will naturally gravitate towards you and begin to tell you about their problems, uninvited. This is because their higher self can perceive the light, which passes through you or radiates from your being. They unconsciously seek that light as a source of assistance. Those young people who are aware, fully realise that they are different; they have the inner knowing of what is happening as they attract others to them, but often feel that they do not know how to help.

In other situations, you might take an attunement, which opens your energy system to light. From the point at which your system has been opened, you continue to channel light. If you are training in healing, you will also be taught how this channelling process works.

In a third situation, you might associate with people of a high vibration and the light within them may trigger a vibrational shift within your own energy system, resulting in a sudden ability to channel light.

When you begin to hold light, you become a vessel that not only channels it continuously, but holds it as a tank holds water. At the same time, you radiate that light from the core of your being. In order to attain this level, a great deal of development needs to take place, a large part of it is to do with the way the subtle energy channels are developed by spirit or higher consciousness as vehicles to carry high-frequency light. Much 'energetic stamina' needs to be developed and this takes time. Just as an athlete must work hard to develop physical stamina, so the spiritual aspirant must work hard to develop energetic stamina. The second aspect to understand is the relationship between Heaven and Earth, or the Masculine Consciousness and the Feminine Consciousness and the parts they play in the evolution of our consciousness in association with the physical vehicle, which has to bear the increased vibration in order to develop.

In *The Keys – Book Two*, we will reveal many aspects of how this masculine and feminine relationship works. For now, we would say that the great majority of people working with energy and light on the planet at this time do not fully appreciate the interrelationship of these two forces of creation and how they function within the vehicle of the physical and subtle human being. One step at a time, we will take you into higher concepts. As you understand them, so your own mind and consciousness will be able to open itself to these incredible possibilities of creation that this knowledge will bring to you.

For now, let us look at some of the descriptive terms used in the spiritual field and align these with what they mean in association with ability. Then you will have a much better idea of the steps of attainment on the path.

Healer

This is the first stage of development on the evolutionary path, that we refer to above when you begin to channel energy and light. This process can occur naturally or can be induced in almost anyone through an attunement process. We might say that this first stage of awakening is a natural right of all humanity. What you then do with the gift of this power is entirely up to you. As we move into the new Age of Aquarius, ever more people will begin to awaken naturally, channelling healing energies because of the speeding-up of Universal Consciousness. This is the birthing age of the healer. So think of all those who came before this time: how their magic was not accepted and how they were often ridiculed. The healers of the previous generations were the first to be illuminated with the fire of God, yet the great majority, still in darkness, were not ready to see who they were. We are now entering the age when many healers will awaken and many will also be born with these gifts.

Those taking a conscious decision to step onto the path have much to learn, but the light within them usually creates the desire to progress. For others, though, the light awakens denial and they begin to resist it. In some this resistance is a natural process and is created through fear, the original darkness that is within all human beings.

The Healer has much to do, learning to stand in the flowing stream of channelled light and allowing it to do its work as *they* work to assist and uplift others. By far the biggest lesson to learn at this stage, is that word, 'allow'. The more you allow the light to flow, the greater will be the result of its healing qualities. However, there is a bit of a double-edged sword here, for at the same time as 'allowing' the light to flow, one also must learn to observe what is happening as it brings about change. The key is to observe without becoming a part of the process. Allow the light to flow, but observe without entering into the process of driving or manipulating the light in any way. Observe that you are the chosen vehicle. Observe how God uses that vehicle to bring light through. Observe how the light touches the other person in the healing session, but ensure that you remain detached from the process.

This is very easy to say, but not easy to learn. A good guideline is that if you pick up pain or symptoms from your client, then you are doing more than just observing. It is a fine balancing act. It is not just a case of standing and holding out your hands and allowing the process to happen, for that will not entail any growth. But, by the same token, it is exactly about standing there, holding out your hand and allowing the process to happen, with detached observation of the procedure. Then you will learn and progress.

Summary:
Take the very first steps in learning to 'be the vehicle,' 'allow the flow,' 'observe the process.'

Energy Worker

The role of Energy Worker is a natural progression from being a healer. As you learn how to channel energy successfully, without suffering any side effects of absorbing unwanted energies, the next level is to learn how to work with energy in a hands-on way. Let us say that when you begin to channel energy, it should pass right through you without you touching or interfering with it. You just channel it, like a drainpipe channels rainwater. When you are ready to progress to energy worker, you deliberately 'handle' and manipulate energy for the positive benefit of the destination that you are targeting.

We fully realise that this seems like a complete contradiction of the act of being the 'vehicle' and 'allowing' the work to be done through you. Quite simply, it is. However, the difference is all about permission from a higher level, to progress.

Universal Consciousness wishes you to advance as quickly as possible, but all humans will progress at their own speed. It is not a race, but at the same time, it is important to push yourself, so as to take advantage of the energies of these times. Let us explain.

God wishes you all to become God, but you can only learn how to become God one step at a time. So, the first step is becoming accomplished in the first step. Universal Consciousness will not allow you to progress until you become proficient at each level, with a full understanding of everything you need to know for your own journey. Remember, all interactions with others are teaching offerings and, therefore, your clients will be your teachers. When you have learned everything you need to learn, then the Universe will offer you more challenging work. When new and challenging work comes, you will know that God is preparing to take you to the next level.

Rods: As you move up to Energy Worker, as we say, you learn how to manipulate energy. A good way to begin is by learning to dowse with rods and work with the earth energies. The earth energies are very strong and powerful and will punish you very quickly if you get it wrong, which is a great way to learn how to get it right in the shortest possible time. It is like learning about how fire burns when you first get burned by fire. You learn quickly.

Some people open very naturally to working with the earth mother and her many frequencies of energy. Try working with a dowsing teacher or organisation, like the British or American Societies of Dowsers. These organisations run many courses with excellent professionals. You will learn about Earth Healing, Geopathic Stress, Sacred Geometry, Earth Acupuncture, Geomancy, Dowsing for Water and many, many other aspects of working with the earth. You will learn how to feel the different energies and manipulate their river-like flows for the benefit of humanity and the Earth Mother.

Pendulums: Dowsing with a pendulum will enable you to develop questioning and investigative techniques to probe deep into the energy systems of both humans and the earth and eventually into any form of consciousness that you might wish to consider. There is so much you can learn that you could fascinate yourself for a lifetime, most easily. However, as you do learn, so you will be taken up again in your vibration and evolution when it is considered by the Higher Consciousness that you know enough at that present level of development. I have found in my own development that I have had to leave things behind that I enjoyed because it was time to move on.

Energy Tools: You begin to work with crystals and flower remedies, colour frequencies and an almost limitless list of tools to help you to work with energy at one level or another. Each type of energy tool you work with will develop you, opening your inner being to change.

With rods and pendulums you begin to become 'hands-on' with energy, to feel it in your hands, to begin learning to let it pass through you without touching you. You become a part of the energetics of nature. As you work with energy, you become so attuned to it that you see and perceive it at many levels. Seeing and Perceiving are interchangeable terms. As you develop your latent abilities you will begin to literally 'see' beyond what we call the visible spectrum of light. Some people develop the ability to see subtle energy with their actual physical eyes, but more often than not it is the development of inner sight that allows you to see into or perceive the subtle realms. However, this inner sight manifests in a different way with each individual. Some people will develop a very visual image of what they might be working with, such as a chakra or an earth flow. Others will develop an inner knowing, without really having a visual image. So, when we use the term seeing or perceiving, you will learn to apply this in the way your own abilities open up to you. Some people receive verbal guidance, perhaps just the odd word or sentence, or a complete commentary. Some develop feeling, known as clairsentience. They can then feel what is happening within other realms, especially the emotional realms. Some develop all of these different ways and more—and they might all function at the same time or individually, depending on what the inner guidance wishes to impart to you, and why.

Summary:

Dowsing with rods and pendulums opens up a myriad of opportunities to learn how to become hands-on with energy. Note that we do not use the term light, but only energy.

You learn to work with, interact with, and manipulate energy for the benefit of humans and the earth.

You learn how to see and perceive energy on many levels.

Light Worker

As you continue to work with energy, energy continues to work with you and, a little at a time opens you to ever-deeper vision. Eventually, you learn to see beyond energy into consciousness and light. Of course, the whole Universe consists of consciousness and light and the energy is the driving force than enables everything to happen. Consciousness and light are the potentials, the ideas; energy brings those ideas to life.

As you develop these greater faculties you will find that your whole life begins to change. Well, we might say that you have already experienced much change on the path to this point, but as you reach the Lightworker stage, the God-consciousness begins to work with you in greater depth, actively pushing you to develop further.

If we look at a chakra (as you will see in some of the later illustrations in *The Keys, Book Two*), a certain part consists mainly of energy, but then you get into the conscious part. When you see into consciousness, you begin to see how things work, to see the driving force behind behaviour, the hidden aspects of how humans function in spite of themselves.

You begin to see and perceive how the deeper aspects of consciousness manifest in the actions the person takes in life and how it is really the deeper consciousness, which they are slaves to, responding and reacting to their own deep inner stimuli, but having little control over their own lives.

At this point of development, God is trying to take you into the first levels of what is called, The Illusion. This is where you begin to see into the engine room of reality and the ugliness of how it is all out of control as a result of the development of fear as a weapon wielded by one person, or nation, over another. This is also what is known as The Fall, or The Fall from Grace, where humanity became separated from God-consciousness.

Of course, God-consciousness is active in every atom of creation, but each atom is driven by one of two forces, either love or fear. A Lightworker begins to see into and have an understanding of love and fear.

Summary:

Beginning to move beyond the coarse vibrations of energy and learning to see into consciousness and light.

Beginning to see and perceive the driving force of The Illusion, which we consider to be Reality.

Beginning to see beyond The Illusion and into Truth.

Beginning to understand the nature of how humans create Reality.

Co-creator

We could say that we are co-creating right from the beginning—as a healer and even before that, co-creating even in ignorance and chaos—but we are really referring here to co-creation on a much higher level. The true meaning of a Co-creator is one who has attained the ability to manipulate consciousness, through higher guidance, for the benefit of the whole of creation.

So, Co-creation is working with consciousness in the way an Energy Worker manages energy. As you might imagine, this opens up a whole new realm of possible experience and it is at this point that many humans begin to sabotage themselves on a most powerful level. Deep unworthiness, a condition programmed into humans at the deepest level, begins to assert itself. There is also a second human programme, Poverty Consciousness. It is active at every level up to this one, but at this level it develops a higher form of activity.

Unworthiness and Poverty Consciousness are the overwhelming programmes of humanity. We say overwhelming, because that is what they do to you. They overwhelm you to the point of paralysis.

At the level of Co-creator, God is holding out his right hand and saying to you, 'Here is my right hand, take it and learn how to climb out of your poverty'. However, the deep inner programming of unworthiness and poverty consciousness both reply to God in the same way, saying, 'I'm not ready.' And, God replies, 'But you are; that is why I offer you my right hand.'

As a person enters the phase of Co-creator, they often stumble heavily. Stepping up into this level often requires that many changes are made to life. This level often necessitates a complete identity overhaul and a positive affir-

mation to change almost everything you know about yourself and some
things that you don't know.

What we mean by Poverty Consciousness is outlined in the words of the
teacher Jesus, at the head of this chapter and repeated here for your conven-
ience.

> When you Know your Selves
> then you will be Known,
> and you will be aware that you are
> the sons of the Living Father.
>
> But, if you do not Know yourselves
> then you are in poverty,
> and you are the poverty.

What the teaching is trying to explain is that when you reach a certain point
in your development it becomes incumbent upon you to delve deeply
within and learn who you are, *Know your Selves*. As you learn to *Know* who
you are, you begin to touch that light of God within. And as the light of God
within touches your life, you begin to feel the pain of the separation from
God, but also the fear of letting go of the ego-self. The fear is always the master up to this point. The fear and the ego-self are the poverty of separation
from the God within, the poverty of which Jesus speaks. The fear is what
prevents you from stepping up to the next level, because as God holds out his
right hand to you, the light begins to illuminate the darkness within, which
is the fear and so the fear becomes stronger and in the process of becoming
stronger it holds you in poverty even more robustly.

The level of Co-creator is the test. This is when God says, 'OK, I've given
you lots of lessons, I've given you lots of power to play with, now I'm offering you the ultimate power. I am offering you the door to my kingdom, but
in order to enter, you must Know your Selves and let go of everything that
you are.'

Summary:

Well, how do you sum this one up? This is the opportunity of a major step
forward on the spiritual path.

Many, many opportunities will be presented to you in order that you can
let go and move up.

You will learn how much you *don't* want to walk the path any further.

You will discover how much you are too afraid to step into the House of God

But, you will also learn how to do many more things that you could do at any of the previous levels. You will advance and you will become ever more aware of your denial of God. For every step forward you take, the denial will also walk beside you.

You will also discover that the rest of the journey is up to you. The only time God will assist is when you cry out for assistance and use your deepest intent to open yourself to that light of God-consciousness, which is burning at your centre. From here on in, you only rise further by your own efforts. It is at this point that Jesus will have gone into the desert for 40 days and 40 nights, in order to offer God the rest of his fear, the rest of his poverty of the separation from God.

Messenger

As you step through the lessons of Co-creator, you learn how to become a Messenger; a Messenger of God. When you attain this level, you have learned how to Co-create with God, you have learned how to accept the gift of power, although, there is still a long way to go. Most of all, you have learned how to conduct consciousness as a conductor conducts an orchestra. You have learned how to conduct energy and light without touching it. You have learned how to conduct the Universe and place your own consciousness anywhere in time and space. Or, you are in the process of doing so, assisted by God. For, once you have passed through the testing times of the Co-creator phase, through finding the courage to surrender, then you will find that God lends a hand again.

The phases of development of Co-creator and Messenger are closely connected, because as you learn to find the courage to let go, your energy system begins to develop to a point where you connect to Heaven and Earth at a much expanded level. As this development occurs, so it is that you begin to hold light. As you can see, we have come a long way from when we were learning to heal and channel light. At last you begin to develop to a point where that light is awakened within you at your core and also poured into you from the Heavenly Father as you are created and transformed into a vessel, which holds light. The Earth Mother is the key to the process and she develops you in an energetic sense, so that you can actually hold the light.

Shall we say that the Consciousness of the Earth Mother and the Heavenly Father begin to become one with your own consciousness. There is a merging so to speak, and as the three aspects merge, you each become more of the other. As the process unfolds over some period of time, you begin to hold ever more light. As a result of becoming this reservoir of light, you begin to be aware that the light is radiating from you. The light you radiate is the Light of God and it continually touches anyone who is within your vicinity.

Another teaching also comes into play at this point and here God asks you to find more courage than you have ever needed before, more even than when you entered the Co-creator phase.

> Jesus said,
>> 'What you will hear in one ear
>> and in the other ear,
>> that proclaim from your housetops.
>> For no one lights a lamp
>> and puts it under a bowl,
>> nor does he put it in a hidden place.'

What the above teaching means is this: *What you will hear in one ear and in the other ear,* refers to the teaching heard in your outer physical ears and the guidance heard in your inner ear, the heart. The meaning continues to express; *what you have heard, 'and know' from your inner guidance … that proclaim from your housetops,* which is like saying, now find the courage to spread the good news (spread the Gospel—in those days there was only word of mouth as the means to spread the news.) The next reference to the lighting of a lamp explains, now you have attained this inner level of enlightenment, that you should not hide it, but go out boldly into the world and have no fear of speaking of it. This is about God saying to you, now that I have illuminated you, as you desired and requested, go forth and spread this light. Honour my gift to you and radiate the message and the light into the world and do not be afraid.

As you learn how to become The Messenger, you go beyond having to be a worker at any level. You identify the work that needs to be done, either healing or evolutionary work, then merely ask and it is done for you. You ask in the full knowledge that it will be done. There is no question or doubt that whatever you choose to instruct God to do for you, based on the Universal Laws that you will have learned during this long journey, God must do for you. Your command must come about; that is Universal Law.

Summary:

This is the level where you begin to Hold Light.

You begin to be more bonded to the Earth Mother. More light is poured into you from Heaven.

A Messenger begins to conduct consciousness and the Universe as if it was an orchestra.

You merely ask and the work is done for you.

Mystic

Well, at this point you might be wondering what more there can be, and the answer is lots.

By the time you are stepping into the role of Mystic, you have forgotten most of what you learned in the earlier stages of the path. Most of your inner vision and perception is switched off — by God — as you don't really need it for most of the time. God is placing you in a position of total trust, or we might say, total surrender. You surrender everything and learn to stand in that place of being where you know that should you need an answer; it will be forthcoming from within.

Both the Messenger and the Mystic begin to do God's work at a very high level, unlocking the truth within people and transmuting the fear of separation. They do this work merely by being. Merely by being in conversation, the work is done. God has prepared these people and he then sends the seekers of truth into their midst so that the light that they radiate will touch the seekers of truth in a way, which accelerates their evolution. We might say that whenever you seek an audience with a messenger or mystic, it is through Divine Guidance that you have been placed before them. It may be that you need just a few moments of that light to help you on your journey, or it maybe that you are ready for more serious work.

Again, both Messenger and Mystic can see into many realms of consciousness. When you can work with consciousness you are working with the source of all issues and human conditions. The boundaries are very blurred between these two levels, there is a lot of crossover of ability, but essentially the Messenger begins to transform into the Mystic at a point where they can 'see or perceive' the light of God at the centre of another human being. When you can touch this point, there is no deeper point available to you. You can see and perceive into the deepest level of any person. You can also do this with anyone, anywhere in the world. There is no boundary to your ability to see and perceive. Time, Space or Distance are no object. You are becoming one with all that is.

As development into full mystic capabilities continues, then you begin to Co-create with matter, not just consciousness. You can begin to manipulate atoms, transmuting from one form to another. Some might call this the phase of The Alchemist, those who change base metal into gold. However, when you reach this point in your ability, you have no need of gold and therefore, the ability is useless to you. You have no use for gold because God provides everything you need and, in fact, you need relatively little because you are fully cleansed of fear and ego.

There are many writings about the Mystics; we do not need to tell you more. When you get to the stage of Messenger, you will be well on your way to understanding all we have said and you will have so many gifts and talents that you will not want for more and of course, that is when they are bestowed upon you.

In times past, the Mystics were way ahead of everyone else. Only a few humans would seek out the sages and their teachings. The times are now changing very quickly. Messengers and Mystics will be born into the world in number and others will attain this level of development through diligent application to the path. We might say that God was always present in advanced physical form through the lives of the Mystics and in this next phase of the development of human consciousness, God will become ever present in thousands of people as those who have been chosen to carry this light will begin to develop to a very high level, in order to serve the Great Plan.

Summary:

Messengers and Mystics are closely related. Their abilities merge as the Messenger grows in stature to become the Mystic.

For the most part, their gifts are removed from them. They don't need them any more because of the level of light, which they radiate, but should they have need, then the gifts are 'turned on' by God.

They can see into many realms of consciousness.

They can see into the deepest levels of consciousness of humans. They can see the light of God within anyone, anywhere in the world.

Your abilities go beyond Time, Space and Distance.

You can unlock the Evolutionary Possibilities of anyone who desires it.

You can begin to manipulate matter in a Co-creative way.

Overall Summary

We have enjoyed sharing this information with you. Now you can clearly figure out where you are on the path. If you are reading this book, you are not yet a Mystic, that is for certain. A Mystic would not be attracted to it, nor would they need its information. However, you could be approaching the abilities of a Messenger, even though you do not know at this point. This is because of the acceleration as we enter the light of Aquarius.

Many are awakening in these rapidly changing times who may well skip most of the learning process of the early part of the path. They may not need to serve a long apprenticeship as a Healer, Energy Worker, Lightworker, etc. Some of you will be developing at a very deep level and will suddenly flower as a Co-creator or even be ready for training as a Messenger. You may suddenly find yourself knocking on the doors of the places of serious learning without a track record in the subtle arts. How and why would this be?

It would be because times are changing so fast, because you have worked diligently in many lives at all these earlier levels. Therefore, you might find that suddenly you begin to awaken with the inner knowing that you are here to help humanity in some way. And, it might be that stepping into a high source of light suddenly awakens within you a kind of blueprint, at a vibrational level, which launches you into a career as a Messenger without any prior training. Again, how can this be? It can be so because of the changing nature of the times and the urgent need for transformation. It does not mean that you are missing out on things you need to know, for you already know them at a deeper level from previous lives.

Messengers work at unlocking the evolutionary potential of others and when you work at this level you work under the direct supervision of God-consciousness. You will discover that as you find the courage to step into the role of Messenger, then God will bring the answers you need. You will be able to learn how to conduct the Universe, how to command God and how to receive his blessing upon those whom you work with to uplift.

More, we cannot say at this point, but as this series of books unfolds, you will understand much about your untapped inner power and how you can step into working at a very high level because of who you have been in previous lives and who you are now. Are you an Accelerated Master? Are you a Chosen One?

PART FOUR

Birth of a New Light

24

The Second Wave of Illumination

As we enter the Age of Aquarian Light, the first major wave of the illumination, which began to surge through humanity in the 1980s, revealing the energies of Reiki, closely followed by many other modalities of healing energy, is still going strong. Many other aspects of light of similar frequencies are continuing to move forward into this new century, pulling in their wake ever more people into the flow of healing light and beginning a world-wide process of awakening and illumination. Times are changing so fast now that I thought it would be good to recap quickly, to gain some perspective.

In the 1960s, there was a conscious shift, pushing the youth of the day to, *turn on, tune in and drop out*, to challenge the ways of their parents, to seek something new. The old ways no longer satisfied the new consciousness. Using the Mayan Calendar as our guide we find that the conscious shift of that period was taking around 20 years to complete a cycle. This means that in each 20-year period we saw the consciousness of humanity go through a complete cycle, or shift. Every 20-year period saw people growing into new light. Under normal circumstances you would be exposed to certain family values and social conventions, depending on the culture you grew up in. This was the 'primary programme' or 'value model' to base your life upon. So, what causes people to change, or desire something different, especially if they see that the existing model has brought their peers or their parents security, success, stability and happiness? What causes them to reject what has gone before? The answer is a conscious shift. Since the 1960s, the acceleration of the conscious shift has been brought about by the influx of new and different frequencies of light, which illuminate the consciousness in a way which drives desire for something different. It awakens and enlivens the 'seeking' gene within us. Of course at the time this 20-year shift period was seen as, 'the generation gap'. In the late 60s, those at the forefront of seeking were experimenting with mind-altering drugs in an attempt to find what they were looking for, or what they felt was out there, but just eluding them. Humanity was seeking to go beyond its current limitation by opening the mind. It stumbled around in the dark a little bit, often destroying that mind in the process. But this is how pioneers work. They just keep moving forward and trying new things. You can't stop the forward momentum.

Twenty Years On

As we entered the 1980s, the most amazing thing happened to human consciousness. I really don't think that many people see it for what it is, because it crept up on us with such subtlety, as do all things spiritual. For the very first time in human history ordinary people had the power to open the consciousness of others with spiritual light. The universe was giving birth to a new level of reality. The healing rays had arrived. The desire to seek and use them had also arrived. This ranks with the birth of agriculture and the industrial revolution as one of the truly great historical shifts, one which is visible on many levels of society and in many countries of the world simultaneously. If the 1960s, saw the shift towards a revolution in consciousness and a rejection of much that was accepted as the norm in society, then the 80s, were the beginning of personal transformation. The factor common to the two eras is the challenge to the perceived truths of the age. Lies began to be exposed as lies and this continues. Lies cannot hide beneath an influx of higher light, for it illuminates the darker aspects of human consciousness, revealing their processes of illusion and how they try to mask truth. As you begin to move up the spiritual ladder, it becomes impossible to live anything but total truth. As the heart begins to open and function at a higher level, it won't allow you to deceive yourself or others. This just becomes an impossibility as you realise the true meaning of instant karma.

My own life is a good case in point to demonstrate the incoming wave of the 1980s. From a position where I was completely afraid of anything psychic, even something as insignificant as reading my astrology in the local evening newspaper, (which as we all know is very much a generalisation of the sun-sign only, rather than a serious individual natal study) I found the first wave of illumination bringing energy into me, which for want of a better description, created a total emotional breakdown within my own energy system. It was accompanied by wild and bizarre sensations in the body. Huge pressures filled me, a kind of fire burnt through me. This was the beginning of the awakening and it lasted for about three years, the middle year being the most intense. All manner of desires were born within me to find out what was going on, but at the same time I was extremely afraid. Eventually, I met a person who explained that I was having a healing awakening and that I was here to learn how to be a healer. Arms and eyes raised to the sky, I remember asking many times, 'Why me, Lord?' Clearly, I didn't choose this path, it was thrust upon me and so it is with many others at this time of planetary awakening. However, once I had become accustomed to what was happening and begun to work with it instead of against it, I realised that this life at this time was perhaps predestined. My evolution and that of my work have been continuous. Today, I absolutely know that I possess the most amazing and unique gifts and have been brought through the most difficult, but phenomenal learning experiences, (which I did not seek). They were thrust upon me so that I could learn whatever it is that the higher consciousness wants me to be the bearer of; for the benefit of humanity. My inner knowing goes way beyond what we generally perceive of as reality at this time and as this series of books unfolds, I will share the journey with you. And, of course, although, this journey may have been thrust upon me, we know that I agreed to it before incarnation.

Acceleration of Time

As we passed through the Harmonic Concordance of 1999, consciousness took another major leap forward. We now see a complete conscious shift occurring every 360 days, as opposed to every 20 years. New waves of consciousness are now bringing awakening more quickly within and around the planet. Those of you who work spiritually may notice this quite clearly. My own methods of working have been changing annually for many years now, which is a good indicator that you become a different person at some conscious level every 360 days, or each year. Observing the Mayan calculations, those of us who are already working with spiritual light will notice quite clearly that we do indeed seem to be learning, practising or unfolding into new and dynamic processes from year to year in this period. In 1999, the Universe shifted gear. When you shift gear in a car, the beast begins to accelerate and that is what is happening now. Year on year, the acceleration is increasing. The next major gear shift is due in 2012, although there will be other lesser shifts before that time. There was one in 2005, 2007 and 2008, for example. They are getting closer together and as I write this in November 2008, Guides have been showing me that the next acceleration will hit us five months ahead on 7th March 2009 — and it did, with some force!

The autumn equinox of the year 2011 is approaching at great speed. My Guidance and the Higher Consciousness, which works through me is constantly telling me that there is 'no time to lose.' The urgency and regularity with, which I am told this keeps me on my toes. I constantly ask myself, how can I increase my speed? The Guidance will not allow me to be complacent for a single moment. At the beginning of 2007, they said, 'Don't plan any holidays.' True to form, I barely had a day off that year. My working day is more often than not at least 12 hours, such is the level of information, which they wish to impart in driving projects forward to help others step into higher light and greater levels of perfection. When we flip through the autumn equinox of 2011, the time period per conscious shift will begin to reduce from 360 days to only 20 days. Imagine that for a moment: a conscious shift every 20 days. The mind will, for certain, rebel. In fact you will find that the mind is too heavy, dense and slow to accommodate such a shift, so you will need to begin abandoning it and living in the moment, with intuition as the guide. Don't panic though. It will be a process. The Universe knows how fast we can adapt to change, but for certain, it will be pushing us to move just as fast as we can. Those of you who have been working with energy and light for many years will already have experienced many shifts and know how bumpy the ride can sometimes be. Those of you who can already relate to the shifts we have been making annually during this 360 day shift period, since 1999, might be quite alarmed to think that we will be changing even faster within the next few years. Truly, none of us knows how it will effect us, but affect us it certainly will and most of the effect will be about learning to let go.

Allowing

We learn to think in childhood as people talk to us and push us to develop the process. Some experts say that thought can only be processed at 24 'frames' per second, based on chemical and to some degree, mechanical processes within the brain. I remember the very first 'rays' of intuition that I experienced many years ago. As they arrived within me, I noticed how they appeared instantly and in a kind of complete form, as opposed to thinking a stream of thoughts and then arriving at a conclusion. Intuition does not rely on mathematical functions and processes. It is a stream of consciousness, which comes directly from the Divine Source. Intuition is a part of our animal nature, as natural to us as any other survival instinct. Unfortunately, over a period of thousands of years most of us have allowed the left brain aspects of thought to override the right brain intuition and we are now firmly patterned and programmed to function in a particular way. However, it is interesting to note that all the truly great scientists acknowledge intuition as a huge part of their ability, yet, bizarrely, this is not taught to aspiring scientists. You only have to read some quotations from Einstein to understand that he was very connected to and guided by God-consciousness and was absolutely aware of it.

Healing Energy and Evolutionary Light

Most of the frequencies of light, which have been bathing the planet and opening the consciousness of humanity since the 1980s, might be described as healing energy—energy as opposed to Light. We call it light, but for the most part it is energy. We can call all frequencies, which enter us light, but there is a radical difference between energy and light and in the way it is delivered to us, which we will explore later. When you understand this difference you will be able to distinguish the two clearly. It will make perfect sense when you see it.

The First Wave brought us many individual aspects of healing and further aspects have appeared on a regular basis since. However, as the Second Wave began to flow, from 1999, onwards, the stakes have been raised dramatically. The new frequencies now entering the planet are truly light as opposed to energy and they interact with you very differently. The new light frequencies are evolutionary in their nature. The healing rays are relatively calm, even if very powerful, in their effectiveness, but the evolutionary rays are a major driving force, a huge leap forward in what they can do for you and in turn for your clients, in terms of spiritual awakening and transformation. The healing rays work with you and for you in a gentle teaching way, while the evolutionary rays are driven through you in a manner, which can often bring transformation very quickly, but at a cost of periods of great inner turmoil and emotional pain as you transcend the challenges they present. They can open you so quickly that you do indeed begin to realise that there is no time to waste. Not only that, but when you work with the evolutionary frequencies of light you begin to be governed more by the Spiritual Laws than you are with the healing rays. Understanding the Laws and then observing them becomes paramount in your life, your work and your success. You will find that, even if you do not know The Laws, they will reveal themselves to you as you begin to climb the evolutionary ladder.

As you are touched by evolutionary light and by the speed of the unfolding Universal Consciousness, you will often find yourself in chaos. Everything goes wrong. Perhaps you are even unable to do what you have always done in terms of your work. This is when you will be guided to consult a spiritual teacher for answers and then you will begin to understand why everything is, indeed, going wrong.

The Second Wave of Light

The Evolutionary Rays of the second major wave of transformational light are the 'real' wake-up call, not only for those of you who have already begun to walk your path, working with energy and light as your guide and means to progress, but for the many who have yet to start. However, those stepping into healing for the first time, would find the power in the evolutionary rays much more than they can tolerate, except for one major point of understanding. The evolutionary light is governed much more by Higher Consciousness than are the healing rays. With the healing rays, you can get away with making all manner of blunders and are forgiven, but with evolutionary light, if you make an error of judgement, it will keep banging on your door with the same message until you understand and learn from what is being presented to you.

Evolutionary light is primarily provided for *your* evolution. You don't merely channel it, as you would healing rays, like Reiki, for example. It is served upon you in a measure that you can tolerate, though this measure might seem at times to be extreme in what it begins to do to you and for you. At the same time that it is being served upon you, it is also given, so that you may use it for your work. For those who have already walked some of the path, these rays will teach you that transformation is not a game any longer. Healing and transformation are moving out of the kindergarten into the adult world. These are major energies and when it is your time to be called to step up into them you will begin to discover what true evolution is all about. Rather than using your gifts and talents for others along with the energies you either channel or manifest, it is now time to begin to follow the maxim, 'physician heal thyself.' The process of stepping into evolutionary light is about what it can do for you, not your clients. The evolution of your own consciousness, rather than your clients, becomes the primary focus and through this your abilities become elevated so that you can help more people. It is a complete switch around.

The First Shift of the Second Wave
In a long career, I have done a great deal of healing work and taught and lectured on many deep and complex esoteric aspects of the nature of subtle energies. In the early days, the work coming my way was very much to do with rescuing people from psychic attack and dark forces. It was quite bizarre really, as I didn't advertise anywhere, but I was busy all the time. People would come and I would ask them how they found me and frequently they had no idea. Higher Consciousness was obviously sending them so that I could learn and thus serve my apprenticeship, for without work to do, how are you going to learn?

As well as general healing work and a great deal of psychic rescue work, my natural gifts had first opened up with an ability to see into earth energies, such as ley lines, vortices, spirals, Hartmann lines etc. This had led me into

Earth Healing and Geopathic Stress Investigation, then later Geomancy. I loved doing this work and even at an early juncture I had amassed a wealth of earth energy knowledge, consuming courses as fast as I could find them and noting how the energies of the teachers seemed to be unlocking me. I was not so much learning about, but experiencing energy. Using dowsing rods and pendulum as my intuitive amplifying tools, I was permanently measuring, tracing or following some energy or other, even if it was only the aura of my office chair, whilst I was sitting on it. I had an insatiable appetite for energy matters. I was driven. Something was awakening within me. It was a process of remembering and becoming. I began to realise I was becoming.

Those who are familiar with my work will know that since my healing awakening in the late 80s, my evolution has been a continuous flow, never ceasing to take me forward, constantly pushing me into new work. No level of transformation has been easy though. Sometimes I have been thrust into very deep and dark places as I have learned how to go beyond my present limitations. Often, the higher consciousness has taken away my memory of who I am and what I do as a means to help me let go of one level, so that I might attain the next. I began to realise early on that what the Universe seemed to do was throw me into a deep dark hole of turmoil and then say, 'learn how to climb out of that'. Sometimes it was a long climb, many months, or even years, and all through this inner turmoil they kept on sending the clients. So, I was always working on two levels at once: helping to move the clients on, whilst learning how to climb out of the next hole. I can tell you that the process leaves a scar. Even though, I might be going for a good length of time, in the flow, so to speak, I can't help but wonder and touch into fear occasionally, at the thought of when it will all be thrust upon me again. However, there is an upside to all of this. I came to realise that the reason I had to go through these phases of difficult transformation was to obtain the understanding of the process. With this experience, comes the knowledge and then the wisdom, so that I might recognise where a student might be on their path and thus help them through their process without them having to go through what I did. A close associate and fellow teacher, Anne, pointed this out to me many years ago, saying, 'Dave, you go through this so that we don't have to,' I've come to observe, she was right.

A Further Opening of Vision and Perception

In the early part of 2002, it came to the attention of Denise and myself that the energies within and around me were changing again, but in a huge way compared to previous events and very quickly too. My vision and perception were opening up dramatically. We pondered these changes and considered that they were perhaps taking us into some kind of teaching role, where I could begin to impart more of my considerable knowledge, particularly in the area of psychic attack, its forms and manifestations and share the knowledge of some of my effective abilities and techniques in resolving these issues with others. Perhaps I would even begin to unlock other practitioners to the point where they could do what I could do.

At this time, a typical healing session was conducted *through* me rather than *by* me. The client lay on the healing couch and I sat on a sofa. Usually, within about ten minutes of the session beginning, we would both be completely unconscious. More often than not, this unconscious state was in fact an out-of-body experience. We would remain this way for at least an hour and often longer. It was clear to me that I was being worked upon at the same time as the client in a process where we were each acting as healer for the other. I became aware of how spiritual energy, light and consciousness entered the earth realm. I began to realise that it can only enter through some other form of consciousness. Of course this is obvious on one level — when we channel energy for healing, it passes through us — but this was working at some other level. It was not mere energy, which was entering the room. I was not channelling it as a hands-on healer might channel it. This was extremely high consciousness, choosing to work with the people occupying the room. I became aware that the universe was sending specific people with certain patterns of consciousness to me so that it could use them in certain ways to bring about *my* transformation, whilst at the same time whatever was within me that the other person needed was being activated. Shall we say that there was an exchange taking place? This was not the case with every client, but I began to understand when the exchange was happening, although, I didn't understand why at that time.

I was taken into such deep places that it is impossible to describe them. When I was returning to my body and beginning to regain consciousness my whole being would shake violently as my consciousness attempted to regain a foothold into what was, essentially, my life. Whatever or whoever was conducting these sessions certainly took everything to the limit. I began to realise fully that my consciousness was being removed from my being so that it was not damaged by the intensity of the energy and light being brought to bear in the healing sessions.

I only saw two clients a day as each session was usually between two-and-a-half to three hours in length and a session didn't end until The Guides said it had ended. I always regained consciousness before the client and they were often unconscious for around twice the period I was. There was a distinct pattern. Clients either needed one session or around three sessions of this amazing transformational energy. Most needed only one. If more than one, they needed a space of around three months before the next session to allow the light to unfold within them. Of course, if people only need one session, you need a constant flow of clients to keep you in business. This did not seem to be a problem for the Universe as I always had a waiting list, which was often around six months in length. For around half a year at one time, it stood at nine months. I didn't do any advertising. In fact, I've never advertised myself personally. However, sales of my first book, *Dancing with the Devil as You Channel in the Light* began to accelerate in 2001, at the same time we were developing our first website, both of which, eventually, brought a steady trickle of seekers and still do today.

Losing the Gift

A few months after these amazing new abilities of being able to see and perceive at much greater depth had arrived, the Universe, in its wisdom, decided to take them away again. I began to notice that my vision was being obscured. It was as if someone was putting a sheet of slightly misty glass in front of my inner sight. My vision was decreasing by the same amount every day. I could still do the work, but I had to work harder in order to see the issues and understand the deeper meaning of the client's problem. It was a case of summoning more energy at first, which was becoming debilitating. They were making me work harder, for sure, or perhaps it was me that was making me work harder. I wasn't certain. I found this change of fortune fascinating, rather than alarming and wondered what it was all about. By the end of the week when this process of reducing vision and perception began, I estimated that within four working days I would be able to see nothing within my clients. I found great humour in this new game that was being thrust upon me, this new hole that I was being slowly lowered into.

I began work the next Monday morning and my visual ability was again reduced. I couldn't help but laugh. It was as if the laughter had been planted in me; as if it was not mine, but it felt good. After my morning client, I was now counting down the sessions to spiritual blindness and I knew that by the Thursday afternoon session my vision would be totally obscured. Gone. Blind for all intents and purposes. The Thursday morning came and sure enough it was indeed hard work. My afternoon client walked in, sat on the sofa, didn't even give me an opportunity to speak and said, 'I'm not going to tell you anything and I want you to tell me all about my life!' Well, I had a huge laugh silently to myself inside. So this was the time of my examination, the test they had been preparing me for. It was a great game the Universe was playing. I made the client comfortable on the healing couch and sat down on the sofa. Within minutes we had both been taken into deep unconsciousness and when I returned to my body, an hour or so later, I sat with my pen and pad and wrote non-stop for another hour. When my client came round I read out what I had written and she said, 'Perfect. How did you know all that?' Well, at that point, I didn't know for sure that I did know. I was following my feelings and coupling them with many years of experience, of knowing how it feels when you've found the right issue. Most importantly, I trusted that I knew, but this time with no vision to confirm the truth. I began to realise that having inner vision is almost like cheating, everything becomes so easy. When you can see the issue it is easy, but if the sight is taken away and you have nothing but your feelings and your inner knowing, then it is impossible to cheat.

Knowing without Seeing

A couple of months later, the vision was slowly reinstated. The Guides explained that I was being taught a process called, 'Knowing without Seeing'. In order to learn how to know without seeing, you have to have your vision removed. Once I had mastered the shift to a degree where The Guides were satisfied, they began to give me back my gift of sight. When the vision came back, I found that I didn't really need it any more, but it was a useful aid to confirm what my newly developed Inner Knowing was showing me. Today, several years down the road and with a lot of development under my belt, this ability is really quite amazing. I can see into anyone anywhere in the world, even without seeing or talking to them. I can only do this if it is appropriate, though. I can't use it for spying, or any covert operation, so to speak. So, all you military and government people who might read this, don't bother calling me up. This gift is for the redemption, enlightenment and evolution of humanity, not the control or destruction of it, through fear.

Do you remember what I said earlier about only being able to stand in truth? Well, when you are given gifts as amazing as those I am using today, great responsibility comes with them. In fact, you are not given them until you have learned this responsibility. If it is appropriate for me to perceive or see into somebody, often all I need is one word from that person in order to make the connection. At other times, I know the issue or reason they are calling before the phone rings. However, most of the time it is important to build up a picture of the person's life to date, so that I can outline the repeating patterns to them. It is not just a case of calling me up and receiving an answer to your questions, it is about understanding the deeper aspects of your inner drives. Difficulties in life are arrived at through a process and the clients should be helped to understand that process to see where all the wrong turns were made, so that we can put you back on the path and empower you to move in the right direction.

Clearly, all this sudden change, the influx of new abilities, then the removal of them again to teach me how to access deeper and greater abilities, was leading up to something and upon waking up one morning in May 2002, I had a blazing vision before my eyes.

25

The Birth of a New Light

As I woke one morning in May 2002, I had a vision. The vision was of a cartwheel, lying on its side, in a blazing yellow and white light. It was as if the wheel was on fire, but with light rather than fire, if that makes sense. I was at the hub or centre of the wheel and at the end of each spoke was another person. I wondered at the time whether these people might be other healers or light workers. Later, as things unfolded, they turned out to be anyone with a particular vibration, not necessarily those who had trained in healing or light work.

I asked my Guidance what this was and was told, 'It is The Wheel of Light. You will develop it. It will take two years before you are ready.'

A Direct Connection

That was the sum total of the message, leaving me bewildered as to what it was all about — the normal form of communication from The Guides at times. They get my attention with something profound and then, a little at a time, they feed me the rest of the story. Within a few weeks information was indeed coming in. One of the first aspects of The Wheel, which I began to understand was that you could connect other people into it, in what The Guides were calling a 'Direct Connection'. They told me that this was a pure 'Trust Process' in which a person would 'Request a Connection' and through their own inner knowing and trust, would receive spiritual light in return. I was also told that this was a 'Very Advanced Spiritual Process', a process where spiritual light could be available to anyone who had the courage to step into it and trust. Much later, I was to understand that this trust process was an aspect of The Law of Reflection. In return for this trust, the individual would become empowered ... a little at a time, I presumed.

I began to receive impressions that, whatever The Wheel of Light was, it was most certainly unique in our time. To express this information, the Guidance was being very visual, rather than communicating in words or emotions. I was being shown a kind of radar screen, which was scanning the whole world, looking for other objects, but there were none. I took this to mean that there was nothing else out there like this, or had ever been, which was available to humanity before. Over a period of time, I was to learn that this assumption was correct. As soon as I had understood the information and the means of connecting others to The Wheel, even though at this early stage I didn't really understand much more than its name and the fundamental idea of how it might function, I began to make plans to make a 'Direct Connection' with a third party.

In fact you can't really plan anything like this, the Universal Consciousness will decide when it is to take place, but you need to put yourself in that place of possibility in order for it to happen.

The Wheel of Light Experiment

The only way to truly find out if The Wheel of Light functioned as the Guidance and insights were indicating, was to test it. Even after all these years of working with The Guides, I hear them sigh when I say, I am going to test their information. I am sure they just sit back and laugh at my miserable human frailty and lack of trust. In reality, I do trust completely, but I just like to see how it works. This is part of the excitement of putting a new spiritual gift or idea into practice.

This testing process goes back a few years to the time when I first created some essences. I had collected the energy signatures of about a half dozen sacred sites and then created essences from these signatures. Once I had them assembled, I then sat in a still space and channelled information about each one and what it might do to help people in need of healing, evolution or whatever. When I had all the information, I didn't know if it was right or not as I hadn't produced anything like it before. I hadn't been channelling in this particular way very long, so I was still in the process of learning if I could trust what I was receiving. Was the information my own wishful thinking, or was it genuine guidance? I engaged in a consultation with a respected reader to get another perspective on the efficacy of the essences. During the consultation the channelled guidance offered this simple pearl of wisdom when I asked how I could be certain that my channelled information was correct. 'You must approach the subject matter with Intelligent Testing!' Since that time, I have always approached everything with Intelligent Testing. That way, you find out what works and what doesn't and then you can fine tune the bits that do not come up to expectation.

The only way to test a Direct Connection to The Wheel was to connect someone into the energy. The Guides suggested I use a well respected friend and colleague, Anne, but without telling her, as it needed to be a blind test. I

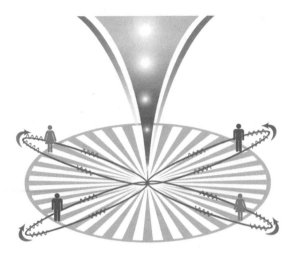

The Prime Force pours into
The Wheel of Light

asked for the permission of Anne's Higher Self and the experiment began sometime around late June 2002. She was totally unaware of this connection, until just before I told her, about 17 months later, in early November 2003.

August 2002

By August 2002, much information had been given with regard to the working process of The Wheel of Light and I found my energies were continuing to unfold and change. I began to radiate energy from my being, which opened other people in a profound way. I could feel how this form of radiated energy changed the energy of other people who were in my vicinity. In particular, I had witnessed abilities in three different people begin to unfold rapidly after merely being in the same room for a short period, yet I had done nothing consciously to effect this change within them. What is more, their light bodies began to develop and metamorphose into something I had never seen before. Whatever was unfolding within me and radiating from me, was doing so in a manner that indicated that it was extremely conscious of its own self and knew exactly what it was doing. I was becoming aware that I was merely the vehicle for something, which was growing in intensity and working through me.

Holding and Channelling Light

I felt that these people had been opened in this way so that I could see and understand more of what was happening. They were signs that showed that amazing transformation could take place with very little effort if the time was right for the individual. It was as if I was the light and they were moths who had been drawn to the illumination: once having fed from the nectar of that illumination for an appropriate period, transformation within them began.

At the beginning of this present transformation process of my own, back in May, when the first images of The Wheel of Light were given to me, Denise and I thought that the whole process was to bring together healers, light workers or facilitators of energy, commonly working at a high level, in order to shift them to a new plateau. It was perceived that we would all link with each other through the structure of The Wheel via this light, which I was now radiating. We considered that this union might be to deal with complex cases of psychic rescue or to help others learn how to deal with dark energy matters, which of course was what the universe had been training me in, these past many years. Or, perhaps it was to connect others so that the Light would support them in their own processes. Those people who could then step into this Light could be trained by us in the techniques I had developed through my ability to see into these realms. Therefore, the possibilities were extremely exciting, especially as the guidance had confirmed many times that there was nothing like this light on the planet. However, ultimately, this perception of how we would use this new light would prove to be wrong.

One Year On

In May 2003, a year on from the first revelation of the blazing cartwheel, we were still wondering how it would develop, often asking the Guides, 'How will it work? How will it unfold?' Also, because I was so busy anyway, with my regular healing, rescue and repair work, not to mention geopathic stress investigation and earth healing, we were concerned that we might not have the time to do the training we perceived would be necessary for this project. However, we figured that God must have a plan to take all our concerns into account. Surely, He must know what He is doing? The Guides kept quiet as they often do until there is something to say, which is backed up by action. They occasionally reminded me that they had said that it would take two years to bring this to fruition and at this point we were only one year down this creative path. Anyone who works spiritually knows that patience is not only a virtue, but an absolute necessity, for you will not unfold until the time is right and the universe decrees that it is so. The Guides show you a carrot and say walk round the world three times, learning and experiencing constantly, then you can have it!

Many Levels and Frequencies

More often than not, it was when a limiting question arose in my constant probing that we got an answer or explanation to calm our concerns and put our minds at rest. For example, after the Guides told me to put the unfolding insights of The Wheel of Light on the website, we received many requests to be considered to work with it, even though at this early stage nobody knew what this journey was all about. It's bizarre really. It is like saying to people, 'Do you want to join this club?' And, when they ask what the club is all about, you can't tell them because you don't know. But, the Light attracts those who are ready to see it and this, essentially, is why The Guides give these directions. If the people see the image or read the channelled words, they will get what they need in terms of transformational energies merely from that simple act of viewing the image and reading the words. The Light radiates from these sources. We were to learn so much more about this process over the next few years. What The Guides were really doing at that time was spreading the Light freely, while I was still being prepared for what was to come.

One request in particular came by email from a young man. He was completely enamoured and drawn to working for the light, but said that he realised that he probably wasn't good enough because he hadn't done much healing work. He had great humility, but I felt he was also putting himself down a little. That night, I did some deep thinking, praying for answers and asking for guidance to the following question. I said to God, 'This Wheel of Light thing? It can't be right as I see it at the moment. It can't be right to refuse anyone at all from working with these energies. Just because they lack experience or cannot work at a high enough level should not mean that there is not a role for them to play in the evolution of man and the planet at some level. To pick and choose who comes forward would put these amazing energies beyond the reach of so many. This can't be right! This would make us elitist and I cannot see the Universal Wisdom in being elitist.' Very soon, the answer came back.

The Guides Speak

'They will not be excluded. There will be a place within the numerous layers and frequencies of The Wheel of Light for everyone who desires it, at whatever level they are at. But one must remember that these are extremely high energies and that some people will not be able to receive them directly without taking some evolutionary steps in other ways first.

What is developing through you is unique and we understand your frustration at trying to figure out what is unfolding, but we ask you to be patient and to trust. When something like this is unfolding into Earth for the first time in the history of humanity, we have many bridges to cross in creating the right platform to enable its success. These are extremely high energies and your own being needs to go through much transformation to accommodate them. You are the bridge into Earth, which we are constructing and when this bridge is complete many will be able to walk across it in many different ways. Just allow the time to pass as we bring the developments to you and all will become clear.'

That made me feel a little better, but there was still more information we needed at this time. How would the training be done, for instance?

The Infinite Flow

Again, The Guides came through and showed me the image of The Wheel and how my energy and consciousness at the hub were connected with everyone else at the end of each spoke. They showed how the light flowed through me and streamed into the others and how the energy and consciousness flowed between us all. My energy was linked permanently with everyone else, and theirs with me. The Guides said to me, 'Draw it on paper.' When I drew the flow out on paper as I could see in in my higher vision, the image hit me immediately as the symbol for infinity. The flow was infinite. We were being linked into an infinite flow, which would support anyone who was connected into it. The Guides had made me draw it as they could see that I wasn't understanding the full implications of how I was being brought into, or made a part of, some kind of infinite flow that would then feed others. However, this did not mean that we fed from each other or drained each other. The flow of light is not the key component. The key component is the consciousness, carried by the flow. The Guides called this consciousness, 'The Prime Force'.

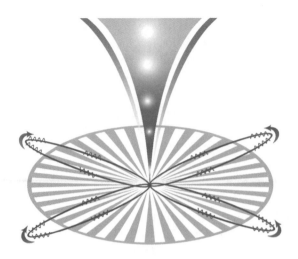

The Prime Force
This is a constant transmission
of evolutionary consciousness

Energy and Consciousness

As they continued to show me the components of The Wheel of Light, it became clear that there were three main aspects.

An infinite flow of energy

The Prime Force, which is the Consciousness of Evolution

The Guides or Guiding Consciousness of the Wheel of Light Energies

The Infinite Flow of energy, is like a road or highway, which carries vehicles. The vehicle is consciousness, called the Prime Force.

The flow of energy is controlled by Universal Consciousness in a balanced way and this provides the highway for the Prime Force to travel upon. The Prime Force is the constant transmission and flow of a form of consciousness with evolutionary expression, which is facilitated and managed by The Guides or Guiding Consciousness of the Wheel of Light Energies. Evolutionary expression means that this is a light for evolution rather than healing.

To put this another way, there is a balanced energy flow, which is infinite, streaming through all beings who are connected to The Wheel. Upon this flow of energy travels a consciousness, which begins to unfold each person in an evolutionary way at the precise level at which they are ready to receive.

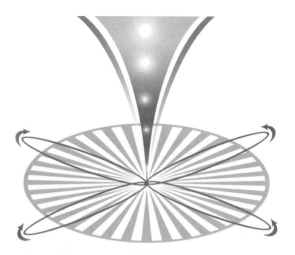

The Infinite Flow of Energy
This passes through everyone
connected to the Wheel of Light

No Training Required

Finally, The Guides answered the question about training.

The Guides Speak: 'You will not need to train anyone with this Light. The Light brings its own teaching through the higher consciousness, which is of itself. The evolutionary energies passing through those who are connected to The Wheel will bring their own teaching. In fact, what will be brought is, 'Illumination' of the inner being. The light will begin a process of developing a person merely by having a connection to it. The light will begin to reve their inner Self. The Prime Force, as channelled through you and distributed throughout The Wheel to those who have a connection to it, will unfold their own natural, but unique abilities, their hidden gifts and talents. Therefore, no wrong turns will be taken on their paths. As each individual unfolds they will begin to discover their own deeper selves. You, David, are a doorway through which the Infinite Flow passes into Earth and those who see or experience this light at whatever level will be drawn to connect with it. This Light will awaken the Seekers of Light. Those who work with this energy and light will find that they begin to develop ever-increasing levels of ability. This will be reflected to them in the clients, which the Universe sends them for their own education. As your clients change, you discover that you are moving to ever-higher levels of ability. The Universe tries to bring you clients who challenge you, for it is through the challenge that you will both learn and evolve. The process is one of development and then reflection. As you unfold, then the Universe will send you the type of work for which you are specifically suited and, therefore, you continue to evolve through your work with others.'

Evolution

I had known for many years that I had an ability to bring about evolution within others, which is very different from facilitating healing within them. Also, an ability to see the spiritual potential in those who are ready for true evolution and a gift to help them unlock their inner power and realise that potential through the consciousness shifting to accommodate a higher vibration. The conscious shift is the key. Many times, even before this Wheel of Light phase of development began, I have allowed this evolutionary consciousness, which is radiated from me, to flow into others within the healing sessions and then see them spontaneously surge forwards both in terms of spiritual development and life change. In the days when I practised my healing work, many had sought me out after seeing friends' or relatives' lives change after connecting with the energies, which were delivered. In other instances, I was guided to work with people through a process The Guides were referring to as a Program, using different processes along a time line, as determined by The Guidance. This then brings about their evolution in a controlled way, allowing them to attain different levels of their potential along the path. Sometimes there are stages where we would do a number of different Programs at different times, several months apart, focused on different issues. The Guides would show me how long it would take to achieve what was needed and how many different Programs would be needed in order to bring the person to that level of attainment. This Program-type work was most definitely focused on evolution of consciousness, rather that rescue, repair work, or even healing. There was a distinct difference in the energies used and the guided approach.

I mentioned earlier that the majority of my clients only needed one session to move them on. These were the people who came for rescue, repair or healing essentially. But those who came for evolution, or in fact, those who were offered evolution by The Guides, were the ones who usually had up to three, or occasionally four sessions several months apart. This would then unfold them into a much higher vibration and allow them to attain their potential in that universal time frame. This seemed to be some kind of 'bringing them up to speed,' approach. Once up to speed the vast majority aligned with their work easily and found their groove in life, so to speak. From that point on, I would find that if they needed anything else, then

Riding the Wave of Time

The Fundamental Plane of Eternity

strong guidance came to them to get in touch. A pattern emerged where quite a number of people would return a year or so later for a touch of acceleration. Those who were really being driven by the Universe tended to come back once or twice a year and this kept their vibration in line with what they needed and allowed them to receive guidance, which helped their focus. I was to eventually understand that these people were being accelerated to the speed of The Wave of Time—pulled up the back of The Wave to then surf on the crest.

A Life Mission

I used to be well read in spiritual matters, until I began to realise that I didn't need to read much more; or, shall I say, until The Guides started to knock me unconscious if I tried to read spiritual books. I came to understand that the time we were moving into had not really been written about; that although, the words of the great mystics have a truth that is timeless, these modern times had not been seen before and new things would be delivered to mankind for his own evolutionary salvation, based on the vibration of the present times. I was forced to stop reading as it was a limitation.

I had a lot of experience and worked with many teachers in the early days, until my own guidance seemed to take over in directing the development of my own work. I absolutely knew that there was nothing like The Wheel of Light process active in our world at this time. In fact, I knew that it was so advanced as a concept that most people were not ready for it. The introduction of The Wheel of Light was a creation process, a sign that the Universe was moving very quickly to bring new things to help us through the coming evolutionary phase as we approach what is known as the end of time in the Mayan Calendar, in 2012.

Sometimes, I think I must be a slow learner, in fact, I know I am. Something can stare me in the face and I don't see the meaning of it. There is no doubt that if I had stopped and looked back at my pathway, it would have been clear that I had been chosen to bring to earth new information and understanding about such matters as psychic attack, earth healing and the way we can unlock the potential within the human energy system. I knew that I could see and perceive at levels others couldn't. At one time, I was very active in the dowsing community, but as my perceptions unfolded, I could perceive and understand things that my contemporaries were not ready to receive. It was a case of the flat earth syndrome and so I was forced to move on. It might be timely also to remember that I hadn't chosen this path in the beginning, it had been thrust upon me and everything, which has happened since has also been thrust upon me, rather than me seeking it. I learned merely to remain open and see the subtle signs and opportunities for the next direction which, would be offered.

I began to realise that the ever-burgeoning abilities unfolding within me had at their heart a great purpose, the Evolution of Human Consciousness. I didn't really know it at this juncture, but, the unlocking of evolutionary potential and raising of vibrational possibility was becoming a major theme of my mission here on Earth. Things were most definitely shifting to a higher gear and I was already in a league of my own, where my abilities to see into energy were concerned. God, or someone under His command, was preparing me for something quite special and indeed unusual as I learned to push back the barriers of limitation within my thought processes. In fact, what began to happen was that thoughts would appear within my consciousness as if they had been put there and these thoughts were always of the nature that I could do things, which most considered were of the realms of fantasy. I found myself always putting them into practice and discovering their truth. I would then show others how to do the same things and it would work. That was truly testing the process: discovering that if others could achieve amazing results with the same process, then I was most definitely not fooling myself.

The gift of The Wheel of Light was beginning to show me that we had a tool for transformation, which seemed to hold what appeared to be unlimited potential to unlock and empower others. It had pushed me into unbelievable territory where my spiritual work was concerned. I felt that I was moving beyond healing and into something else altogether, though I was not sure how to describe it at this point. The feeling was right and the journey, which unfolded, unbelievable.

26

The Devic Essences

I had worked with essences since the mid 1990s, but around 1998, The Guides were pushing me to begin to create my own. I spent a couple of years researching the ins and outs and Sue and Simon Lilly of Green Man Essences gave me a lot of help in putting it all into practice. I had met Sue many years earlier, on a week long Geopathic Stress course in London, facilitated by Jimmy Scott, the father of Health Kinesiology. When I began to move on from crystals to essences in my work, it was Sue and Simon's essences that I used first and then also began to use others from different essence producers

During the mid to late 90s, I was doing a lot of geopathic stress investigation and earth healing and was highly connected with the nature spirit consciousness. This type of work was my first love as it was earth energies that were the first frequencies outside of the visible spectrum that I began to see after my awakening. Compared to people, the earth is easy to work with. She doesn't argue and welcomes any attention you might care to lavish on her. You just sit with her and she tells you everything you need to do in order to bring about the healing. So it was, that The Guides began suggesting to me and then later pushing me to begin to obtain the energy signatures for essences from ancient sacred sites, such as stone circles, cromlechs, etc. As I was connecting into the nature spirit realms, or realms of the Devas, in order to co-create these essences, I called them the Devic Essences. After all, it was the Earth Mother in concert with many levels of nature spirit consciousness, which were yielding what I required. I was later to understand that it was in fact, a combined form of the masculine God-consciousness working in co-creation with the feminine Earth Mother, which brought forth the vibrations for these essences and indeed, they were being given specifically for my own personal transformation, rather than for clients, although, they were used for both. Also, I did not realise at that time, how important the essences were going to be in the grand scheme of things, until the Universe instructed me in how I would eventually begin to unlock the evolution of human consciousness within spiritual seekers, using these as Keys of Transformation.

I work with essences for my own continued transformation on a daily basis. I tune in to them several times a day to ask is there something, I should use to help attune me to whatever I might be working on at any particular time. The most important times to tune in are, first thing in the morning and last thing at night. The morning essence is always to prepare me for what the day may bring. Then it might feel appropriate at any time during the day to check again and finally at bedtime, it is a good idea to ask again and if an essence comes up, then put the bottle under your pillow so that the energy can be working within the aura during the night. Today, as I am writing this book, I was told that I didn't need anything in my morning session. However, when I had been writing for a couple of hours, I took a break and after I felt rested, clear and ready to resume, it felt appropriate to ask again if an essence was needed. The Guides selected one for me and I took it without thinking; other than to notice that it was a Devic Essence and not one from one of my other ranges. In fact, it is not often that a Devic Essence is selected for me these days, but so as not to keep you totally in suspense, it is because these essences have been the tools to unlock my own evolution and as I have moved on, then new essences have been created with higher and more advanced vibrations to cater for my continued journey. Therefore, the earlier essences do not often come up for me in the present, although, they are still very valid for others who are still aspiring to a higher vibration.

As I began to write this piece about the Devic Essences a strange synchronicity occurred. I suddenly realised that the essence the Guidance had selected for me this morning was the very first one ever made. The Trippet Stones No. 3. I felt them chuckling at my realisation and then they suggested that perhaps I should share the reading with you, also. You can't do anything without them knowing and they often throw a little synchronicity into the day just to show you they are always there and ready to help with come kind of confirmation. When I re-read the information for The Trippet Stones Essence, it was perfect for what they needed to remind me of and at the same time help to illuminate you, if you are indeed seekers after truth. At the time of the creation of the essence, they had worked with the Earth Mother and the Nature Spirits in order to guide them in what I needed for my own evolution at that time. This particular essence has great power for anyone who is beginning to advance in their work with energy and light. As you read this series of books you will come to understand how the essences were the keys to my own transformation and as such, they have the ability to unlock the spiritual evolution in others, in the same way. We begin with the details of how, when and where the co-creation took place, followed by the reading. Please note that merely reading the information can bring a certain amount of the light into your being. Linger on the words and contemplate them for the maximum effect. I hope that you enjoy the experience.

Trippet Stones No. 3

Location: Neolithic Stone Circle, Bodmin Moor, Cornwall

Weather: High cloud with sun breaking through, warm with a gentle northerly breeze.

Details: Three separate energy signatures were received from the very same spot at the same time at the Trippet Stones. They were taken on the ground, n.n.west of the centre of the stone circle by about six feet. There were two earth currents flowing across the circle. This location was close to the edge of one of the earth currents, whilst being in the full flow of the other.

Time: 11:15 a.m. Sunday 6th August 2000.

Group: Spiritual Evolution

Keynote: Brave New World

Opening the Doors of a New Reality:

This essence both transmits and connects one with an extremely high needle-like frequency, a brilliant, burning white light, which comes down through the crown chakra directly into the heart chakra. This is the light of personal truth from a soul level. The light allows one to receive the clarity of truth at the core centre of the being, the deeper heart. This allows the stripping away of misconceptions about the reality of all existence and where one stands within this time space continuum. It strips away the anchors to doctrines and belief systems, allowing the person to become free to explore their spiritual self. Connects one with a cosmic driving force, which pushes forward the speed of human evolution in spiritual terms. Helps make ready the spiritual aspirant to receive the truths, which will spur them on in their own seeking of evolution, quickening the pace of learning at a universal consciousness level.

Clarity: It is particularly useful when trying to unfold and understand new perceptions about the nature of what we perceive to be reality. Especially in the realms of working with subtle energy, whether as a healer, psychic, geomancer, or whatever calling you

may practice. As one casts off the weights, which hold your consciousness in physical reality, this essence will help bring clarity
and understanding of the part God-consciousness can play, if we
will trust and allow it to manifest within us and within our work.

Receiving Wisdom:

Anyone on the path of spiritual evolution may take this essence at
any time it feels appropriate to help and enable the understanding
of your individual path and your individual truth.

The First Essence

This first Devic Essence was in fact one of three individual energy signatures, which were all taken at the same time. I think that The Guides were in
such a state of frustration that it had taken me two years to get to the first
sacred site since their original indications that, that was the direction I should
now be going; that they didn't want to lose any opportunity to bring forth
the energies and light, which were needed. Therefore, I was instructed to
place three separate glass vials in three separate places within the stone circle
of the Trippet Stones. Thus, we have three essences numbered 1, 2 and 3, but
all received at the same time. So, you could say that things started with a bang
in August of 2000, and everything has been going bang ever since.

The Holker Great Lime

In late 2002, The Guides were also insisting that I begin to bring my attention to old trees. The older the better was the brief and, therefore, much
research was entered into and the locations of certain old trees noted
throughout the British Isles.

On the 11th May 2003, just a year on from the first Vision of The Wheel of
Light, Denise and I found ourselves on a mission to locate the Holker Great
Lime Tree at Holker Hall in Cumbria. Once in the grand gardens of Holker
the search was underway for the Great Lime Tree. I was confident that it
wouldn't take long to find it as limes are amongst my favourite trees and old
limes are huge and very distinctive in their growth pattern. However, the
search for the Holker Great Lime was bizarre to say the least.

We walked around the whole of the gardens and we couldn't find any sign
of it. We walked around a second time and it was again nowhere to be seen.
This was reputed to be a 400 year old tree. I knew exactly what it would
look like. The trunk would be huge, formed of great castle-like buttresses
with a mass of low growing smaller branches, forming a nest around the tree.

It would be difficult, if not impossible to hide a tree like this. It was becoming clear that the old tree did not want to be found. We set off round the gardens a third time and encountering a gardener, asked the location of the tree. He told us that it was in the stand of lime trees near the main path. Well, we had already looked through this stand of limes, but we persevered and visited them again and still couldn't find it. This situation was ridiculous. I kept saying to Denise, 'This tree must be huge, yet it is avoiding us.'

Still searching, we wandered off the path and into a back area used by the gardeners for storage etc. There was no sign of the lime tree here either. But, there was an interesting old beech tree. Not an ancient tree as such, but completely hollowed out by the erosion of time. A wonderful specimen. I had a good look at it and we both spoke a few friendly words to it before leaving and re-entering the gardens. We had not gone more than fifty yards or so, when this beech tree opened my consciousness and dumped a mass of information into me. It is impossible to adequately describe the feeling of this process. It is, as if a kind of computer download has taken place into your being, the vastness of which ensures that you are completely speechless as you try to understand what has taken place. It is not like being given a message, or a little bit of information, it is like a complete encyclopaedia has been dumped into your mind. You instantly know that there is so much information that even in a whole lifetime, you might not be able to use it, even providing that you could access it. At this point, I was not confident of even understanding the nature of the information, but I knew it was within me or within my reach, but it was not readily available. It was as if it needed to be unzipped or unlocked. Weeks later, I was still trying to put this experience into words and when I bumped into Sue and Simon Lilly at the Buxton Festival the following June and told them about it, Sue said that they had had exactly this type of experience some ten years previously and were still working with the information.

Clearly, we were not meant to find the lime tree until we had encountered the beech tree and received whatever information it had chosen to reveal. The only thing, which I truly understood at that moment of intense communication was from the essence of a message, which came with it. This was along the lines of, 'Humans are only just beginning to touch the consciousness of trees' and it was indicated this reference was to do with, 'the way humans make their essences.' It continued, 'The consciousness of trees is vast in comparison to your knowledge and understanding of them.' This insight or message was hinting that there was so much more to come for humans in their interaction with trees, that even those of us who were working with the essences of trees still had no idea of the possibilities, which might present themselves. It would be three more years, before I had a taste of what was meant by this and truly it was a magnificent experience when it came and I shall write about this in due course.

Within five minutes of the encounter with the beech tree, we had located the elusive lime tree, would you believe? The situation was truly amazing. We had walked past it at least three or four times in our earlier search. It was only some 22 feet from the main path through the gardens and could be seen clearly from the path. It was standing within the group of lime trees, which we had already investigated twice. There was even a large sign on the path pointing directly at it. It was impossible not to see this tree and we were both amazed that it had eluded us in this way. Truly it would seem that it had cloaked itself in invisibility until we had received what we came here to receive. And, yes, it was a huge, buttressed specimen, just as I had imagined it would be.

Send Him Forth into the World

The method, which The Guides were employing is a little like saying, if we send him to Egypt he might encounter the pyramids, or if we send him to the coast he might encounter the sea. In this particular instance, they were trying to bring me to a particular tree, which was not one we might be looking for, but by ensuring that I didn't find the one I thought we were looking for, they brought me, eventually, into the incredible light of the old beech tree. I have learned much since that time in the way trees are used as messengers and in fact we might remind ourselves that the Buddha found enlightenment under a tree.

The information given by the beech tree that day was clearly gestating until the moment was right to bring us into a new reality where trees were concerned. Three years later, in 2006, the most amazing connection to the Universe would unfold through the Rectory Oak Tree, which created both the Extreme Essences Range and the Essences of Time and Space. These are essences, which have fully moved the genre of essence creation into a new league and truly do expound the virtues of essences as being The Keys of Transformation. We will speak more of the Extreme Essences and the Essence of Time and Space in due course.

27

Expanding the Understanding

New things about The Wheel of Light project were coming to me almost daily. I was always working something out based on a little insightful clue from The Guides. They were leading me along a path and teaching me many lessons at the same time. There seemed to be a carrot-and-stick pattern to it: they would show me something we were working towards in the future and would then lay down a lesson I must learn first in order for it to come to pass. I will share one of these lessons with you now. The way it unfolded was truly fantastic in what it delivered over the following two to three years, eventually coming to have connotations for the whole of humanity.

Sitting in the Garden

In August 2003, I was taking a break of several weeks to recharge my batteries. We had been incredibly busy that year and had a waiting list nine months long—over three hundred people waiting for appointments. Very often you have to ask the question, 'What is God up to here? What is the grand plan?' From Monday to Friday, I was seeing ten clients a week in one-to-one sessions during the day and in the evenings, I was working on distant clearance cases and psychic attack. It was a 12-hour day of solid energy work. Most of that time I was experiencing that howling light pouring through me at a level, which seemed at times like it might just burn me out completely.

While sitting alone one day in the sunshine at the retreat, a gentle voice spoke up, 'Do you want to sit in the garden all day and earn £50,000 a year?' A simple question you would think and one I didn't need to reflect on too much. It certainly attracted my attention. I was about to reply that it seemed like a good idea, when the voice continued, obviously having been watching the machinations of my mind, 'Do as we say, and it will come to pass.' Well that certainly aroused my thought processes. For the life of me, I couldn't think how it could be achieved, but I wrote it down as it had been given to me so clearly in that moment of quietude. The question implied that I could sit in the garden and do nothing yet earn this large sum of money. I bet you are wondering whether it did come to pass? We'll come back to the subject later. What I can tell you now, is that the question was not so much about me earning the money, more to do with learning how humanity is trapped within poverty consciousness and then developing something that would help them transcend it. Since that time my life and work have been an even more phenomenal journey than before.

A Process of Integrity

Ever concerned about getting the job right and acting on the guidance correctly, I wanted to ensure that whatever was unfolding had integrity, which should not be a problem if it is coming from the Divine Source. I continued to ask daily about all manner of aspects of this unfolding mystery and the phenomenon called The Wheel of Light. There seemed to be no end to the questions arising in my mind. As we had never seen or heard of anything like the process of The Wheel before, I asked The Guides the following, 'How will people know if this is real or right for them and how will they be able to trust it?' After all, the subject of a Direct Connection to a stream of Spiritual Light involves total trust, which is way beyond the capacity of most ordinary folk at this point in the human evolutionary cycle. The level of trust needed would, I considered, be beyond even some who were well versed in spiritual matters. Consider for a moment that most of you reading this book will have some knowledge or experience of healing, metaphysics and deeper spiritual matters and practices; some of you may even have experience and understanding of the Spiritual Laws and quantum physics. But take yourself back to when you didn't have this knowledge and experience. For example, I can remember when distant healing was a strange concept to me.

When you have worked in the spiritual field for many years, you begin to forget the early part of your path. You forget the amazing things that happened as you learned to go beyond what are normally considered the limitations of reality and also as you achieved great and interesting things with healing energy. This came home to me quite forcefully some months ago, when I bumped into an old housemate in a supermarket. We chatted for maybe half an hour and she told me all about a near-breakdown she had gone through recently. I mentioned something quite casually to her about healing or astrology, I can't remember which and was astonished when she retorted, 'Do you believe in all that stuff, Dave?' Now this is a well-educated, intelligent and worldly-wise woman who has devoted most of her life to the arts. Very right brained, you might think, but, even though, she had been through a difficult trauma and the normal medical route had not been able to offer her anything other than anti-depressants and an appointment with a counsellor; declined because of the three month waiting period, she had not considered exploring other avenues for help. If this scenario did not awaken her to other possibilities, then I don't know what would. If the mention of a fairly well known healing practice still raises the eyebrows of the average person, then the concept of distant healing is, perhaps, not yet a subject for many to contemplate.

Distant healing challenges many people; to say to someone, 'if you request a Direct Connection to this energy it will begin an evolutionary process within you,' might be a little too advanced for our time. When we are in a one-to-one healing session with a practitioner, we experience their presence and also the presence of the energy they channel and any doubts can usually be allayed by question and answer, or even demonstration of the energy by the practitioner. But, think for a moment about taking your own journey, in isolation, with nobody to consult and with just the energy for company. Try working out what is happening within your energy system and consciousness. It takes a great deal of trust to take the necessary leap of faith in a process you may have never heard of previously, let alone one which seems to be a little far fetched in its concept. It certainly does help if you have a fair bit of spiritual work under your belt and are perhaps sensitive, perceptive and intuitive. But, I guess that is who it is meant for.

I know the concept of Direct Connections, an advanced spiritual process, is ahead of our time, but by the same token I know that it isn't ahead of its time, because it is with us now. Now is the time, in terms of the cosmic consciousness shift, which will bring new and exciting things for us to experience on our path of eternal transformation, providing we are unlimited enough in our approach to experience them.

The way I have been shown how to use essences is also ahead of its time. It goes against the grain of everything that the traditional essence producers and practitioners have been taught. The difference is that I have been taught every step of the way by Guidance, rather than on the traditional pathway with human teachers. We are all changing fast with the new energies entering earth. If you choose to stick rigidly to what you have always done, then you will always get the same results. It is a time of going beyond our limitations, so if you are given guidance, follow it and it will open doors you could never imagine. It is always one step at a time with me, never a huge leap. Always an idea or an instruction first, then I unfold it and see what it brings. It has been a long path, but one absolutely grounded in practicality and common sense.

Developing Essence Programs

The Guides had also been pushing me to develop our work with the essences. Although, I had been using them for a few years, placing them upon the client where guided to do so, during the previous few months, I had been able to see the light being channelled into the bottle, activating the vibrational energy as the bottle lay upon the client's body, or around them. The Guides were describing this use of the essences as healing. When we sent an essence to a person by post, to work with them at a distance, The Guides would give very definite instructions as to the way it was to be used and this distant work they termed an Essence Program. In some instances, after a healing session, they would insist that the person take an essence away with them. I knew that this was not just for normal use, but that The Guides were going to drive some kind of light through the essence as the person took it in a daily regime. The Light would drive the vibration of the essence deep into their being. So, rather than the light radiating from the vibration of the essence, it was being driven with an intent to penetrate deeply.

There seemed to be an increasing desire from The Guides to push the development of this distance working method, but in 2002/3, it was most definitely still in the experimental stages. Without doubt though, the results were absolutely phenomenal. For example, a badly damaged aura or torn chakra envelopes normally took the most intense amount of energy to repair and usually a good two to three hours with the client lying on the couch and me unconscious on the sofa from the intensity of energy and light which was being brought to bear. The waves of energy used during these sessions were at times extreme. I had always known that, because of the level of energy needed to bring about repair in this type of case, it would be impossible to do at a distance. However, one day such a case came up. As I used my remote viewing ability to analyse the situation over the telephone, I could see the whole pattern of damage and also the trauma that this person's life had been subject to this past couple of years as she had tried to find help for the problem. The woman lived on the south coast and I was in Manchester, so quite a journey would be involved if she came for a healing session. As we were making arrangements for her to travel up, The Guides suddenly said, 'She doesn't need to come'. I asked her to hold on a moment, while I checked something. I asked The Guides, had I heard them correctly? They repeated, 'She doesn't need to come. You can do this at a distance.' I asked her could we just suspend our conversation for a few moments and I would call her back as I wanted to spend some time in my own energy to double check something. We, the Guides and I, put the telephone down and I then asked them to explain.

From experience, I absolutely knew we could not repair such damage to the fabric of the subtle energy system at a distance. When this type of work was done, the amount of energy brought through my being was so powerful and intense that it rendered me completely overwhelmed and energetically flattened. I used to see The Guides working and they would show me that the repair process was like high intensity welding with light. In fact, the intensity was such that I was often surprised that the energy did not melt or somehow destroy the subtle energy system rather than repair it. The process often reminded me of what Robert Oppenheimer said when they were preparing to detonate the first nuclear explosion, 'There may be a risk of igniting the earth's atmosphere.' But they still went ahead.

As I put down the telephone, The Guides said for a third time, 'You can do this at a distance.' They were not going to tell me how though. I had to work it out for myself, but as was their usual *modus operandi*, they gave me guidance and then confirmed everything, once I had understood the method. I called the woman back and told her what we were going to do, that I had not done this before, but that my Guides were telling me that we could do it this way and so we should try. I sent her an essence and we agreed a day and time when she would begin to take it. We then arranged to keep in touch over the next few days. From the first day she noticed a distinct improvement. The improvement continued and after about three or four days, the improvement was such that we chose not to communicate again until the bottle of essence was completed. I continued to monitor how she was doing remotely and, after three weeks, The Guides told me that the repair was complete.

Within a couple of months of that first energy system repair to be performed at a distance, I was doing ever more of this type of work. It was as if the universe suddenly sent me a whole bunch of cases so that I could test out the new procedures. We were suddenly doing the most amazing and complex energy system repair work at any distance on people with torn auras or extremely damaged chakras, who were perhaps suffering extreme anxiety, panic or fear attacks as a result. The first case had taken three weeks to repair, but the time limit was reducing and in some cases minor energy system damage was being repaired in as little as a couple of days. Clearly, I had gone through some kind of shift to enable this sudden advancement.

Essence Programs were then and still are, ahead of their time, but even those seeking healing or spiritual help with little or no experience of spiritual matters, have stepped into the process with trust. When the process is explained, light is transmitted into them, or rather, if they are open, then light is absorbed by their own Higher Self as it desires to know and seek whatever might be able to help it to move forwards. As the light is received, people seem to connect with the concept immediately. They connect with their heart, not by the left brain analytical approach and they instantly have 'the knowing' that it is right for them. Regardless of whether it seems impossible or bizarre, that inner knowing overrules all fear and doubt and they step into the light and therefore, into transformation.

Clients are not sent to you by the universe if you cannot help them, unless there is some lesson there for you. Therefore, trust that your clients have been sent to you specifically and the universal consciousness will shine its light through you and upon them in answer to an inner call. Trust that everything is unfolding exactly as it should. I have found that there are very few people who are not ready to walk the path that I offer them. Sure, there are one or two who are too challenged by the concepts and walk away, but often they return some time later. It is not my work to 'sell' a process. It is my work to be available for those who are ready to receive what is offered. If they are ready, then they will know it in their heart and that is when transformation takes place.

How Can People Trust Direct Connections?

I was beginning to step from working hands-on to working more at a distance with Essence Programs, but the concept of Direct Connections was even beyond the new Essence Program idea that I was being trained in. In order to get a better understanding, I needed to find out how people would know that this was a genuine opportunity to become connected to a high evolutionary light. I asked The Guides, 'How will people know that this is a good thing? How will people know that it is genuine? How will people know that it is real? How will they be able to trust it?'

The Guides Speak

"The children of the Lord who will benefit from this movement of energy we call The Wheel of Light will '*absolutely know*' it is part of their pathway. There will be no question in their minds. Their consciousness will speak to them and they will just 'know' that they have to be connected to this source. All truth comes through the heart and those with the heart open and ready to see the truth at this level will feel the truth within them speak."

"Also, this movement of light will be calling to those who have journeyed together in the past. They will know this light as the next part of that journey. They will see it and realise what they have been waiting for. They will awaken to it as soon as it is time for them to discover it."

Lack of Trust

"The Wheel of Light is a gateway, which is being opened into Earth at this time, and its Light will call out to the children who are meant to pass through its doors. Many lessons will unfold for each individual through a Direct Connection. One of these lessons will be trust."

"*Lack of Trust* is a great limiting factor in the evolution of human beings. There is great fear around trusting that you are protected; trusting that you are guided; trusting in many things, which are of the nature of creation and the process of moving forwards. This is because of the fear of ridicule, which has been programmed into so many for so long. A fear of ridicule develops a fear of trusting your own Divine Self, a fear of trusting the guiding God-consciousness within you, a fear of trusting your heart. Many feel the guidance and goodness and then deny it out of fear. Trust is about learning to open your heart. Without opening the heart, evolution cannot take place. Therefore, those who are fearful will not trust The Wheel of Light, or for that matter, any other source of high spiritual light. Quite simply, this is because their evolution has not reached a point where they can step into the unknown in trust. Those whose evolution is approaching the highest vibrations of spirituality in Earth at this time will hear the call within them and then step into the light."

"The doors of evolutionary possibility will be opened, but only those who can perceive the pathway will enter. Throughout history, there have been those who could see and understand the hidden meanings in the messages of the teachers and the light, which radiated from them and those who just could not understand and would continue to question. The time is now with us where many are opening up and then learning to understand and in that process they are also learning to trust. These are the ones who will be called to The Wheel of Light, who will see it clearly for what it is and request a Direct Connection. These are the ones who are truly ready to take the next steps on the path of the evolution of human consciousness and who are beginning to perceive the speed of the shift, which is upon us."

"If The Wheel of Light calls to you, then you will feel it in your heart. If you feel the call in your heart, then you will not question, and you will have no fear of trusting in the process."

The Guides
September 2003.

November 2003

By November 2003, The Guides had given me an enormous amount of information about developing Essence Programs, which you will read about in more detail later. The Programs allowed us to do a whole range of work with people, from rescue and repair, through to full blown Evolutionary Programs. At this point in time, I was seeing that Essence Programs were a kind of stepping stone, which would slowly bring people through different levels of advancement, by raising the vibrational rate in a controlled way until they could attain the ultimate evolutionary step, which was a Direct Connection to the Wheel of Light. It was becoming clear that Essence Programs and Direct Connections were integrally linked.

However, as I write this in 2008, about five years later, the acceleration of light, which is now entering the planet has changed and advanced so dramatically that it has already pushed many thousands of spiritual seekers much further along the road, to a point where their vibrations are much higher than might have been perceived at the time I was being developed to unfold these new processes. Those who are here at this time to experience an evolutionary mission are unfolding so quickly that I know the majority don't even realise what is happening to them. We will look later at why this is so.

By being brought into the light slowly and evenly, many of those who might have needed a year to two of preparation are now in a position to request a Direct Connection without going through those stages. As Universal Time goes through its process of evolving the consciousness of humanity, the Higher Consciousness now upon us is providing a platform, or good foundation for those who are ready for more intense or serious spiritual advancement. The incoming universal light is awakening them at such a level that they are automatically being guided to find the Spiritual Light, which is most appropriate to them for their next stage of evolution. On one level the Universal Shift is awakening them regardless of their own efforts and at another level it is awakening them so that they have no choice, but to realise that they have to take the initiative in following the path of evolution, discovering for themselves what is out there to assist them.

Satellites

In November 2003, when completing a one-to-one healing session with a client who had travelled from Sweden, The Guides closed the session with one of their little-gem one-liner parting shots. 'She will be a satellite!' What is a satellite, I thought? As usual, this was the first part of a picture, which was yet to be shown to me and I had to wait for a few weeks until they gave me the next part. I knew at the time that this had something to do with The Wheel of Light, but at this point had no idea what it meant.

The Guides began to give me little bits of the Satellite puzzle and I built this up until I had a complete working hypothesis. It became clear that a Satellite is someone who can form a bridge between me and a third party, someone with a special ability to carry and relay the energies, which I hold and channel. It is a little like a seeding process: they are connected through me into the amazing grounding connection into earth, which allows them to then carry this light.

The Guides Speak About Satellites

'Satellites are people who can act as a kind of 'relay station', carrying the consciousness of the Prime Force from the co-creator and the grounding channel (Dave) to the end user, for the purposes of healing and evolution. The best way to utilise this function is by using Vibrational Essences to help carry the energy.' (It was becoming clear now why I was being encouraged to pay attention to working on the creation of new essences.)

'For example, if the co-creator is in the United Kingdom, one might then have a Satellite person in another country. This person need not necessarily be a practitioner as we understand the term, but can be a link in the chain. If they are both, then all the better, they do not have to be. All they need is a certain conscious capacity to act as this 'relay station', a carrier of the Prime Force.'

'This is like distant healing, but at a much higher level. With distant healing we know that we can connect with anyone anywhere on the planet and bring an energy change to their situation. With The Wheel of Light energies carried by Vibrational Essences, the power one can bring to a situation is enormous in comparison with traditional distant healing, for what is unfolding here is a new paradigm in the creation of conscious links across time and space.'

'Satellites are very special people, with a unique ability not only to channel the consciousness from the co-creator, but also to amplify and support the co-creator's energy and consciousness in a non-intrusive way, without any energy loss to themselves.'

'The Satellites are not merely a bridge or a relay station between the two points of contact, but will be a very important interactive support structure for the energy and Prime Force, which passes into this world through The Wheel of Light, allowing that unique healing and transformational consciousness to reach more people without the energy drain on the co-creator, which usually accompanies such work. This energy drain is not caused by something being out of balance, but is created by the heat and friction of the energy passing through the co-creator. This will be addressed as the plan unfolds and new methods are introduced. The co-creator will become ready to adopt them from the perspectives of energy consciousness development.'

'Like the Indigo Children, the Satellites are special people with special gifts and they will begin to come forward to be used by the Divine Universal Consciousness in association with those with the advanced spiritual ability to evolve others. Their role will be to assist in passing on the evolutionary energies to those who are ready to receive them, supporting the co-creator energetically at the same time. Quite simply, they are channels, but with unique and advanced potentials, but yet they might not know this until The Wheel of Light calls them.'

The 'Direct Connection Experiment' Continued

You will recall that back in June the previous year I had embarked on an experiment with The Wheel of Light energies, connecting them to a colleague without her knowledge. The Guides had said right at the beginning that it would take two years before I would be ready to work with the energies of The Wheel. We were now in December 2003, about 17 months after I first connected Anne to The Wheel. We need to bear in mind that in the early days of the connection there had only been a relatively gentle flow of light. I was not yet capable of holding the rays to a sufficient degree for it to flow fully. By now though, Anne was becoming aware that something was afoot.

Anne's Development

I had recently been working more closely with Anne. I was pushing her into new work and also pushing the envelope where her abilities were concerned. She commented that she had begun to think, a couple of weeks previously, that I was, 'up to something', just when I felt it was time to bring the experiment to her attention. Needless to say, the experiment was a great success. Things changed enormously for Anne. Gifts and talents unfolded and she found the Universe bringing her work, which had previously been far beyond her capability. She found that something was guiding her to solve these difficult cases and bring much needed relief to the sufferers. Shall we say that the Universe brought the challenge and Anne rose to it and as is always the case, when you rise to the challenge you transform and transcend.

Not only was Anne developing at an incredible speed through her Direct Connection to The Wheel of Light, we also discovered something new. The Guides who were facilitating The Wheel of Light Energies were also training

Anne's Guides and her Higher-Self at the same time. Anne commented that what had amazed her most was the high level of protection and inner strength she felt in all her work and that this had given her a far greater degree of confidence to look at cases, which were once too frightening to even contemplate. She found she was able to transcend fear. In the ensuing months she was to be tested on this as ever deeper and more complex demonic possession cases came her way as if to prove to her that she really had made this enormous shift. I think Anne's observations are important to enable you to obtain a different perspective from my own, so I have included them here. You will observe how effective the Direct Connection was, even though, Anne was unaware of the connection.

Anne's Observations

When, Dave asked me to join him in June 2002, to visit a client who had some demonic attachments, little did I realise what an impact this event would have on both my life and spiritual development. In the past, I had been with Dave during some of his healing sessions, therefore, with a little trepidation and a great deal of curiosity I happily agreed to go.

After three exhausting hours Dave completed that first session, which was remarkable to say the least. The energies in the room were almost tangible. I felt that my main contribution had been to provide Dave with an additional energy source to use and lend support to The Guides in locating and removing several unwanted and harmful beings, both in the building and attached to the client. Later that evening, when Dave shared his vision and insights regarding 'The Wheel of Light,' I was fascinated.

The Importance of Confirmation

During the second visit to this client, Dave frequently asked me what I was sensing, I was delighted to find that when I had described what it 'felt like', Dave, using his inner vision, had drawn an exact replica to confirm this. Once again, this was a very intensive session and I began to understand why Dave's energy was so depleted following these treatments. When he informed me that this had been one of the most complex, multi-layered and multi-faceted cases he had ever dealt with, I felt extremely relieved I had been with him and not met this on my own.

The third visit was equally dynamic. Dave encouraged me to verbalise what I felt was happening and I was amazed to find myself describing things I never knew existed. Again, Dave produced drawings to confirm what I had described.

My only previous experiences with unwanted energy sources consisted of a personal demonic attachment, plus a few incidents with clients and colleagues with what I would now describe as 'energy clouds' and 'lower level entities'. Nevertheless, when dealing with these I had always, with his prior permission of course, asked for help from Dave's Guides.

Over the next few months, I noticed that the incidents of clients presenting with dark forces seemed to be occurring more often and perhaps more importantly, were becoming more complex. One evening Dave telephoned and said, 'I'm closing down my energies and will be away for a couple of days,' He had never done that before — or since! Imagine how I felt when later that evening the client who I had been working with during that day, (doing what I thought was a normal healing session), telephoned me in desperation for help: she was experiencing a very powerful psychic attack. My first thought was to ring Dave. However, once I had recovered from the initial shock, I asked my Guides. 'Can we deal with this?' Once I was told yes and recognising the level of protection I felt, I calmly and confidently seemed to just know what to do. Something was very definitely guiding me. The next morning when I telephoned my client to confirm that all was well, we were able to reflect back on the event and discuss the guided insights that had been given to me, I was astounded in what I had been shown and what had been accomplished. Since that time, my Guides and I have been sent increasingly more challenging cases to deal with.

The shift I was experiencing was so incredible, literally on a daily basis, that I can still hear myself saying to myself, 'I can't believe this is happening to me.' Immediately the answer came back — 'Believe it!' When Denise asked me to help with some of Dave's workload, I just accepted with a deep knowing and trust that I would be totally protected and safe.

More recently, whilst Dave was talking about the Wheel of Light and the new developments and insights he had received, I slowly began to realise that something special had been taking place. I have always known there is a deep connection between us, however, over the previous 18 months or so, this has reached a new and different level, a sense of somehow being connected to an immense power source that transmits through Dave.

I can honestly say, whatever cases I have faced and some have been more than a bit daunting, once I have started to work, I have always been confident and reassured that I was fully capable and protected. I feel that it is important for me to say, that this was from a position of absolute trust and not fear."

Anne Betts, December 2003

Anne was my teacher and mentor for a number of years and that period was a most important part of my apprenticeship with subtle energy. It is through Anne, her patience, understanding and natural caring nature, along with her healer friends, that I learned so much about how to sense subtle energy, in particular via the meridians. Week after week, month after month, for a couple of years or so, we met every Friday and practised all manner of techniques, which involved interacting with each other in a subtle energetic way, usually holding acupuncture points and feeling the energy move. It took me a while to develop my sensitivity to the energy, but eventually I began to become a part of that flow. These days, I often work with my own acupuncture points and meridians. When I go for acupuncture, which I love, my sensitivity is such that I can tell were the needles need to be placed. We did some valuable work in those early days and I might add here that I met Anne on that same geopathic stress course in London where I met Sue Lilly. Great and lasting friendships were made that week.

The £50,000 Question

Just in case you were wondering did that £50,000 a year materialise, well, to tell you the truth, I forgot all about that question from The Guides and carried on doing what I do best, which is following the Guidance implicitly and keeping my nose to the grindstone. A couple of years went by and Denise and I were sitting in the garden in the sun one lunchtime, between telephone clients, as by this time I had moved beyond seeing clients on a one-to-one basis, when that question was suddenly given back to me. I asked Denise did she remember it. How could you forget? And, then I said to her, 'Do you know how much money has passed through here in the last three months?' She said, 'No.' 'More than enough to break that £50,000 barrier,' I replied. Without even noticing it, the Universal Flow was pouring an ever increasing amount through our work and had taken us beyond that psychological marker which The Guides had set up a couple of years previously. The flow has continued to stay above that marker ever since.

However, there is something very important to understand here, because this work is never about money, it is about learning how to attract and attain the Universal Flow and that is what The Guides had been teaching me during those two years. Although, it's true we were not sitting in the garden and earning a fortune for doing nothing, we were still working very hard and still are, but the nature of that original question was to catch my attention, which it certainly did. The Guides were giving me a reference point to show that if I truly followed the guidance to the letter, then great things would come to pass, and they did.

That flowing stream continues to grow, but it is not about taking all the money for yourself. In fact, most of the time I hardly have anything in my pocket, but that is because we *allow* that stream to flow in the building of our

school and other projects. The key to attracting the Universal Flow is all
about learning how *allow* the energy to flow and this is what The Laws of
Evolution explain and teach. The flow allows us to invest in many and varied
projects to bring spiritual light to the seekers of truth, like this book for
example through the good works of many people who were involved in the
production of it. So, many people benefit from the flow we are creating.
Allow the flow to grow deep and wide so all can bathe within its light.

Learning how to step into the Universal Flow is not a five minute teaching. It takes time to understand and feel your way in, but having learned how
to do it, I now teach others the way and of course, if you can show that your
guidance has worked and you have done it yourself, then students can have
trust in the processes that you teach. The larger picture is all bound up with
the major Poverty Consciousness Programme which is sewn into the consciousness of all of humanity. This is a big subject which I may explain later,
possibly in the next book. Dissolving this programme is all tied up with
learning to live by The Laws of Evolution, but also in understanding how
humanity has separated itself from God-consciousness. Although you can
work it all out yourself, it helps to work with a guide or teacher to facilitate
the way for you. My teacher was that direct guidance which was given to
me, which I could have ignored, but instead, I trusted it and it worked. The
other most important thing to understand about the Flow is that the money
is just energy so you must treat it as such. You must ensure that it flows
constantly, like water. It is not my money to hoard, as it then doesn't flow.
The more you learn how to expand the flow of Universal Energy through
your heart, the more of that flow passes through you and you always find that
there is enough for everything you need.

28

The Day After Tomorrow

Over the winter of 2003, The Guides were bringing me ever more into the amazing light of The Wheel. They were showing me how things worked and directing me to draw pictures and produce images to put on the website, so that others could then view these and see what was developing. The importance of putting them on the web was, firstly, so that the light of The Wheel could radiate from the image into the lives of those who viewed it, and secondly, because the diagrams would enable people to get an understanding of how the process worked—within our three dimensional reasoning.

Sweden

In March 2004, we tested the Satellite theory through our friends Lena and Ian in Sweden. We first made the acquaintance of Ian, who had read my book, *Dancing with the Devil*, some years earlier. Ian had a lively interest in all things metaphysical, especially earth energy matters. Ian, originally from the south of England, had met Lena at a seminar in Italy, or as Lena puts it, she manifested him from a list she had drawn up of the requirements she desired in a man. On visiting her at her apartment outside Stockholm, Ian discovered some very serious spiritual goings-on in the home and suggested that they should get in touch with me to see could I explain what was happening. Lena at that time was so depleted she could barely walk down the street. To give you an idea of how busy we were, I actually called them on New Year's Eve, the only time I had a slot. The problem was a resident spirit feeding from her energy. We sorted that problem via some distant energy work, then, later in the spring, Lena came over to England for a couple of healing sessions when I was still practising in Manchester. Her second session saw the completion of the repair to her damaged energy system, damage caused by being drained by the spirit entity over a long period. At the end, The Guides said 'She will be a satellite!'

We were probably now about a year on since The Guides had declared Lena a Satellite and an opportunity had come our way to try the process. We connected the Light through her, supplying an Essence Program to a third Party client through the direction of The Guides. It was a long Program, of three months, in three stages, but using a Satellite as a relay station to carry the energies into another continent was producing equally brilliant results to those I had experienced with my clients in Britain. The Program created such an amazing conscious shift in the client that her husband then wanted a Program for himself. This began to open up a vast picture of working more powerfully at a distance than ever before, through the amazing power of The Wheel of Light and the Essence Programs together.

We had not yet reached the two year mark, which The Guides had originally given to get The Wheel up and running. Their words at the time were. 'It will take two years before you are ready.' If I was still not ready and we were achieving such amazing results, what was still to come, I wondered? I was still working in my practice in south Manchester on a one-to-one basis with my clients, but we were now working more often with Essence Programs in complex cases at a distance. We had also tested out the Satellite theory and everything was very successful on that front too. My insights were constantly confirming that this was only the beginning and that there would be many more developments to come. The time had flown by and all of us who were involved in the project had learned so much. I was bathed in ever increasing amounts of this Light and the shifts were so intense that I changed the way I worked several times in a month. The rate of development and new knowledge being brought to me was incredible.

The Burning Out of the Old

The important thing to note is that at some level it was becoming clear that I had been selected to be developed in order to carry this Light. In fact, if I go back to my original healing awakening in the late 1980s, it was not something I *chose* to do at that time. The healing mission was forced upon me and it was a very difficult time, which I could only describe as a kind of death and rebirth, or even a total emotional breakdown, which then allowed a different person to emerge from the shell of my previous self. It was most certainly a breaking down of the old me and a rebirth of a different me. That process was accompanied by what I can only describe as a kind of fiery purging of one's system. There was great pressure in my body and mind at times, almost to the point at which I thought I might burst spontaneously into flames. It was incredibly intense and quite frightening, too.

It was a time of great confusion and even when I began to understand what was happening to me, by consulting many different people, I still didn't want it. Every step was very much against my will in the beginning. I was accelerating in knowledge and ability way beyond my peers and it was becoming clear that whatever was going on and willing or not, I had been chosen for some kind of journey. Certainly, I knew that whatever was taking place through me was unique and very powerful. The constant stream of clients who were delivered to my door was very much my education and apprenticeship on the one hand and the opportunity that forces of higher consciousness needed to create for their purpose, on the other. I was being burned by this Light. The constant stream of clients was the means by which this transformation could be served on me, as they, the unknowing partners in this subterfuge, provided the perfect layers of consciousness, which allowed a two-way process of giving and receiving to be enacted. It was a fascinating process, when you begin to see how it was working and gain an understanding of the higher principles involved in bringing it.

It became clear that the development of this first phase of The Wheel of Light and the frequencies of Light, which comprise it, were at this early stage nothing more than something to burn my channels open. The Guides began bringing the powerful stuff through me as far back as the late 1990s. That is when I first began to lose consciousness in the healing sessions. It was a power, which was barely tolerable on most days, leaving me exhausted by the end of the day and most certainly wrecked by the end of the week. People would say to me, 'You must be doing something wrong if it burns you out like that'. I constantly questioned this, but the truth was that I was not engaged in the healing process for the most part anyway. I was just a bystander witnessing the hurricane of Light, which was being thrown at the client, through me as the vehicle. It would even happen when I was not in healing sessions. Sometimes, I would be in general conversation with someone and I could feel The Guides using that person's consciousness to bring me some form of Light, which I needed for my continuing transformation. On one occasion, I was sitting talking with a friend and within about five seconds we were both completely unconscious, taken well clear of our bodies, whilst some operation was carried out.

Eventually, I became confident that I was not doing anything wrong and as I began to understand more of what was being created with The Wheel of Light, I became more comfortable with it. This didn't mean that I wasn't still the subject of preparation by those upstairs who had plans for my little old life, but I had come to the conclusion that whatever I had to go through, I always seemed to be able to take it and recover relatively quickly, between a Friday afternoon and a Monday morning. I was pushed to the limit, but never quite beyond it as I began to understand that this incredible energy was being used to literally burn open my being at every level. The process forced my vibration to rise and in turn created a vessel, which could hold light. I began to learn how most anyone can channel light, which is the easy part. The trick is to be able to ground the Light, then you can hold it and radiate it. If you can't ground it, then you can't manifest with it. It is as simple as that. Grounding is the key to the manifestation process. I will teach you about this in the next book.

A Trinity was Born

It was an early April morning and I had to abandon working in the garden as it had begun to rain. I settled down indoors to catch up with some essence work. I was preparing the bottles, boxes, labels and getting the Mother Tinctures ready, in order to create some new stock bottles, when The Guides suddenly said, 'We have a transmission to make … Enlightenment.'

There was a sense of urgency in the energy of the message and even though the terminology was new to me, the energy that came with it made it clear that I was to be given a vibration for a new essence and it would be called Enlightenment. In fact, within three hours, three new essences were birthed: *Enlightenment*, followed by *Awareness* and, finally, *Quickening*. Nothing like this 'direct delivery' had ever happened before with this kind of intensity. There was a kind of manic speed to everything that was happening. A great pressure built up in me, which reminded me of my original awakening many years before. The energy was running through me like a train. My brow chakra was whizzing round and information was coming so fast, as I tried to make notes, whilst simultaneously working on the new arrivals. I was in a panic that I might lose the information before I got it all down on paper. It was craziness in action, with no time to think.

Because I was on such a high from the amazing energy that accompanied the arrival of these new essences, I completed the Mother Tinctures and made up ten stock bottles of each essence immediately. However, what The Guides didn't tell me until a few days later, after I had labelled them all as part of the Devic Essences repertoire, was that these new essences were *not* Devic Essences. They were to form the nucleus of a completely new range, a vibrational vehicle called The Wheel of Light Essences. What unfolded over the next few days made it obvious, but my enthusiasm to play with these new toys had got ahead of me. I was surfing along on the wave of energy, which had brought them in and in my enthusiasm I had created thirty bottles and printed ninety labels, which were now completely useless. It pays to be a bit slow sometimes, but my haste could not detract from the fact that these new Wheel of Light Essences were a turning point in Essence Creation for us and another piece of the Wheel of Light Puzzle firmly in place.

When recording an energy signature to make a new essence, I always take fundamental details like time, date, weather etc., but it wasn't until I was tidying up the details in the computer later that afternoon that I went to the calendar to see what date it was. I should have known because the Jehovah's Witnesses had called at the door that morning and read me a couple of passages from the Bible, but it hadn't really registered ... as it often doesn't with me, at the time. I am the original absent-minded professor. As I looked at the calendar, I realised it was Easter Monday, day of celebration of the resurrection of Jesus.

What's in a Number?

Later in the evening, as I sat finalising the day's work, my energy now much calmer, I couldn't help, but ask questions of The Guides about this mad, ferocious, energetic day and I could hear them giggling in their amusement at my mental musings. They put my trust and patience to the test sometimes, but they won't ever reveal to me the information until the appropriate time. It is always on a need to know basis. They must consider that all this mental questioning helps to keep the mind fertile, I think.

Why did this phenomenon happen then? It was the first time a 'transmission' had been made in this way. Why a Trinity of Essences? Three essences within three hours on the 3rd day, when Jesus rose again to life. 3 plus 3 plus 3. What does it mean? From experience, I know that when The Guides want to say something important, there is always some kind of intensity to get my attention and there was plenty this day. Also, there were only three weeks to go before the date set by the Guides to complete the evolutionary cycle, which was the unfolding of The Wheel of Light energies into our Earth realm, or, to put it another way, the period of opening me to a stage of completion where I could then move forward with it. You could say that this three week period is another 3, making 12. Try fitting this around disciples? Also, in numerology, 12 reduces to 3!

When there are answers that I still need to find, there is always a burning fire or a kind of pressure within, driving me to seek the truth. The Guides keep that pressure going so that I know there is still work to do. I knew that these numbers were no coincidence, so I looked to Linda Goodman's book *Star Signs* for some clarification. Let me tell those of you who might not have discovered Linda that her work is phenomenal. I was introduced to it right at the beginning of my path and it doesn't matter how far you ascend, there is always something in there for you. It is full of magical pearls of wisdom that only a true master can understand and reveal and when your vibration is at the right level, you then begin to perceive them.

So our first number is 3. This is the number of optimism, movement and expansion, the holy trinity of the mind, body and spirit. It is the foundation of a great ideal and travel is an absolute necessity. Travel and America, was to become a bit of a focus shortly after this and continued for some time with regular commentary from The Guides.

Our next number is 3 + 3 + 3 which, equals 9. This is the number of completion. Three essences as a complete entity, arriving on the eve of a two year cycle, completed the first phase of The Wheel of Light, or perhaps this was a sign that I was reaching completion of this phase of my own development so that I could undertake this work with The Wheel of Light.

And then we had the number 12. For the number 12, I shall quote from Linda's book. '*12 is the educational process on all levels, the submission of the will required and the sacrifices necessary to achieve knowledge and wisdom, on both the spiritual and the intellectual levels. When the intellect is sacrificed to the feelings, the mind will be illuminated with the answers it seeks. Look within for the solution. Attention paid to the requirements of education will end suffering and bring success.*' This, of course, fitted perfectly with the evolutionary nature of the names of the three new essences ... *Enlightenment, Awareness and Quickening.*

I worked with the information in her book for another couple of weeks, on and off, while the fire continued to push me. Then I read one particular word and the fire cooled, instantly ... *Jesus!*

Linda says that Jesus' name is the most revealing and strangest she has ever calculated using numerology. The numerical values of the word Jesus add up to the compound number 18. When you add 1 + 8 it equals, or reduces to, the single number 9. The word Christ does exactly the same and if you then work with the words Jesus of Nazareth, the most common term to describe the man, it again adds to 18 and reduces to 9. Bizarrely, the words Jesus Christ together, also adds to 18 and reduce to 9. So, the number 9 is the inescapable number of Jesus and is also the alpha and omega, the beginning and the end, the thing, which encompasses everything that is. The totality. Unity. The Source.

Signs and Signals

I had been waiting for a sense of completion to emerge for The Wheel of Light, as I sometimes found myself thinking I must be imagining this whole process of spiritual unfoldment. The Guides have put me in many situations over the years, saying that what might seem the most bizarre and incredible things can be achieved if I listen carefully and follow the guidance exactly. Doubt and questioning are only human and important too, for they show that we are thinking about things, evaluating potentials and testing theories, but the Guidance has never been wrong. If they say, 'you can do this,' then I always can. Or, if they say, 'such and such will happen,' then it does.

Our work is always about bringing more light into the world and that is the first thing The Guides said to me after they announced the arrival of Enlightenment: 'Bringing the Light Closer.' We must all draw our own conclusions from our own experiences, which then become our truth. Does it matter that we try to evaluate anything that is given? I don't think it does, but our feeble human selves do occasionally desire a peg to hang something on, some kind of momentary attachment for security purposes. What was given that day when the transmission of those three essences came forth, is open to conjecture. I only know what I know from experience. When the fire instantly cooled upon reading that one word, then I knew what I was meant to know and as I write this today, there is a very powerful knowing, peering over my shoulder and a presence which, is unmistakable in its loving intensity.

At the time I was working out the numbers and looking for the answers, I could hear The Guides nonchalantly saying, 'These are just signs; signals; things, which give you something to think about.' Yes, they are always giving me something to think about, just letting me know in a subtle way that there is so much more to whatever is coming through than meets the eye. But often there is no explanation, because it is trust that they are constantly trying to teach, and trust works on many levels. Just when I think I have learned to trust, they put me to the test again and I discover that the levels at which we must learn to trust are endless and it is my understanding that once you perfect it, then you can walk on water! Mmm, a bit of a way to go yet, then. However, it is good to remind ourselves constantly that lack of trust is one of the main causes of us limiting our potential. The other is fear.

> They came to Earth in a raging fire of light,
> A complete entity in their own right,
> Separated not, from the hearts of each other.
> Given from above for our Earthly brothers.
> … and Sisters too, of course!

> David Ashworth, 20th April 2004.

The Closer I Get, the Further Away I Seem to Be

As we got closer to May 2004, the date the Guides had said we would be able to begin utilising the growing potential of The Wheel, the energies coming through grew bigger, more powerful, more intense and more effective. One might almost describe them as elaborate. I felt I needed to know more, so that I could explain how The Wheel worked to those who were interested. Well, the truth of it was that the means by which we were achieving these amazing results just didn't make sense to me. I had worked in healing for a long time, with some great people, seen, felt and experienced all manner of fantastic things of an energetic nature, yet there was so much, I just could not understand at this juncture in The Wheel of Light adventure.

I am used to seeing things through my gift of sight, but when I connect into the energies of The Wheel, I can't see anything of it. It is as if it is deliberately blocked from my vision. I receive all the information I need in order to do the work, but this is given at a deeper inner level, a level of Inner Knowing, which leaves me in the position of 'Knowing without Seeing'. I just know that what I am being told is correct. Well, perhaps this is okay for me, because I am working with this light every day and so I have a great deal of knowledge of it and trust in the guidance that has been with me for years. But, what about others who are being introduced to it for the first time? They need to be told something of what it is and how it works. The closer I get to the Light of The Wheel, the further away I seem to be for an explanation. Eventually, no doubt, to put me out of my wretched misery and probably to confirm that I was seeing things correctly, The Guides spoke on the subject.

The Guides Speak

'David looks to us for explanations in his awe at the things we tell him he is capable of with this stream of consciousness we call The Wheel of Light. He becomes frustrated when we say we cannot show you. He tests our explanations of the possibilities to prove them. Again, we see his frustration that he cannot put into words what he perceives, understands and knows within his heart. We see his need to explain to others, but cannot because the Light is indescribable in your terms. We constantly have to give him the same message and we would like to repeat this message for yourselves.

We cannot explain to you the power in this Wheel of Light. Just look and you will know it.

We cannot explain the power, which can be carried and transferred to you through the Wheel of Light essences. But try what we say and you will see.

We cannot explain the sheer size, extent, or un-encompassable vastness of what has been unlocked and is unfolding now into Earth through this channel.

It is not possible for you to understand it. You have no frames of reference to map it or compare it to. It is impossible. You will just have to trust what we tell you.

We might also add that you cannot understand the nature of what we are. We might describe ourselves as Guides beyond Guides, Guides from a higher dimension. But we might also say that we are not even Guides at all, but a form of changing and flowing consciousness, which can take the form of many things. It is not important how you look at us or how you see what we can do, with and for you. It is only important to you know within your heart your own truth.

These are very advanced energies coming to Earth right now and they will not speak to everyone, for there are many who are not ready for this level of attunement and attainment or the unfolding process that it will begin with humanity. But, those who are ready will hear this Light speak and when it does you will perceive a message, which will leave you in no doubt as to what you should do.

If you are called to The Wheel, you will not be able to put into words what it does for you. You will simply know that something has changed. You will know that something has moved you. At the same time you may even think that you feel the same and nothing has changed, but you will 'know' for certain, within your heart, that you are not unchanged. If you touch this Light, if this Light touches you, then you will be changed.

This Inner Knowing is the awakening of the God force within you. It is the ignition of a spark, which begins to spread like a small controlled fire, warming your soul as it gently opens your perceptions and changes your vision. You will be confused. You will say to yourself, 'how can I feel that I am the same person, when inside, in the deepest parts of my being, I know that I am not?' This is the nature of true evolution.

Like David, you will be frustrated, because you also will not be able to explain or express what touches you. But, as he has had to do, over many years, you will learn to trust that Inner Knowing, which calls you and if you follow your heart in truth and listen for the messages which Guide you from within, as he continues to learn to do, then you too will unfold into your finest potential.

Our Light was drawn to David for he has gifts that even he doesn't know about yet; nevertheless, through the most difficult times he has been able to continue to trust and walk the path. Many beings work with and through him and they are all drawn by the same elaborate canvas that we saw, which is his ability to be limitless in his vision of his potential, but with a great ability to serve. It is David's ability to look and trust and try, where others would walk away in fear of failure, which makes him different.

Those of you who can become this limitlessness, can rise like a star in the heavens, which sprays radiant light to all those parts of the planet that need it. As this light falls to Earth, it will speak of you to those who are listening. Then, like David you will become one who can help to raise and free the consciousness of others, so that they in turn can bear the torch of their own radiant Light into your world.

Together, this is all about uplifting and empowering others. The power behind The Wheel of Light is to empower others. David's work is about empowering others. To open them. To push them forwards. As a human, the more you work to empower others, then the more power is granted to continue your own personal journey, so that you can bring ever greater gifts to humanity.

The Guides

April 2004
Well, that little download from The Guides answered all the questions without answering any, you might say. I still can't tell you what it is or how it works. It just is. But, I think when you read the words of The Guides there is a light and power in them, which comes through as being all-knowing, or certainly knowing at a level, which is way beyond our understanding as humans. It goes beyond mind and communicates with the heart. I do hope that you have enjoyed reading their words here and that they touch you in the way that they touch me with their light. What you find with words like these, which are 'given' is that every time you read them, you absorb more of the light that they radiate and as you absorb that light over time, it brings illumination so that you can see and perceive beyond the words and go some way into the source and in turn, the source helps your understanding and knowing through its radiance and in turn you then learn to trust ever more of what is revealed to you.

The Day After Tomorrow
The only essences we had used in our experiments with the Essence Programs up to that time were the Devic Essences. Eventually, I began to understand that the Devics had been conceived and created with Essence Programs and distance work in mind, but within a couple of years, I began to see an even bigger picture of why these essences had been given. We will come to that in due course. However, some three weeks earlier, we had been presented with the new Wheel of Light essences, The Trinity.

The first time the Guides selected a Wheel of Light Essence to use in a healing session with a client was 29th April 2004, two days before the 1st May 2004, the time that The Guides had said, two years previously, that I would be ready. Ready for what? I really still had no idea, but certainly lots had unfolded in the previous two years. I assumed that when I was ready then The Wheel of Light would come to some kind of completion and would be switched on as an entity in its own right, rather than us dipping in and out of it as guided so to do. The fact that we were on the eve of May and

The Guides were telling me to use Wheel of Light Essences for the first time in a healing session seemed good confirmation that we were on track and indeed that this was another step forward.

Healing with Wheel of Light Essences

As that healing session began, the effect upon me was phenomenal. I was taken so far out of my body, at one point I actually thought I might die and that feeling continued for some 15 to 20 minutes. I was literally trying to hold on to life, but at the same time, trying to let go of everything that I knew that rooted me in the physical world. I was trying everything I knew and even things I didn't, in order to surrender to the experience and let go of any fear, which was rising due to the intensity. I was so far out of my Being, I thought I might not fully come back in again. The impact on me, as the vehicle for what was coming through, was like being flattened by a road roller, with every last ounce of life and energy being squeezed out. It was almost impossible to breathe, such was the pressure on my physical body. Words cannot describe the power, which came through into that room in that healing session. We had used Quickening and Enlightenment together as the essences to open the door into the client's consciousness and the result was some kind of driving force, like a hurricane, powering its way through my now enfeebled body as it sat slumped, relatively unconscious on the sofa. I fully realised that the reason I had been removed so far from that withered form of myself was so that my delicate consciousness would not be damaged by the intensity of the light passing through my subtle channels. As a Being, my energy system was intact and visible to me from some vantage point distant from that room. I was watching what was happening to my energetic body, my aura and chakras, but my consciousness was removed from this reality, observing the process from afar, but at the same time experiencing the depletion, terror and fear that whatever was happening was way beyond my control and the only thing to do was submit to it and experience whatever was coming forth. Normally, I would be completely unconscious in a session like this, but it was as if I had been placed in some kind of suspended animation so that I could witness the effect on myself, whilst being absent from myself.

If this was a taste of things to come, I knew instantly that I couldn't take it. It would kill me in no time at all. There is no way that a human energy system, or delicate consciousness could stand in the direct line of fire of this incredible force of light without being incinerated. For certain, nobody could last a week in this kind of energy.

29

Unfolding DNA

After that first amazing experience of using Wheel of Light Essences in a one-to-one session, things really began to change rapidly. From that moment, I began to go through a deep shift and I could see into issues more deeply than ever. And, as always happens when your consciousness and vibration go through a shift, God sends you clients to challenge you on the next level, so that you can continue with your learning process. As I worked on evolutionary sessions with certain people, two things in particular began to happen. Firstly I was able to see and perceive the subtle energy system in much more detail than before and secondly, when we were specifically using The Wheel of Light energies with people, I could see how the light began to change the structure of their light bodies. Those clients who were already healers or lightworkers began to change very quickly. In some instances their light body was not only responding to the light and changing, but changing dramatically as it unfolded into new forms.

12 Strand DNA

As I observed this phenomenon, my searching and questioning mind went back to what I had heard and read over the years about DNA developing in some people from 2 strand into 12 strand DNA. I couldn't remember if it was being unfolded within people, if they were being reconnected with it, or what exactly. My logical mind had struggled with this concept for a while, in fact probably for six or seven years. I was thinking that if these people who claimed to have the 12 strand DNA were actually tested, what would show up on their scans? Would we find that they did indeed have 12 strands of physical DNA, which could be viewed by an electron microscope, or would it still show 2 strands? There was lots of information around on the subject if you cared to look for it and for certain, there were teachers and practitioners claiming that this was the work that they performed. I had no reason to doubt any of it, as I keep an open mind on all subjects and investigate them if necessary. I have always taken the view that most people don't tell lies and even though a subject might stretch the imagination a little, that doesn't mean it is not true. Clients know what they are experiencing and just because it might not fit any known model, this does not mean it is not happening to them. Many times clients have been afraid to tell their story for fear of ridicule, which is very sad and a true reflection of how the limitations of human perception in general push people away. How is humanity ever going to get anywhere with a closed mind? It certainly will not evolve unless it becomes more open to possibility.

I had not done any real research into this 12 strand DNA scenario, merely kept it in my mind for when the time might be right to gain an answer. That time came one day when I was looking into the structure of cells, at the same time researching the work of Fritz Albert Popp and his discoveries of the emanation of frequencies of light from the physical body. I was deep into the questioning process of both cells and DNA with The Guides and as I delved ever deeper into the cell at a physical level with my higher vision and then deeper than that into a subtle level, I suddenly began to see the light around the strands of DNA. I was quite startled for the moment. It was at that point that I was prompted by The Guides to ask the question, which had lain for so many years at the back of my mind. They said, 'You are now in a position to see what you need to see.'

As I looked at the DNA structure, I could clearly see the double helix, but this paled into the background beneath the light, which was radiating from it. It was the light, which carried all the information and transmitted it to each part of the cell. Each cell has its own nucleus, where the DNA is located, therefore, each individual cell within the body is generating and radiating this information source. I was fascinated by the light I could see, then, suddenly, I saw the 12 strands. I should be clear at this point that I was not looking into a client, but working via remote viewing of the subject matter as presented to me by The Guides. So, you might say that I was in a classroom situation and The Guides were providing examples for me to see.

Forget the physical structure of the two strands or double helix of DNA for a moment and concentrate upon the light, which emanates from the strands of DNA. As I viewed the light, it occurred to me that the source of the information within the light is not merely held within the double helix, or even within the body at any level. The light within the cell is like a radio receiver. It receives information from a higher source than mankind and then transmits this information into the body.

This was something of a revelation. What I was seeing was a picture where each and every person on the planet is working through a kind of electronic blueprint held in a higher place. Someone, or something is watching each and every one of us every moment of our lives. It is as if we are radio-controlled, but only for our own highest good. We are monitored and watched over. Let us use those simple terms, which make it easy to understand. Let us call the place where these transmissions come from, Heaven, and let us call the one who does the monitoring, God.

The Explorer

I could see that for the most part we are on a sort of automatic pilot, walking through life and its experiences as they are brought to us. We are all individual and we operate on a unique emotional, mental and spiritual programme, which, has been predetermined by our soul or larger soul group. The soul provides the programme within us, or — another way of looking at it — the soul sets up the receiving station within the cell and determines what frequencies it will receive from the transmission source, based on our vibration. Lessons and experiences are pre-programmed into our lives, based on what the soul is ready to experience in its own growth cycle. At this level the soul has free will and decides, based on many criteria, what will determine the personality of the person acting out the programme. Imagine you are a fragment of the soul, let us say an explorer for the soul. The explorer and the larger soul agree what is to be learned and experienced in a human life and when this agreement has been made, the programme is launched into a human life, which satisfies all the criteria for the soul mission of learning and experiencing. The explorer is born through a woman into a human life in the earth realm. All this learning and experiencing is focussed on one outcome, which is growth for the soul. The explorer experiences the mission and the guiding programme ensures that the explorer meets with the experiences desired by the higher consciousness of the soul. Upon returning to the soul after physical death, the explorer, as a fragment, merges once again with the greater soul being. What we need to understand here is that the spiritual aspects of our Selves are a fragment of that greater soul and so we are essentially serving ourselves as we are an existing part of that larger consciousness we call soul.

Meanwhile, God, or the ever-present omnipotent consciousness, takes a back seat and allows the soul to manage the explorer's mission into earth, but He watches your life and monitors your progress. God is ultimately the source consciousness responsible for the quality and accuracy of the transmissions you receive within the DNA.

Since I first saw this, I have occasionally touched into deep consciousness, where it is possible to see that, perhaps, we have no free will at all, or that we have no choice, which, is a different thing. We are programmed from birth to death. To see or touch into this level of reality can be extremely frightening and traumatic, but you get used to it after a while and go beyond the fear. However, at the same time as being in the programme, or receiving the pre-programmed signals at the light level within the DNA, (which, in turn, illuminates our lives at whatever level we are ready to receive) there is also the illusion of choice. It appears that we make all the choices we want, but those choices were already programmed into us and the pathway from each choice to the next was also programmed, so that eventually we will find the right path and reach our destination, whether in this life or a subsequent life. When you touch into the life-programme, believe me it is very scary, but a little at a time you begin to accept it, even though, you might try to distance yourself from it. However, once you have seen something for what it is, then you can't un-see it again. It becomes a part of your experience and knowledge. But, the key words to observe and understand in all of this are 'will,' 'free will' and 'will power.'

The will is located in the heart, along with desire. Will and desire are partners, bedfellows and act in unison to help us overcome what we truly desire to overcome. The desire is stirred by the God-consciousness within you and is the signal that it is time to act. Once desire speaks to you, then you can activate your will (at will) to take action to fulfil your desire. The thing to understand here is that the desire is not yours. Yes, you feel it, but it is the God within you that activates it, so really desire is stimulated by God to help you find the right path, to point you in the right direction to attain what you need to, for your learning experience.

We have the will and we can use it either to tackle the challenges we face or to allow the challenges to overcome us until such time as we choose to summon that will to work on the experiences, which we are meeting in life. The will is ours to use. The will gives us the mechanism of choice. On the one hand, we can say we have plenty of choice, but in the larger picture you could also say that there is no choice, because we are all on a predetermined path of the evolution of consciousness. We are merely given a choice as to how quickly we walk that path by means of using the will.

Changing the Programme

God is like a loving parent, watching his children grow and learn. But, because we do have free will at a certain level, we can actually request that the programme be changed. Unless we do this, then the programme stays on automatic, as given to us by the soul prior to incarnation in a human life. If we go back to the beginning for a moment, the soul decrees the experiences to be enjoyed, then the personality enters Earth through a woman; we grow and function as a human, until eventually the physical structure ceases to function and we return to unload (or download) our experiences into the soul temple, or hard drive. The soul then integrates the experiences you had in life as the explorer and moves accordingly to the next level or phase of its evolution.

During this process of life, we are given a number of choices. The first is that you can live out your life, or your programme, on automatic pilot. Let's face it, you must know lots of people who seem to drift though life without a care in the world, or drift through life without appearing to change in any definitive way, or indeed drift through life going from one crisis to the next without ever solving any of the issues being presented to them. These are the ones on auto-pilot. At some level they are bringing back information and experiences to the soul, which are desired, but without pushing the enve-lope, so to speak. The soul is non- judgemental about the journey into an Earth life. If evolutionary progress is not made, then that is just fine accord-ing to the parameters that the soul works from. Indeed, there are certain times in the Great Cycle of the evolution of consciousness when it is not so necessary to push the evolution and there are also times when it is appropri-ate to do so. Entering a new age is one such time, when things are speeding up and, therefore, a time when we should be searching for that edge to go beyond.

The second scenario is that, by using the will, you can modify the programme. By using the will to achieve what you desire to experience, you begin to take over the programme and as a result of using the will in this way, you draw the attention of the God-consciousness and He sees your effort and upgrades the programme. He begins to respond to what you desire to experience. He begins to transmit different information into your DNA and you begin to become more of the pilot of your life than the passenger, content to progress on auto-pilot.

The third scenario is that in certain soul agreements, you are programmed to go through experiences of serious transformation by a process of awaken-ing into the light of higher transmissions. When this happens, you initially work to some degree to an auto-pilot-type programme at some level, but then the will becomes active and you begin to question and to seek answers to life, the universe and everything — to coin a phrase. These types of people, where the will is active, are usually very intense, or driven. This is the reflec-tion of the intensity of the light within them. So, we might say that there is a background programme running, which ensures an ability to survive, then the secondary drive is mobilised and this is the will to achieve or attain, or the will to drive the life forward in some definitive way in order to experi-ence what is desired, which is usually an awakening experience. And, of course, we must not forget that the desire is initially stimulated from the God at the core of your own being. Simple or complex? Well, it is a bit of both really, but in order to get your head around it, you need to experience it in a form that you can comprehend. Everyone who is on a spiritual path of awakening will pass through this and touch it at some point. Then you will know.

When you touch into learning experiences as profound as these, as I have said, it disturbs the balance of the inner you. It shocks and frightens, but that is the nature of all evolutionary processes. When you face fear and pass through it, then the fear no longer exists for you, it is no longer a limitation on your life. That is true evolution. When the fear is dissolved, it is replaced by Light and so you carry more Light. But little revelations like the one above come and go. They become a part of your reality as you touch them, live them and go beyond them and then they almost cease to exist. They are not important any longer. They are only presented as a hurdle. Once you have learned how to jump that high, then you let go and move on. For example, I wrote this down as I experienced it at the time. If you asked me to explain it at any time in the future, I would have to re-read it and reconnect at that level of consciousness so that I could perceive it again. In short, you just move on and let it go. It isn't important any more. You can't change the truth of the situation, but you can use your will to continually transform. That is the nature of the evolutionary journey. Just keep moving forward, but by all means record what you have seen so that it might help others to understand when it is their turn to observe the phenomenon.

The Chosen Ones

We have not finished with programmes yet. Coming back to The Chosen Ones, we often find these people tend to experience great difficulty in early life. They can find themselves in situations where they work extremely hard and seem to get nowhere, or for example, they might battle with substance abuse or homelessness, or suffer personal catastrophe after catastrophe, like major car accidents and from an early age feel like they don't fit in. This very real hardship is designed into the programme as a kind of guidance system. It is telling them that they are on the wrong path, but they tend to keep following it until something occurs to change their direction. When they eventually find the right path, then everything begins to run more smoothly and success comes to them on many levels. However, they often do not find the path by themselves, it is forced upon them through an awakening process.

People with this particular programme have often brought great challenges into this life, to help them learn through adversity. Through this learning process they transcend and constantly find themselves on a path that reveals more and more amazing experiences to them. The experiences are definitive of awakening and transformation. Through constantly opening to ever-higher levels of conscious awareness, where mystical experiences are often experienced, these people eventually begin to understand the programme and how it works. They are then able to almost 'command' the programme to bring what they want, within certain tolerances. As you learn to understand the programme and have the courage to play with it, exploring what you can achieve, you are often given great power to effect change for other humans. However, you are only ever given the power as you learn to use it appropriately.

This group tend to be fighters and use the will in great measure in order to bring new experiences. Even though, they might not know what those experiences will bring when they arrive, they know they will learn great things from them. By using the will to command the programme or co-create with the programme, God constantly comes into their lives and brings the experiences that, although, often challenging, evolve their consciousness by the greater amount. These people are not merely explorers, they are absolutely on a mission. They may become the leaders of their age, sages and guides to a multitude. Even though, they may not know and understand this at the beginning of their awakening journey, they become more and more attuned to it as they progress through life. As the will is used to constantly question, so God constantly changes the programme, transmitting new information to help them find the answers that he places before them. These people are true co-creators with the God-force.

They have been called The Chosen Ones, chosen for a mission, but also by agreement at the highest level. They are often on a non-spiritual path when the awakening is forced upon them. They have been prepared in many previous lives and then, at certain appointed times, they are awoken by having the light poured into them. This was my own experience and when the incoming light began its work it took me through an extremely traumatic process, which can only be described as a kind of breakdown, a death and rebirth, in order to carry light. A process of forced illumination, the initial period, as I have said, was around three years, but it has never really ceased since then.

Whatever we are and however we respond to our programme, we are always an expression of the soul's evolution under the direction of the higher God-consciousness. Therefore, when we come to Earth and find that we have gifts and abilities, which might appear to be different from the norm, such as psychic ability, intuitive ability, healing ability, or whatever, we often find that we are connecting in to our programme at a higher level than the average person. If we choose then, through our free will, to push the boundaries, they will be pushed. When we reach out and ask God to help us evolve, He comes to our aid, looking at our programme and adjusting it accordingly. He adjusts what we are able to receive by transmitting frequencies of light that begin to change us. A little at a time, we then move forward as our physical vehicle adapts to hold more light. As we hold more light, then our reality changes.

Uploading a Newer Programme

As the God-consciousness begins to transmit an update to your programme and it is received within the nucleus of the cell, within the double helix of DNA, these light transmissions begin to change your life. New information is received and so new learning experiences are brought to you. As a result, a little at a time, your perceptions of reality change. You begin to see through the illusion and then stand in a new truth. When I reached this point in the remote viewing of the DNA and the information streams of light, I didn't need to see any more. I had seen all I needed at this point in my development. I had enough to take on board and process for a while. From experience, I knew I could trust that what I had seen was the truth. My interpretation of those images may be a little simplistic. I tend to bring things down to the lowest common denominator, as it helps me understand the process and I find that others also understand things easily if presented simply. The important thing to understand here is that we can ask for our programme to be changed, modified or enhanced. However, don't think you can just do this without working on yourself too. The God-consciousness is there within us to respond to our requests, to respond to our lives, but there has to be true intent and desire to improve yourself and to evolve, and subsequently help the lot of mankind to evolve through your additional knowledge. The truth in your heart is always where the programme can be seen and felt most keenly. When your heart is true, then you will be able to receive evolutionary transmissions from the source with ease. The more adept you become at receiving them and interpreting them, the more you are forced to live in truth.

Receiving the Twelve Strands

As I looked at the light radiating from the double helix of the DNA, I asked God, what is all this business about 12 strand DNA then? I was told to watch carefully and I was shown that the physical structure of the double helix remains unchanged, but the strands of light begin to multiply. The double helix is apparently the perfect transmitter for any number of strands of light and strands of light equal information. For every additional strand, which develops, additional information is received at a cellular level and then re-transmitted into our physical being and into all the subtle levels of our being at the same time.

The strands of light, which radiate from the DNA structure appear to start multiplying in no fixed pattern at all. You might be given one extra strand, maybe two, as is appropriate for your work on evolving yourself. In fact, there is no limit to how many light strands you may have, although 12 strands does seem to be a current limit, simply because we are held in a certain energetic space based upon our evolution as a planetary group. The group of humans on Earth at present can be divided into two simple levels as far as evolution is concerned. Those who are not really awakening yet, or evolving into a new reality and those who are. We can also take this back a stage to soul groupings. There are soul groupings, which are more advanced or evolved than others. The whole picture is like a garden coming into bloom, with all the plants and flowers at different levels of perfection, intensity and luminosity.

Although, I am shown that there is no limit to how much light we can receive and carry, there is a kind of limit, because we have not yet figured out that we can ask for more. Unlike Oliver, who was berated and beaten when he asked for more gruel, God looks at us and says, 'How much do you want?' We are only ever limited by our own limitation. However, we can't expect to become super-humans overnight, or is that placing a limitation on it? Seriously, with light comes power, with power comes responsibility and we have to learn how to handle this power and responsibility. God keeps hold of the reins, just like a caring parent with their toddler and as we learn how to use the light and power, so He lets go of the reins a little. Just consider for a moment that it took two years from my vision of The Wheel of Light to reach a point where I was ready to hold that light. Recall the intensity of the light the first time we used the Wheel of Light Essences with it. This is an indication of how long it can take to evolve your being to a point where it can receive the higher transmissions.

What is most important to understand about the speeding up of the evolution of human consciousness is that the rules are changing by the minute. Just because it took two years for me to attain a particular level between 2002 and 2004 does not mean that others would take a similar length of time. Because of the speeding up of the light transmissions bathing us all, we all have the opportunity of greater acceleration. That two year period was a limitation based on what my being could handle and hold in terms of light at that time. If I ask The Guides how long it would take me to make that same journey in our present time frame the answer is twelve months. So, we can see that as light unfolds throughout the planet in this Ascension Period, as we enter the Age of Aquarius, we can achieve so much more in much less time. And those of us who are already receiving higher transmissions are unfolding constantly, whether we realise it or not.

If you want illumination, just ask for it, but be aware that a lot of learning experiences come with it. When we get smart we realise that once we are up and running, reins-free and gambolling through the playground of life, instead of having fun all the time, we should turn some of our effort into finding out what we can do with our light and power. Once you have been granted light, then you will not be allowed not to use it. We will all develop different talents and abilities as we become illuminated and although, it is absolutely fine and in fact we might say imperative, for us to have fun and enjoy using and sharing our gifts, there is nothing to stop us asking for more. God says more will always be granted based on your ability to learn. Ask and you shall receive, seek and you shall find.

30

From Rescue to Evolution

I was doing ever more evolutionary work as The Wheel of Light continued to unfold within me. To put it another way, certain people were coming and The Guides were showing me the evolutionary potential within them and how to unlock it. It might be pertinent to share a typical case of the time, so that you can judge how the work was progressing and, later, you will be able to see how far it has advanced from this stage. Typically, where a person is awakening spiritually, it can take around three Programs to accelerate their vibration to a point where Universal Consciousness begins to pull them along. However, this case study was a little different. The person had huge spiritual potential, but was at the time struggling at a physical level.

You will see, in the fifteen months from August 2003 to November 2004, how The Guides progressed this evolutionary case from a very difficult beginning, when the client was seriously ill at a physical level and brought him through to a position where he could unfold his inner gifts and talents.

Just to remind you, in the healing and evolutionary sessions at this time, the client would lie on the healing couch and I would sit on the sofa. There would be a period when we would both be deeply unconscious. Then, as I began to emerge from this out-of-body state, The Guides would give me the words to write down for the client, describing the work being performed on them. This was the period where we began to move from working at a one-to-one level, to working at a distance with Essence Programs. Today, all work is done at a distance and I haven't seen a client in a one-to-one session since the end of 2005.

In the reading, you will notice how The Guides often switch from speaking to me to speaking to the client. At times, they will be showing me images, as clear as seeing them on a movie screen and describing what they are doing and what will happen; then, within a sentence, they will address the client directly through me. I have left the channelling in this form for authenticity.

Mr. D. One-to-One Session on 1st August 2003

The Guides Speak: Firstly, with D, even though we see physical debility, this is more of an evolutionary process and problem than anything else. However, his situation is very difficult at this point and initially we must approach the issues delicately as a Rescue Situation.

D struggles with his physical body because his essence is extremely spiritual. Now, this is different to what we might call a high vibration. Let us say that D has a high vibration, but it is not as high as the essence of his spiritual self. So, what we have here is a situation where an extremely high spiritual being is inhabiting a body, which is not compatible, because the vibration within the lower bodies, such as the individual levels of the aura — the Lower Mental Body, The Emotional Body and the Etheric Body — is too low in terms of its vibration. Yes, this is confusing, we hear you think.

What we might say is that D has a high vibration, but a person's vibration is limited by many things: attitudes, diet, beliefs, thoughts and actions within the physical world. Now, we do not criticise D in any way for the path he is walking at present. At one level, everything is going as it should, but there is always room for improvement. So, we say that as vibrations go, there is room for change and we will work on this today. However, the struggle with the physical life and this major life-threatening illness comes because the spiritual connections, which pour through D are far more advanced than the body he currently occupies can cope with or relate to. So, it is a bit like trying to wear a pair of shoes, which are two sizes too small. You can get them on, but they are painful and uncomfortable to wear and you become so limited in your movement that you cannot function at your best.

With D, we have a situation where the spiritual being wants to move a lot faster than the physical being is capable of doing. The spiritual being is being held back by the density of the bodies, which comprise the lower self. Therefore, there is always pressure in the lower self, driven by the ideals of the spiritual being. The spiritual being is always trying to take D. higher, but he is limited by the vibration of the physical and lower bodies.

The Solution

Today, we are going to have a look at raising the vibration of D. There is much potential within him to do this, but we also say to him that it is time to let go of certain thoughts and conventions and 'be ready' to move forward. He has to be willing now to trust, so that we can create the situation, which will allow necessary changes to occur.

This is about trusting at a new level. Just allowing the Universe to take him forwards. He has to put out his own individual message to the Universe so that it can bring him what he needs. It is no good holding a vision of what he wants, he must put himself in the hands of God and say, 'Here I am Lord, please guide me and open me for that which you wish me to accomplish for you.' Then he must trust that the Lord is indeed unfolding this plan for him.

He will be placed in positions where he has to make decisions and he will be full of fear of making those decisions, but he must remind himself that God is putting up the signposts and he must follow them, whatever challenges seem to be in his way. Also, it is imperative to remember that God is indeed within him and he is also that God-consciousness itself.

D's gifts at present are limited by his circumstances. Time has been marching on and he has not addressed the situation until today. Now the work can begin. It is not until one reaches out that the helping hand can be effective.

The first place we are working today is in D's heart. In here are some of the answers he seeks, but as yet he cannot see them for there is too much density of energy in the heart. We want to create a pathway where his mind can see more deeply into his own heart. Not until we can do this will he begin to understand some of the things we say to him.

Secondly, we are working in the sacral chakra. In here there is a kind of anchor holding back his creative power, which in turn holds back his whole life. This is linked to the base chakra and the creative energy within the base chakra also. One fuels the other and together they push through a link into the heart. This link will be activated at a deep level and then the energy entering the heart from this source will begin a process of transformation. This is where the journey begins.

At this juncture there is no point going into any other aspects of the deeper consciousness or of D's personal issues, for we cannot access these in any meaningful way until we get the light in this heart moving in a way, which flows without resistance. Until we fuel the heart with Light, there will be no illumination and therefore, you will continue to labour in darkness.

Now, to answer some of your questions. The dream you had, in which a lion is looking for his courage, is all about your doubts around protection and guidance. Again, this is linked to the inner fears. There are a number of these. The first is the uncertainty about life and the process of dying, which of course, is strongly in your perception because of your physical illness.

This is a difficult question to answer for nearly all of mankind. The energy of Earth is so dense that it roots us here and when we are rooted, we tend to learn to belong. When the time comes to leave, then it is often a great struggle because of the way we have attached ourselves to this place and others within it and also the experiences of being here. We say to you right now, do not struggle with this issue, but try to become free within your mind. Allow yourself time to be free of all Earthly pursuits, like work and family and make space to become lighter within your being. Allow the heavenly energies to penetrate you without the worries of everyday life getting in the way. You are a being who struggles in this density of earth and, therefore, you must make an effort to find space where you can lose some of that density.

Much of the fear is caused by confusion. The confusion arises because you don't really know who you are. This arises because of the conflict of vibrational rates within you. You are more like two beings than one and the two beings don't have the same goals. They are often working against each other. This is what we hope to redress with a change in your vibration, bringing the two beings into greater harmony with each other, so that both will begin to walk the same path.

In this session, Light has been poured into you and We will now work with that Light within you for a period of 23 days. This healing process will then continue for approximately 7 weeks. At that point, we may be able to effect further changes. We suggest taking the essence of Pipers No. 1 to assist this process.

There is more work, which can be done. However, it is difficult to project a timeline on this at present, as it depends in the early stages on how quickly the heart can respond. The response is determined by the consciousness, which holds it, to a certain extent, and so, as you can let go and allow your consciousness to become free of the shackles, which hold it, then the work we have initiated in the heart will proceed at a faster rate.

Mr. D. One-to-One Session on 22nd December 2003

The Guides Speak: This session with D is very much a continuation of the previous work, therefore there is not much in the way of new information we can give him with regard to the general state of affairs with the energy system and level of debility in the physical, but we will guide you through the process.

Firstly, again we are working on that heart and levering it open a little at a time, in association with the guidance of your own Higher Self. Shall we say that your Higher Self is giving us permission to work and we agree every movement we make with your Higher Self before we make it. At the same time, your Higher Self is encouraging us to push things to the limit in order to help you unfold. We are preparing to push you through new levels of learning and trust. D is in what we might call the 'no man's land' of change at the moment. Even though, he has been unfolding for many years, he is only just reaching a point where things will change much more quickly for him and in a more tangible way. We might say that he is only at the beginning of his path as a healer and Light Worker. Yes, he can do it, but the question is, 'is he doing it?' The answer is, yes, he is doing it a little, but there is room for improvement.

There is huge potential here within D, but we are only at that level where we are laying foundations for his change. A lot of the speed of change is dependant upon himself, too and the way he learns to trust the process and be ready to deal with whatever the universe throws at him.

God works in mysterious ways, is what we often hear and these mysterious ways are often about putting us in difficult positions, so that we can learn to get out of them and by so doing, we evolve our consciousness. Quite simply, we as humans learn through adversity. If we haven't worked through difficult issues, then how can we help others in those same positions? This is the meaning of Physician, Heal Thyself. There are many deeper meanings to this saying of Jesus too, but for now we are explaining to you that many things do need to change and he knows this, but that changing what often seems impossible, or at least very difficult, is part of the effort God wants to see us making. In return for our efforts he sends more of his love to unfold our gifts. As these gifts unfold, he then sends people to use them on so that we can learn. But we have to be ready and waiting for this.

Our message to you today, D, is that you must be ready in your own mind and heart that you are good enough and you have the power to change lives. D must say, 'I am here and I value myself and I am ready to do battle with my own issues as well as the issues of others'. D must think about his worth and his boundaries, for he is ready to move into the next phase. He must make out his plan of who he is and 'know' it deep inside. He must not even question or doubt himself in any way, or God will not support him. In fact, God cannot support him without this self-belief. God will merely sit patiently and send more lessons until the awakening occurs.

D must, with all humility, see himself as a God. He must, with all humility, know that he is guided. He must, with all humility, understand his power and he must, with all humility, use this power to unleash the power within others. This is not using the ego more than it should be used to help you with opening your own eyes to yourself, but it is using the ego as a tool in measured ways to feel that you are worthy.

Here is a mantra, which will help you, if you say this for the coming weeks of this next unfolding healing process:

I am worthy and I am ready to receive what is mine by right.
Help me to trust now Lord. (Remember to address this to the God within you)
Show me the way and allow me to feel your presence in my daily life.

Things will not always be as you would like them to be and they will often feel less than perfect but perfection is only our own illusion. We do the best we can with what we have and we give thanks. Forever give thanks while ever striving to improve what we can offer.

In this session, Light has been poured into you and The Guides will now work with that Light within you for a period of 23 days. This healing process will then continue for approximately 6 weeks.

No Essences Required.

Mr. D. One-to-One Session on 8th September 2004

The Guides Speak: Working with D today, we are looking at his energy system as a whole and it is in a very good state of balance now. Things are working well for D. This means we can go a little deeper, a little higher, as there is now nothing more to fix. We can now move into a pure evolutionary process. We are looking primarily at the central channel and the connections to Heaven and Earth.

Today, we are opening deeper connections into the Earth through the base chakra, to help to ground and strengthen and we are expanding the connections to Heaven, through the crown chakra, in order to allow higher communication to be received more easily.

Within the central channel itself we are smoothing out the flow and suggesting to this part of the energy system that it is OK to move to the next level. We are seeking to allow your own consciousness to make this next move by placing suggestions into your Higher Self. What we want to achieve here is a kind of self mastery, where your Higher Self actually begins to work at a new level, where it makes suggestions to your life that it is OK to move forwards, and helps to guide you in the right direction. *(This is a direct reference to upgrading or replacing the Soul Mission Programme as we outlined in the previous chapter—DA)*. The link between the Higher and Lower Selves is being strengthened and opened to a new level, so that the lower self can more easily hear these higher communications and suggestions.

Sometimes in life, the Lower Self struggles to accept the nature of the unlimited potential within us and the Higher Self fails to push this message, especially when things appear to be going well in life. If things are coasting along without much pressure or adversity, then the Higher Self can become lazy. That is, the subconscious overrules the Higher Self, insisting that no work needs to be done. But we, as Guides who are here to bring evolution to humanity, want to see 'vast evolution' in these coming life times. Therefore, with the appropriate permissions from the highest authority, we plant suggestions in the appropriate places within the consciousness, so that all levels may become more motivated and enlightened towards the unlimited status that we might attain as humans.

Becoming

It is now time to open your being to the point where you enter a faster state of Becoming. So that the evolution is processing within you, by and of itself. You are ready for this. The nature of Becoming is to be open at all required levels so that the Divine can work with and through you as it sees fit, when it sees fit and to this end, you will continually transform and evolve.

It is the nature of the higher energies available through this Wheel of Light connection, which allow this level of transformation to be activated within a human being. When it is activated, you enter a new level of existence where your own inner drive will manifest change at whatever speed you can perceive appropriate, based on your own perception of your unlimited nature. You are in control of your own destiny to a certain degree, but aligned more closely with the creator within, so that between your higher ability to listen and hear, you may be more accurately guided towards the goals, which have been set out for you at your soul level for this journey through life.

As of this day, you are now free, unbounded by any shackles to your old inner self, free to evolve at whatever speed you can accommodate. You are now unlimited.

In this session, Light has been poured into you and The Guides will now work with that light within you for a period of six weeks. This healing process will then continue for approximately 12 weeks.

Peace be with you.

Mr. D. Essence Program, 2nd November 2004

We now move on to an Essence Program, conducted at a distance, rather than a one-to-one session, with D.

This Program has been channelled for you through David by The Guides.

The Guides Speak: In this Essence Program we are bringing in and enhancing the way the Prime Force Light enters the heart chakra. We have initiated and there is now presently developing, a kind of overlay, like a second subtle body, which acts at a higher level than the existing subtle body, but with complete interaction with the original. We call this an Advanced Light Body.

This Advanced Light Body, which is now developing, will be more focused on bringing higher frequencies of light directly into the heart chakra from the Heaven Link, while at the same time developing a greater degree of grounding of the Heavenly Light into Earth. By the same token, the Grounded Light can then be returned to you from the Earth Mother consciousness in a way which will allow you to manifest with that Light in ever new and powerful ways. As this Advanced Light Body develops, you will discover that the heart chakra becomes more connected with both Heaven and Earth and thus more connected with the divine aspects of the masculine guiding principles and the feminine supporting energies, developing a more centred and connected aspect to your whole life and sense of being.

This Program is a pure Evolutionary Program, which will develop many aspects of the heart chakra, whilst at the same time, pour more of the Prime Force into your life and your core Being. You will then begin to develop an ever deeper understanding of the nature of humanity and of the pathway you are on, that of the evolution of human consciousness.

In the above example, you can see how The Guides brought the client from a Rescue and Repair situation, raising the vibration in increments, to a point where he was ready to receive a full-blown Evolutionary Program, performed at a distance. At the same time, they were beginning the process of instigating changes to the Soul Mission Programme for his life.

Advanced Light Body
This was the first time I had seen the Advanced Light Body revealed. Shortly after this period Guides showed me other people who were already beginning to transform and develop the Advanced Light Body as a result of the seeds of light planted in earlier sessions, as The Wheel of Light energies began to be used in earnest and as my own being allowed this light to pass through me. However, I was not able to view them at the time, or indeed explain the process, due to my own vibration still requiring some development. Whenever your vibration reaches a new 'perfect' level, that is, locks in harmonically to what we might term a whole note frequency, rather than being someway off key, new things will be revealed in their entirety. In the next chapter we will look at the Advanced Light Body concept in detail.

Upgrading the Soul Mission Programme
You will recall that the programme cannot be interfered with at any level other than with the direct approval and guidance of the highest spiritual

authority. Therefore, the fact that this work is possible reflects back to that singular name, Jesus, that was revealed through the numerological study I did after receiving the three new Wheel of Light Essences. Also, you will note in this reading above that The Guides state… *suggestions are being placed within the Higher Self.* To understand this process, you need to understand a little more about how the God consciousness functions, whilst working with it-self.

The Higher Self is at the very core of the deepest part of the Heart and is also the deepest part of human consciousness. You cannot go beyond this level, as there is nothing to go beyond. We will look at aspects of the Higher Self and its location in due course. The greater God-consciousness prevalent in every atom in the Universe is functioning and unfolding the bigger picture as per the Great Plan from upstairs. The two levels of God-consciousness, that which comprises the Higher Self and that within every atom comprising the physical Universe, are inseparable from one another and, therefore, each is as the other and they are both as one. So, at a Higher Self level we can say that God is allowing Himself to suggest to Himself that He unfolds and evolves. Therefore, what part are we actually playing in all of this? A good question and I can assure you that if you wish to concentrate upon it, then it will keep you busy for the rest of this lifetime and a few others besides.

When you reach a certain point in awakening or becoming, the picture becomes so big that you can't comprehend it and to waste time in trying to do so is not a good thing. What we might say here is that even before a spiritual path is embarked upon, the picture is unfathomable because our brain/mind continuum has not evolved to a sufficient level to understand the complexity of what we might call The Great Game. Also, you might have come across the saying, *the more I learn, the less I seem to know,* well, this is also the truth. You reach a point in development where you just have to let go of understanding the bigger picture, because you come to realise that it is only a distraction from life and the parts of life that you are currently learning. The practice of letting go is so important to the overall evolutionary process that we cannot stress it enough.

In anticipation of your questions, Dave asks of us, what part do we, The Guides or Guiding Consciousness that Dave accesses, play in this evolution-ary work of providing this outstanding light to the seekers of inner freedom? What part do we play in delivering the light through the process of the Essence Programs? What part do we play, if we have already stated that it is really God who is unlocking God within the core of the human heart of the person being worked upon. How we answer this is to say that it does not matter at one level, because it is too big to understand, therefore, let it go and don't waste time on trying to figure it all out. But, on the other hand, it is important to 'feel' part of this process. The part you are playing, as readers of this work and the part Dave is playing in the transmission and sharing of this knowledge and the part that we are playing of unlocking the God-consciousness within humanity is all the same thing. Do you see, by whatever means we all enter into this process, we are all working towards unlocking the God-consciousness within humanity.

For example, you might consult Dave or any other teacher or practitioner for some work on yourself. As a result you become empowered. As a result your vibration increases. As a result, your perceptions change and you radiate more light into the world. As a result of radiating more light into the world, you assist in the process of unlocking God-consciousness within humanity. No matter whether we are seeking answers or practising our gifts and talents, we are all working together to uplift humanity.

As Dave follows the guidance that comes from within, or wherever, he sees the results of this work as the clients begin to change. Therefore, he 'knows' that whatever he is doing is performing some duty, or right that helps the person move on and improve the quality of life. Therefore, the process is one of uplifting humanity. That is all that is important to understand. If when you follow the guidance it uplifts others, then that is how you judge that it is coming from a true source. For it is the work of God to guide his own consciousness out of his own darkness and He plays this game through the lives that we choose to live. Therefore, do not get hung up on the whys and wherefores, but do the work and judge your work by the results in ordinary human terms. If an Essence Program helps a person to overcome a difficulty in life, then that is God's work in action. Accept the success of it. That is how simple it all is.

You all have the power to open the God-consciousness within you. That is the birthright of humanity on the path of the evolution of human con- sciousness. However, sometimes it can be very beneficial to seek the help of someone who has walked that path before you and knows how to attain some of the answers that you might seek. In this way, you can likely deter- mine a shorter route through the forest of darkness and emerge onto the plane of light.

You can now answer the question as to what part we play. We are instru- ments of God that assist and allow humans to play God in the process of learning how to become God. And when this is done with all humility and an understanding of what is happening at the simplest level, then ever more of God's power is released so that it can be used to uplift fellow humans, because essentially, we are all one and we are all on the same path: the path home to unity.

31

Manifestation of the Advanced Light Body

The Guides Speak: As you reach a certain stage of evolutionary development, a process occurs called Manifestation of the Advanced Light Body.
The action and purpose of the Advanced Light Body is to pour light into the
heart chakra with intensity and sometimes force, in order to drive the evolution of consciousness forward.

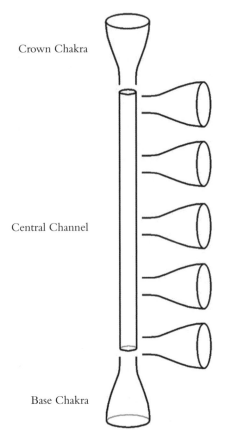

Crown Chakra

Central Channel

Base Chakra

The Fundamental Chakra System

Imagine the fundamental chakra system, with a central channel, which has a crown chakra at the top, pointing to Heaven and a base chakra at the bottom, pointing to Earth and various other chakras attaching to the central channel in the appropriate places.

In the normal chakra system, the heart chakra is protected from a direct or intense flow or force of light by the chakras above and below it within the central channel. Protection is also afforded by the diameter of the central channel and the natural restriction and governance of flow that this provides. We might describe the action of the Central Channel as like that of a feeding trough of energy and light where plants, the chakras, can dip their roots into this moist pathway of sustenance in order to draw up to themselves the power and guidance needed to provide a balanced energy system for the well-being of the human life.

Advanced Light Body

Now visualise a completely different subtle energy system, as we now describe it to you. A crown chakra, which is 'at least' four times the volume of your present crown chakra. This chakra begins above the head as per the original, but it finishes by connecting directly into the heart chakra. The base chakra is a mirror image of this. So, this new Advanced Light Body consists of a giant crown and base chakra, which both connect directly into the heart chakra, so that the only things separating these two main entry points to your being and your life is a small area of heart chakra.

The Advanced Light Body is provided by higher consciousness and appears or manifests to the outside of the existing and original chakra system. This means that the original chakra system remains intact and functioning in its normal capacity, but there develops an additional chakra system, which then forms an overlay around the existing system. This new overlay then functions in a completely different manner to the original system, having a different focus in its role in human life.

Visualise this scenario first of all. The original chakra system is essentially fed from two sources, the Heaven Link or Spiritual Channel and the Earth Link. The flow of light from Heaven enters the chakra system via the crown chakra and the Earth energy enters the chakra system via the Base Chakra. The chakra system, to all other intents and purposes, is sealed. These are the only two routes by which the main sources of uplifting and life-giving energy and light can enter you. Of course, the chakras breathe prana in and out as a way of generally energising, cleansing and balancing the system as a whole, just as our lungs breathe in and out to nurture us with oxygen. However, the real driving forces of life are fed to you through the crown and base chakras *via* the Heaven and Earth Links.

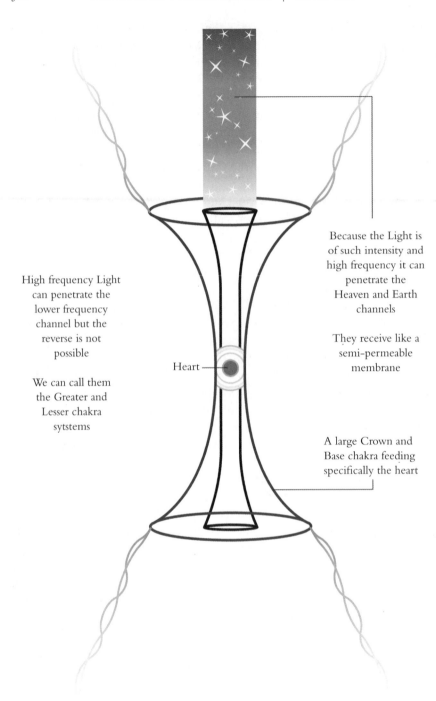

Because the Light is
of such intensity and
high frequency it can
penetrate the
Heaven and Earth
channels

They receive like a
semi-permeable
membrane

High frequency Light
can penetrate the
lower frequency
channel but the
reverse is not
possible

Heart

We can call them
the Greater and
Lesser chakra
sytstems

A large Crown and
Base chakra feeding
specifically the heart

Advanced Light Body

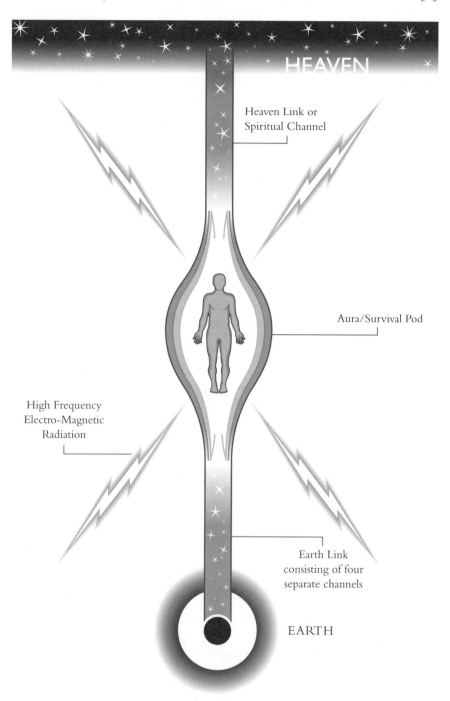

HEAVEN

Heaven Link or
Spiritual Channel

Aura/Survival Pod

High Frequency
Electro-Magnetic
Radiation

Earth Link
consisting of four
separate channels

EARTH

Heaven and Earth Links

As your vibration accelerates, you initially begin to channel additional streams of energy and light, or shall we say a broader spectrum of frequencies. For example, those of you who have taken attunements to various healing energies can suddenly find that within a few months of that attunement, you begin to open up to other frequencies. Those of you who are on a path of acceleration will notice this happening very quickly. As evolution continues, you begin to move beyond channelling and into manifestation. This is a little like when you begin to develop spiritually or through healing, you become more aware of energy and of other levels of reality. You might perhaps begin to see or perceive the colours of the chakras or hear communication. This is a process of 'going beyond' your present limitations. As you 'go beyond', you begin to open to new or advanced abilities. When you begin to manifest an Advanced Light Body, this is a huge leap in 'going beyond.'

Channelling and manifestation are completely different processes and manifestation does not usually begin to enter your life until you have done a fair amount of work on yourself in terms of your own evolutionary development. However, with things of the nature of light and evolution we can never say never, especially as your own Higher Self can begin to accelerate the game at any opportunity or pre-planned point in your lifetime that it chooses. But we can say that there are general patterns common to the unfolding process of most people. When manifestation begins to occur, though, you absolutely know that you are going through some dynamic changes in your life.

Let us just be clear about what we mean when we speak of manifestation. When your vibration reaches a certain point, changes occur to your energy system in order to manage and handle the increased frequencies of energy and light that will begin to work with you and pass through you, not to mention, emanate from you. The sudden appearance of an Advanced Light Body is a manifestation process. That means that it is suddenly born into existence. It suddenly appears or manifests. This is very different from what most people understand about manifesting where you use your conscious thoughts to continually focus on creating a situation in life, which you desire. This is manifestation through deliberate human action through the use of focussed thought, mantra or whatever method employed. An Advanced Light Body is given by God as you reach a point where you are ready to receive it. You could imagine it as like being given a great cloak as a reward for services rendered to both yourself and the Universe.

The Greater and Lesser Chakra Systems

As manifestation occurs, we might say that you grow into the Advanced Light Body. It is always there as a part of you, but it is not functioning and cannot be seen or perceived until the observer's vibration reaches a certain pitch. By the same token, it does not function until you begin to touch a certain frequency of vibration. At that point the Advanced Light Body is suddenly born. It awakens; it manifests; it fires up and begins to illuminate you for the first time. For clarity, we would describe these two systems as The Greater and Lesser Chakra Systems. The Lesser Chakra system is your original chakra system and the Greater Chakra System is the manifestation of the higher level chakra system.

The Greater Chakra System consists of only two chakras. These are a huge crown chakra and base chakra which join each other at the core of the heart chakra. There is no channel to link them, such as the central channel in the Lesser Chakra System. The Greater Crown Chakra and Base Chakra are fed by huge heaven and earth links, compared to the lesser system. The Lesser Chakra System continues to function as previously by supplying all the original chakras in the normal manner, but because of the birth of the Advanced Light Body, you suddenly become more connected to Heaven and Earth.

The Main Focus of The Advanced Light Body

As the Greater System begins to function, it has one main focus, which is to feed the heart chakra directly. The huge Heaven and Earth Links of the Greater System feed directly into the heart chakra via the exterior of the Lesser Chakra System. The Greater System bypasses all the chakras except the heart chakra. The total focus is upon developing the heart chakra by pouring energy and light into the deepest parts of the consciousness of the heart, access to which is determined and governed by the Higher Self. The core of the heart chakra is made up of energetic structures, which are as strong as steel. We will look at the reasons for this in due course, but essentially, the higher vibrational rate, plus the direct feed from the developing Greater Chakra System, pour energy and light into the heart in a way which directly challenges the resistance of this steel-like core.

Although, the Greater System is outside of the Lesser System, it does affect the performance of its inner associate. Because of the intensity, frequency and force of light, which pours through the Greater System, the Lesser System cannot help, but be influenced by the increased vibrational rate that it sits within.

It is very difficult to describe how the one affects the other unless you can see it in higher vision. This is because it functions in 5th dimensional space, outside the physical laws. However, to give you some idea of how it looks, try to visualise the following. See the normal Heaven Link as like a clear plastic hose pipe feeding downwards and entering the Crown Chakra. Within the hose is a flow of electric blue water, symbolising the light. If you then image that the hose dissolves, but the flow of the water remains in exactly the same place, as if held by an invisible hose, then that would describe the light feed to the Lesser Chakra System and the Crown Chakra in particular.

Now visualise a Crown chakra with ten times the volume, pouring silver light directly into the Heart Chakra. As you look through the glass-like structure of this huge chakra, you can see within it, the Lesser Crown Chakra, with its stream of electric blue water. Both chakras are pouring different frequencies of light into the system, one inside the other. Both systems are separate, yet integral, but the higher light from the Greater System influences the flow of light in the Lesser System. If you stand any high source of light next to a lesser source, the higher will always influence the lesser in the direction of ascension. For example, if a group of people go to a workshop given by a teacher who radiates a great source of light, they will all be uplifted merely by being in that presence.

On one level the Greater System enhances the Lesser System to a fair degree, tending to increase the pressure within the Lesser, which in turn forces the chakras to expand more as they learn to spin faster, hold more energy and light and generally function at a higher level all round. At the same time, this process tends to begin to burn the central channel open so that its diameter and volume increase. The result is that the recipient of this manifestation process begins to channel and hold more light.

One of the side effects of this type of increased energy and light is that it pushes the Evolutionary Cycle, constantly raising the vibration and initiating deeper releases from the heart of matter, which you no longer need to carry. We will look at the Evolutionary Cycle in detail in book two.

Therefore, we can conclude that as your vibration reaches a point where the Advanced Light Body begins to manifest around your existing chakra system, your evolution will begin to accelerate and it may speed up quite dramatically. At one level, the Higher Self will be in control of this, but at another level it often begins to push you mercilessly into facing the challenges that limit you. You can feel and perceive them like a wall of resistance that is difficult to pass through. The Higher Self is only interested in one thing at this point and that is the emergence of its own God-self into your life. It will push hard, so that you begin to learn how to 'allow' that God within you to express itself through your life. It is at times like this that you will find that you need to resort to The Laws of Evolution 1 and 2 and get some help with managing the processes, which you are being thrust into.

32

The First Direct Connection

It was now six months since that amazing day when we first used The Wheel of Light essences. Daily healing sessions were continuing, but were evolving through the use of the new essences. To some degree the energies were ravaging me more than ever before, but I could clearly see the different level of transformation within the clients. It was fairly obvious that more of this new light was being used in these sessions, as it could now pass through my system in greater quantity. I was observing my own acceleration through my unfolding vision and perception, too. New and advanced spiritual concepts were being shown to me regularly and I entered into this next phase of my development with a kind of pioneering enthusiasm, always wondering what the next day would bring. There were almost daily revelations in this period, although many of them were fine-tuning aspects of what was already being applied and 'intelligently tested' in both healing and evolutionary work. Then the day finally arrived when we received the first request for a Direct Connection to The Wheel of Light.

Guides suggested the time period for this connection, which was six months. I explained the process to the client and he agreed that it felt absolutely right for him.

Mr. J

A telephone consultation was scheduled and I treated it just the same as any other consultation, although, I knew that this person was particularly keen on the Wheel of Light and he had been sent to me via one of my associates who had said that he was most definitely ready for this higher light. I tuned in as usual to my calm inner space, expecting nothing new or unusual and keeping the imagination firmly in its place, but the door to the intuition opened. As my vision opened and I began remote viewing of his subtle energy system, the light was suddenly incredible. These past months of preparation had revealed many new, exciting and intense experiences, but at this point, The Guides were suddenly turning on something with an intensity that revealed more than I had ever seen before.

The First Session – October 2004
The following text is set in the present tense as it was channelled at the time.

As we look into the energy system, the higher vision is bright and clear. At the same time The Guides are showing me images and pictures as they tell me that they will open the client's crown chakra in a most unusual way. I feel the light pouring through me to illuminate his crown, so that I can see every filament of it. I watch as they effectively change the shape of the crown chakra into that of a trumpet-shaped flower, informing me that they are completely remodelling it. This is an example of upgrading the Soul Programme, mentioned previously. They then show me a picture of a white lily and inform me that this shape is necessary to facilitate a certain type of spiritual energy. The Guides say that they cannot be specific about this energy, as I have never seen the like of it before and won't understand it. I have no frame of reference for it and humanity in general will have no gauge to judge or measure it by, but that this energy is very different from the mainstream spiritual channels of light, which normally connect into humans. They also tell me that it is very specific to this client and The Guides who will work with him and that its purpose is very specific to this particular soul mission.

The Guides instruct me to change my viewing frequency to look into the heart chakra. I go through a yawning process that re-attunes my frequency. They begin to show me a type of golden light, which is usually associated with Angelic forms and forces. This light is very strongly focused around the core of the heart chakra within the central channel, which connects the crown and base chakras together. I sense that there is more to this than just Angelic Light and then I see a kind of pearlescent light also, which again, I have never seen previously.

The Guides then ask me to try to see into two places at once, which is a little tricky, but I allow my consciousness to divide, begin to sink into a kind of fifth dimensional space and experience the expansion of consciousness as it becomes separate from what I consider to be me. It is like trying to watch a movie on a screen in front of you, whilst also watching a different movie on a screen behind and then gaining a complete understanding of both films at the same time. In the physical world we can't do it, but in the world of consciousness we can. We just need to learn how to let go of our learned limiting processes of the physical world. If The Guides say do something, then you know you can do it; they don't ask you to do things, which are impossible, but sometimes they are a little difficult to achieve at first.

I begin to look into the crown chakra and see the heart chakra at the same time, not just the shape of the chakras, but beyond the energy and into the consciousness of each. At the same time, The Guides begin to move my hand on my writing pad and I begin drawing a circle, which encompasses the heart chakra and crown chakra. They are effectively saying that they are binding all the higher chakras together within this circle, but specifically, they are linking the heart and crown in what they describe as an 'Ascension Process.' They reinforce this by repeating 'We are working to bring about an Ascension Process. What will unfold is an Ascension Process.'

Do I really know what an Ascension Process is, I ask myself? It is something people talk about and occasionally one may read about it, but does anyone really know what it is? I fear that perhaps none of us do. Again, I note that, although, I have been unlocking evolutionary potential within people for a long time, whatever is unfolding here is most unusual and from the energetic feel of it, must be of a very high vibrational nature. I have not seen this type of work performed by The Guides previously and they leave me in no doubt that the energies, which will come through to bring about the transformation for the client are so high and extremely fine, that this process cannot be undertaken with anyone who does not have a certain vibrational potential to begin with. It is as if we are moving into a consciousness, which can barely function in the earth realm because of what appears to be its fine and delicate structure, but at the same time *can* function because it is associated with humans. Without humans, it could not work in the density of our earth realm. It would disintegrate. However, because of our physical density and to a certain degree, our complexity of different frequencies of energy and light, especially our grounding connection to earth, we can hold it or anchor it here and then function with it.

The Guides now point me to the lower chakras beneath the heart, and say, 'Forget these chakras, Dave. They are not important in this process. Our focus here is that we are creating a type of Ascension where the higher chakras will begin to vibrate at a much higher frequency. The result will be that the higher chakras will raise, but the lower chakras will stay where they are and maintain their slower, denser vibration for the time being. Although, this may seem to offend the rules, which most lightworkers consider to be the norm, you must understand that we are now bringing frequencies of light into earth, which have never been here before and so the rule book needs to be rewritten.'

We must also consider that it is not me doing this work, but some form of higher consciousness called The Guides or Guidance. The process would change later, as a further expansion of consciousness occurred.

The Guides Begin to Address the Client Directly Through Me

'It is essential to the Ascension Process that these lower chakras maintain their present vibration. They will need to sustain the grounding and also anchor the higher light structures we are now creating within the light body, in order to hold the frequencies of this higher light, which will commence the next phase of your development. The vibration of these frequencies of light is so high that we can only open these connections very, very gently over a period of time. They are also extremely subtle frequencies of light. There will be no rush of energy as the connection is brought into your being, but this light will begin to lift the higher chakras into a new level of reality, where truth may be perceived beyond a certain level of illusion. You will learn how to perceive truth at a higher level, you will begin to unfold into a higher light of truth. As this happens, you will begin to see more of the illusion that many people live under. They continually tell themselves a particular story of how life is, often *not* the truth, but an illusion they paint into their perception of reality and reveal to themselves as their truth.'

'Firstly, we will enter the heart chakra and then move into the central channel. At this point we will leave the system via the crown chakra and enter into the spiritual channel. Most of our work will be to facilitate the changes at this remote point, away from the subtle energies of the lower self such as the chakras and the aura. The place we work will be completely remote from the earth realm. The changes we will integrate will be so fine and high in terms of their vibration that we could not achieve them within the light body itself at the level of density within the chakras or auric realms.'

'Imagine a spiritual connection to the heavenly energies being like a clear glass tube, which ascends to heaven from your crown chakra. We will be inside this tube, but a long way out from where your body and life are. This is a little like going back to source and as we make the adjustments remotely from your being, the energy will filter down towards you like sparkling light or stardust. As it comes down to meet you, a little at a time, very, very subtly, the light will begin to open and activate this Ascension Process.'

I asked the Guides for some information on what an Ascension Process is. They replied as follows.

'An Ascension Process is like moving to a new continent. When you go there you know nothing of it, but often there is a sense of excitement of the unknown. As the energy begins to open and enter the person's life, the person will get this sense of excitement, a sense of going on a journey. This journey, however, is into higher light. It is a connection, which is held there for you. You can then use this connection to find answers to all manner of things both, within and outside the realm of earth.

'This connection is individual to the person and for the most part it lies dormant, but always on hand to be used. We might say this connection is a little like a telephone. If you pick it up and use it, then you can connect to others and gain information, which might help you, but if you don't use it, then it is useless. However, even though you may not wish to use it regularly, it does open you up to a higher reality. It does connect you to Beings of Consciousness who will oversee your advancement and try where they can to guide and advise you, whilst at the same time trying to influence and bring to you events and situations, which will help present an ideal life path before you. You will become much better attuned to receive this information through the connection, than by not having it. This is not like a connection to Angels or Guides, but one which can go far beyond the realities, which humans currently understand as principles, which can help us. Through the Ascension Process you can gain access to other Beings in other realms, in other Universes, in other realities. We might say that there are no limits on where you can connect to or what you can bring back through this process. You will be your own limitation, or you will go beyond that, dependent upon your imagination and courage.'

'No pressure is put on you to use this for yourself or for others. It is something, which has been asked for at higher level of consciousness and something, which has been granted by the same, on the basis that you are ready to receive it. This does not imply that you must use it either now or at any time within this lifetime. It does mean that it will be here for you in future lifetimes though, as once the connection is made, as with all evolutionary matters, it is never undone or revoked. It is a blessing, earned and deserved by Divine right. We might also say that it is like a badge of recognition. You have arrived at this point and this connection into the higher light of the Ascension Process is rightfully yours to do with as you wish. The consciousness of the higher realms sees your vibration and it is the frequency of this vibration that we refer to as the badge.'

The Process

Direct Connections today are very different, but this being the first one, I needed to monitor it to some degree, whilst trusting to another degree, as usual. I also went through the process of just being alert to what is happening, to the point where I know I can step back and just allow it to happen.

The Guides determined that this first Direct Connection would last about six months, with a Start Date of 21st October 2004, and an End Date of 18th April 2005. To give you an idea of how things have advanced, as I write this in April 2008, Direct Connections now take only one month to achieve a similar level of transformation. This is partly due to the speeding up of

Universal Consciousness, partly to my own advancement and the way I have been taught to continually go beyond limitation. There is much yet to reveal about my evolutionary pathway and how I now teach others to unlock their abilities, but this will come in subsequent books. Today, I don't any longer channel the light, but manifest it at will within the seeker, at the appropriate level to bring about the required individual evolutionary process that is required, plus some other quite magical processes, to be revealed later.

As the Direct Connection neared completion, I asked the client if he would give some feedback from the journal he was keeping. The Guides had said that the process was going to be extremely subtle. I needed to know just how subtle. Did he feel anything at all?

Client Feedback

Hi Dave,

'On first being connected, the first few days I noticed that I was quite hot—this calmed down, or perhaps I just got used to it as I don't feel the cold as much now as I used to! I also noticed a significant enhancement of my clairvoyance and psychic ability. I found that nearly every time I spoke to someone I was given a message to weave into the conversation. This still happens, but seems more subtle—and doesn't always feel as if it comes from spirit. (What the client is beginning to notice here is that the guidance is coming from the illuminated heart within.)

I also find that memories of things that I thought I had dealt with years ago pop into my head and won't go away until I've processed them and released old anger, embarrassment or upset. Again, this happened quite frequently at the beginning, but happens less obviously and frequently now. Things that are coming out now are things, which were buried very deep but obviously needed resurfacing. (As he is moving through the Program, the light is dissolving the lesser aspects of old issues. The result is a clearer energy system, which allows the light to go deeper, to bring up the deeper, heavier energies.)

More recently I've been questioning my many values, beliefs and principles and discarding those which no longer seem relevant or helpful. This can have a traumatic effect at times, but once worked through provides a new lease of freedom and life. Open up that closet and get those skeletons out! (This is the illumination of truth as a result of the dissolution of illusion that The Guides spoke about above.)

Also, more recently, I've felt that the Wheel of Light Guides have been communicating with me directly—almost as if they're preparing me for the next step, which obviously they are. Initially they waited for me to talk to them and now they initiate conversation when they feel it's appropriate. (At this point, the client has forgotten that he couldn't communicate at this level previously. Clearly, as his level of vibration rises, he is beginning to take the higher communication for granted—a clear sign of how subtly the light is blending with him, revealing a greater perspective of reality, but without going through the trauma of a difficult awakening process.)

All in all, a fantastic experience and one that I would highly recommend—a real self-awareness experience and one of enhanced positive energy. One cannot help, but be moved and supported throughout the process.'

In love and light,

A.J. London

33

The Fade Out

I absolutely knew that The Wheel of Light was so advanced, so dramatic and so unlimited, that there had never been anything to compare with it at any time in the history of mankind. How did I know this? It is impossible to say. It is just an inner knowing, which comes as a result of the stimulation of some deeper place within, by some inner or outer force; a stimulation where you know that you are witnessing something that others have never seen. It is as if a wave of energy comes over you in a way which lets you know that you are privileged beyond measure to be experiencing the moment. Apart from this, The Guides kept telling me so, as well.

The power and the light of The Wheel was incredible, yet I knew that we were only at the beginning of understanding its true potential. We were only at the end of the first development stage and I could feel and sense that there was much more learning to do. We were merely touching that first point of bringing a new light into earth and the next phase would be to learn how to use it more effectively and allow it to expand. What I did not consider at that time was that there might be another agenda for what I had been taught so far. In my own mind, I was just a healer, using the light to heal with as any other healer might do. But, something quite remarkable was about to happen. My days as a healer were numbered. I would be told in no uncertain terms to lay down that mantle.

The Beginning of the End

As we moved through the latter months of 2004, The Guides effectively switched off the Wheel of Light. That's right. They switched it off.

A part of me constantly considered (not doubted), that the concept of Direct Connections was probably far too advanced for most people. I knew it was way ahead of its time, which of course you cannot say, as everything is created and presented at the *right* time. It is just that the right time for the Universe to reveal these things is often way ahead of man's ability to comprehend or trust them. We only have to glance at history to see that it is littered with great ideas, which people were not ready to accept through fear, lack of courage or lack of vision. I also knew that the present level of illumination and spiritual advancement within the healing world in general was not sufficient to accept these new concepts. Yes, people were awakening and seeking, but put something in front of them that challenges their comprehension or stretches their imagination one step too far and they turn away in doubt rather than step up in expectation. Man's natural response to anything he can't comprehend is usually ridicule. Many new ideas are ridiculed as they challenge the *status quo*. It is this lack of vision and a kind of pioneering mind set of expectation or possibility of positive results, which holds so many people captive, keeping them constantly in a place where they fail to make any real advancement. It is also a natural process based on the programming of humanity in general. Show a person something that appears unbelievable and they don't believe it, and that is where the major elements of limitation of consciousness are founded. How many times do you hear someone say, 'I don't believe it', in that kind of dismissive way that completely closes off their consciousness to any possibility that there might be an element of truth worth investigating? Well, I've been hearing that all my life, so I am well experienced in observing the programmed, self-imposed limitations of peoples' imagination and of course, imagination is the key to creation. Therefore, what possibility do most people have to learn to create if they can't take the first step. That first step is merely being open-minded to possibility. The second step is to become enthused by the imagination as you allow the creative thoughts to fly. Even though, I had a strong level of inner knowing of the truth, the integrity and the potential of The Wheel of Light, I still knew that the leap of faith required for most spiritual seekers was far too great and that the majority of people were just not ready for this advanced concept. But, by the same token my healing practice was permanently full, so clearly this light was attracting people on some level. So, why had they turned it off?

More Understanding Needed

When something is suddenly taken away like this, it raises a lot of questions. Why had I been shown all this potential? Why had I been taught these processes? Why had I been allowed to work and play with this powerfully stunning light? Why was it then all taken away? Had I done something wrong? Had I misused the light? Had I misunderstood the nature or purpose of it? I asked endless questions over the coming months and The Guides remained silent. Sometimes answers are not appropriate. Sometimes, time must pass and then the answers reveal themselves through one's own growth in experience and knowledge brought about by vibrational shift. It would take me a year or so to understand why the light had been switched off.

Big Changes Will Come

A month or so after completion of the development period (June 2004), I was given a very clear message one morning, 'There will be big changes in January' (January 2005). Indeed, big was not the word to describe what would begin to happen. It is impossible to sum up the next part of this journey and, therefore, it will be the subject of Book Two in *The Keys of Transformation* Series.

34

Who are The Guides?

As we learn to work with energy and light, we find that guidance comes to us at some level. Some of us experience this as an external source and some as internal. Your vibrational level determines how you perceive and in fact, receive the guidance. For the most part, those who are new to spiritual work receive the guidance from an outside source and as you develop, it may then become more internalised. For example, my guidance comes in many forms at the same time, such as words or whole channelled pages if I am at the keyboard. If I am working with clients, or students, I receive words, sentences, emotions and most often, a combination of all of these. More often than not, when I'm really in tune, information comes as a stream of images, like watching a movie in my mind, which informs me of the work we might be doing and at the same time the words are streaming through me as channelled speaking, to the client, or student, in tandem to the movie-like imagery. The words are channelled for the benefit of the third party and the imagery is given so that I can understand what is being transmitted. The two forms come together wonderfully, to paint a very clear picture, especially when looking into deep consciousness or past life imagery.

In the earlier period, I used to refer to my guidance as The Guides, because most people easily relate to Spirit Guides, Angels and the like. In fact, at one time, I used to do Spirit Guide readings as part of my work, where I would connect with the Guide or Guides of the client or student, which would usually present itself to me in visual form and then explain its main purpose and how it influenced and helped the life of the individual person.

As we look into the Spiritual Channel, it is possible to ascend through various layers of consciousness, which communicate, or bathe us, with light and information. The first level as we move upwards from the crown chakra is The Guided Realms, the place from which Guides communicate. Beyond there we enter the Angelic Realms and beyond there, the Arch-angelic Realms. Beyond this we touch Christ Consciousness and there are levels beyond here, even, yet they are little use to us in physical form as the light at this level would incinerate us if we were to touch it.

As your vibration increases and the God-consciousness within you, at the core of your heart, becomes more illuminated, the guidance may then begin to expand into a mix of both external and internal guidance. Again, as the vibrations creep upwards you become more aware that a great deal of it is coming from within. This is the point where the Christ Light or Higher Self within the core of your heart is able to communicate with you directly. As this inner light begins to reveal itself, it drives your evolution forwards. When you reach a certain vibrational level, it is as if you have released the genie in the bottle that is the God-consciousness at your core. As this happens, you become ever more connected with the God-consciousness and your inner knowing begins to grow within you. Illusion begins to be stripped away, so that you can learn to discern truth.

As the inner communication becomes more established, 'The Guides' or Guidance reveals much less to you about its nature. Let us say that the source of the guidance becomes a mystery, for in truth the process of communication becomes one of trusting that the guidance will always be there when you need it. This process of receding is in the nature of teaching you to trust.

For example, if we consider the Universal Consciousness, or God as we call it, it is impossible to know God in the sense that you can't explain it to others, for to truly know God is to be God. Shall we say that the only time humans require proof of God is when they stand in separation from God and therefore, in a place of aloneness. But, as we become unified with that level of consciousness within ourselves that is the very nature of God, we become it and it becomes us, therefore, we are not separate from it. At that point we Know God, but only in the measure that we have Become God. This is the origin of the term becoming. We continually become until we become God. This is the journey.

Jesus said,
 'He who drinks from my mouth
 shall become as me;
 and I myself will become him,
 and the hidden things shall be manifested.'

It is a kind of catch 22 really. Those who require proof will never receive it, for God does not do proof. But, those who learn the processes of trust, will, by stages, begin to experience that state of unity with the oneness of everything. You become that oneness within and it becomes you and this state of oneness within cannot be shared or explained adequately. It is a state of Inner Knowing. You either experience God at a level where you absolutely know that you have touched that consciousness at some level and you also know that the consciousness has touched you, or you don't. It is kind of one and the same thing. As you touch it you become it and it becomes you. Therefore, if you *think* you've touched it, then you haven't because to be touched by it brings you to a state of absolute inner knowing and once you have experienced this inner knowing, there is no doubt ever again.

This is why the world has spiritual teachers. They have learned how to touch that place within. Because these teachers have ascended in vibration to the point where they have touched it, they have learned the process of attaining that level. Thus, it becomes incumbent upon them to share that truth and help others on the same path. Let us say that God knows his people, or God knows those who have the knowing and when it is your turn to walk that path, then that same God-consciousness will guide you to the particular individual who will be able to help you to attain the same place as themselves.

As you evolve, the nature of the presence within constantly changes. It becomes all the more encompassing as you become it. Clearly, you are only learning to touch the amount of unity that is possible without you being incinerated by the light. It is a one-step-at-a-time process of unfolding into the light as your system becomes strong enough to attain and hold it. With good guidance, one step at a time, you do learn how to attain the correct level of trust in order to experience the God force merging with the Self. The more you learn to trust, the more light you can hold.

Because we are only human, it is difficult for us to stay in that state of tune required to experience the glory of inner connection on a permanent basis, until we truly do attain a highly enlightened state. Also, we must keep things in perspective. Even when we feel at one with the creative force and even when the light is pouring through us in the most magnificent, illuminating way, we must remember at what level we are experiencing it. For certain, we are not experiencing the whole power that creates Universes, but only experiencing the tiniest fraction of God-consciousness, but enough to keep us moving towards unity.

So let's keep our feet on the ground, shall we and take it one step at a time?

My Spiritual Helpers

Whatever was happening in the early days of the birth of The Wheel of Light and in the healing sessions, which took me out of my body, some extremely potent spiritual essence was definitely assisting the process. Today, I don't really feel or perceive Guides as such any longer as individual entities, but I am certain that everything is still there, but communicating in a different way. It is as if I have been placed in a different conscious space and the guidance from within has now taken over the tutelage of my journey. But those other beings who were Guides in the first instance are still very much involved in the work we are doing on many levels. As I write this, they show me images of themselves coming and going, rushing about, helping many people, both clients and students and always in a teaching role.

The Visitations and Other Phenomena

During the process of unfolding and awakening, a trinity of very strange and often alarming phenomena were visited upon me on many occasions, often commencing during the night when I was sleeping.

The earliest events probably began around 1997, I found that whenever in a deep state of meditation, contemplation or sleep, convulsions began to surge up my body driven by some kind of massive energy release. This still happens today and it is not an unpleasant experience. However, perhaps more alarmingly, a more major type of event began to occur, where I would find myself in a dream situation fighting some unseen force, which appeared to be attacking me. The natural instinctual response was to fight it off. These events were quite terrifying and in my struggle, I would make strange and eerie noises. My partner, Denise, would try to wake me up when one of those events began taking me over. The struggle was immense, it was as if I was being completely subjugated against my will and even raising as much effort as possible to overcome what appeared to be some kind of attack, I was no match for whatever was holding me.

After a number of these events, I began to understand them a little more and it became clear that they were spiritual interventions. Some kind of being or spiritual essence was entering my own being and performing some task. As this became clear, I asked Denise not to wake me, but let me go through the whole process. Even though, I now knew what it was and had some understanding of it, it was no less terrifying an ordeal. I reached a point in my own development where I could sometimes observe these events, whilst being in the midst of them. I would try to resist fighting and allow whatever was taking place to continue, but this is actually a very difficult thing to do. Imagine someone trying to do a heart transplant on you, against your will, whilst holding you down and with no real knowledge of how, or why it was being done. This would be a good analogy of what was happening. For certain, something was entering me and initiating changes within my energetic structure, consciousness or both. Each visitation was in a different place, such as in a different chakra. On one occasion, I almost caught them out, for what I discovered was that they were not allowed to be in my being whilst I was conscious. Therefore, whatever work was being done had to be carried out quickly before I regained wakefulness. What also became clear was that it was the sub-conscious mind, which was doing the fighting and this effort was driven by fear of change.

On this one occasion, where I almost caught this spiritual intervention out before the essence of it could leave my body, I was in a state of awareness that something was happening, but quite relaxed as my sub-conscious was doing the usual and fighting the good fight. I suddenly found myself beginning to awaken, whilst the essence was still deep within my heart chakra. The energy of the being, realising that I was coming round, began to leave extremely quickly through my crown chakra and the faster it went, the colder my head became. I was aware that the being knew that it needed to leave very quickly, but that it was also aware that if it left too quickly it could do me some damage. In particular, it was worried about freezing my brain! The process was fascinating as I observed it unfolding. As the spiritual essence streamed out from my crown chakra, the cold became more and more intense to the point that, indeed, I began to think my head would become frozen. There seemed to be a kind of synchronicity as the last atoms of the essence, which was like a long stream of cold white light, left me literally at the exact second that I awakened. I reached up to feel my head and indeed it was freezing cold. I had a strong sense that much work has been done and they had stayed to the last second to perform as much as possible, but also a sense that whatever was being done had been accomplished, just.

Not So Much Fun When You Are on Your Own

These visitations happened perhaps three or four times a year for several years and continue to this day, only less often, perhaps once a year or so. The most recent was in December 2008. The dream scene was set in an old house, perhaps of Tudor origin, although, we were in the present day and Denise and I had just gone to bed for the night. As soon as we began to drift off to sleep, I became aware of spirits in the room. They began to shake the covers on the bed, Denise remained asleep, but I knew that they were strong and powerful and that I would have a bit of a battle on my hands to get them to leave us alone. I began to use my old gifts of communicating with them, but they did not want to know. They became more boisterous and began to lift the bed up and down off the floor. In the dream Denise woke up at these violent movements, she also woke up at my side in reality too, as whatever was going on in my world was beginning to disturb her. In the dream, I told her not to worry and stay under the covers as I then began to wrestle with them in a physical sense, unable to see them as they were invisible, but holding tight onto their arms.

At this point, the real scenario, as opposed this dream scenario, was that the visiting spiritual essence is pushing deep within me to bring about some kind of change and my sub-conscious, representing what it thinks are my best interests, is resisting the invasion as strongly as it can. During these events, I am always kind of paralysed and that is the nature of the real struggle. It must be very similar to those people who are fully awake through operations, even though, the anaesthetist considers they are fully unconscious. Denise says I make the most unholy and strange noises, but never do any real words come out.

However, in this particular battle, it reached a point where I began to shout for Jesus to give me a hand as these two spirits were extremely difficult adversaries. I was using all my knowledge and skill and although I was holding my own, I could not gain mastery of the situation. Of course, in reality, I was being subdued so as not to gain mastery until the work was done. Eventually, I managed to get the boisterous and enthusiastic spirits out of the window and as they left the building they manifested visibly into a young couple. They were quite angry at having been forcibly evicted and I immediately felt compassion and sadness for them, bidding them to please return, but leave us in peace. I explained there was plenty of room for all of us if we respected each others space, but they continued to drift away.

The spirits left in their misery and I awoke, the struggle being over. Denise was quite alarmed, her hand on my shoulder, as this battle had been raging for some considerable time. She told me that I'd been shouting for Jesus and she was very aware that I had been calling for assistance to help with whatever I was going through. In reality, it was probably him that was inside me! This was the first time I called out any words and was probably indicative of the intensity of the struggle.

As I pondered the dream situation over the coming days, it was clear that whatever the spiritual essence was doing, it was trying to remove some aspect of consciousness, which no longer served me. The image of the old Tudor house was symbolic of my being as a whole, as the young spirit couple were symbolic of some aspects of consciousness, probably both masculine and feminine, or a duality of some description. The imagery of wrestling them out of the window is symbolic of the removal from the body of these foreign invaders who were no longer wanted. Once clear of the house, my being, they manifested visibly, this was so that I could visibly see that something had been achieved.

The battle had been the inner struggle of the sub-conscious mind trying to hold on to something that the spiritual essence considered no longer served me.

Skinned Alive from the Inside

I think this next phenomena began around the year 2000 and it built up to a crescendo over a period of time to around 2006, when it then reduced to once or twice a year during the following years. It would commence just at the point where I would hit sleep, the point at which I passed from wakefulness into the beyond, then it would begin.

It starts with a tingling sensation at the base of the spine, then it intensifies and waves of energy begin to rise up the body towards the head. However, it was a real struggle for each wave to pass through each chakra. As it reaches the heart, it is as if I am being turned inside out. In fact the feeling is akin to that of being skinned alive, but from the inside. So, if you can imagine someone reaching inside you from the top of your head, reaching down to the base of your body, then taking hold of the inner most layer of skin, then tearing it upwards and removing it completely from inside you, then that is something like how it feels, only energetically, rather than physically. Talk about traumatising and quite horrific. It is a terrifying event and it seems to go in cycles. When it chooses to come, it might then happen once a night for a couple of weeks. Each night the intensity becomes stronger and each event can last up to a couple of hours. My whole being goes into severe anxiety and desperation as I try to hold on to dear life through each wave. As the process begins, it would awaken me and I would lie there absolutely connected and focussed at the deepest level of my awareness on what was happening. As the energy rises towards the heart, it feels like the heart might completely stop. It performs all kinds of unnatural patterns. It becomes so loud within that it is impossible to hear anything else, but at the same time, I have to concentrate on keeping calm and allowing it to beat to the best rhythm of normality I can muster. It seems as though, if I don't keep it going, it will just stop. As the wave passes the heart and rises towards the head and the crown chakra, it begins to fizz and the sensations are overwhelming as the intensity continues to rise as the wave passes through. As the energy wave leaves the body through the head, I begin to breathe a sigh of relief and relax a certain degree, but awaiting the next wave with some trepidation as I know that it will be more intense than the previous one. It might take between five to ten minutes for each wave to pass. Once a wave completes its course the next wave is only moments away. As each wave builds up, the terror builds up with it and a desperate attempt at holding on to life ensues as I consider the possibility of surviving the next wave. In each night, there would be a whole series of these wave events perhaps as many as a dozen or more.

Sometime in 2006, I had a singular energetic wave event like the above, but of much greater intensity than ever before. During the process, I reached a point where I knew that I could not bear it any longer, I was certain that I would not survive the next wave. My mind searched for a way to deal with what was happening and suddenly I seemed to step out of my body and become a remote observer, rather than the person who was experiencing the process. Even though, I was observing, I could still feel everything, but not with the same intensity. However, as I managed to step out of my body, the wave passed more quickly than usual, but seemed to take with it, such a great layer of energy that I immediately felt lighter and changed. After this intense event, I was not troubled with this process again for around a year and since that time, I've only had a few minor experiences of this event of much less intensity.

For certain, it seemed like what was happening was that layers of energy were either being removed or stripped out of me at some level. The other explanation seems to be that the electro-magnetic energy of each wave activated my being at such a level that it allowed old energies to leave me.

Death at Any Moment

At the beginning of 2006, a new event visited me, but this time it was not as I was sleeping, but when I was fully awake and going about my daily business. It was like being unplugged from the very essence of the life force. To explain this feeling and sensation is very difficult as you would need to experience it to fully understand it. What would happen is that I would feel the life force drain away and I would become so weak, that it seemed like I was about to take my last breath at any moment. All strength left me, although, at the same time, I could summon it if needed, but there was an inner knowing that if I did summon it, that might be the last thought that I had through the effort involved. When this process began, I would feel it coming on like a funny, odd feeling that perhaps I was a little faint, but then I didn't faint. I just got weaker and weaker in the sense that I could feel the life force separating from me. It was as if I was balanced on a knife edge and given the opportunity to observe my last breath in this lifetime. Each breath would seem like the last one and I would wait with trepidation to see did I have an opportunity to take another breath, until the effects eventually left me. This process could last for hours and in many instances once it began, it would persist all day and not subside until the following morning, upon which I would awaken fully connected again and certain that I was most definitely continuing to live for a while longer. Whilst in this depleted state, I was totally consumed by observing what was happening and trying to understand it. On the one hand trying not to think because there wasn't the energy to do so, whilst on the other hand consciously ensuring I kept breathing and so didn't accidentally fall dead in the next breath through lack of concentration on being here in the present. I just kept hanging on, like on life-support and hoping for the best.

After having such a range of strange effects since being on this spiritual path, within a few events of a new process, I usually begin to obtain an understanding that, although, it seemed like I was only seconds from death, I always got through it and this is what keeps you going, the knowing that, however frightening or horrifying the experience as you pass through it, by tomorrow it will have passed. I've never spoken to anyone who has experienced anything like these events and I certainly would not wish them on anyone else as they are truly scary, but I suppose this is another symptom of this unique path of evolution of consciousness that I seem to be walking.

Who are The Guides then?

Guidance comes from many levels, from both without and within. I would say from my own experience that Guidance almost certainly begins from without and as you evolve and the light at your centre begins to activate, then there is a movement towards that as the source, although, even then, assistance can be brought to you from an outer source. As you can see from my own journey, even though the guidance I work with for the most part now seems to be given from within, from my core, the interventions that happen to me are almost certainly from an outer source.

When working with clients and students in particular, one of the first points that Guidance asks me to look at is the source of their Guidance. They call it the Transmission Point and this is the place where an individual's guidance comes from. As we look into the Spiritual Channel, my Guidance will take me on a journey through the individual's spiritual connections, so that I can figure out at what level they are connected, why they are here in this life and what path they are supposed to be on. We view three particular connections.

The first is the **Overall Spiritual Connection**, which determines at what level the individual is 'hard wired' or carries a 'direct connection' into the Universal Game via their spiritual channel, such as, connected into the Guided Realms, the Angelic Realms, the Archangelic Realms, the Ascended Masters, the Christ Light or beyond.

The second connection we establish is the **Vibrational Level** of the individual. This shows me at what level they can receive communication and whether the communication is developed yet, or not, as the case may be. It is fully possible to have the most amazing spiritual connections, but not receive the information. If the individual has not learned how to allow the communication through, even though spiritual sources will communicate and guide constantly, you will not perceive or receive the information.

The third level is called the **Transmission Point**, the place where communication is transmitted from. The Transmission Point is more often than not a little higher up the spiritual channel than your Vibrational Level, as your Guides are always trying to stimulate you in an upward direction pulling you up the spiritual ladder, as it were.

The viewing of these three connection points identifies exactly who you are and why you are here at this time. It is the knowledge of how these connections work, which allows the identification of The Chosen Ones and the Accelerated Masters.

Outside Intervention

For the most part, I am sure that the majority of people do not seem to receive the kind of intense outside interventions that I have experienced during my own path. Your Guidance comes to you at a level dependent and appropriate to the life mission you have chosen and agreed to at a higher level before incarnation into this life, so no doubt, I asked for some serious pushing at certain points on the path. However, it also seems certain that the more you ask for help, guidance and acceleration, those upstairs will respond to your call, although the way in which that intervention comes to you might be very difficult to understand at times, such is the way that Universal Consciousness brings the opportunity of change to us. Frequently, it does not fit our own reasoning based on our limited experience of things above our present level of evolution. Many times, I have worked with clients who think they are under severe psychic attack, only to discover it is some form of spiritual guidance, which they have not yet understood.

One thing I've noticed over the years is that where students are concerned, the pressure put on them to evolve, once they have chosen to step into this light, can take their guidance to a whole new level in which whoever or whatever is working with and through me tends to then work with them, accelerating them in a way which can be very powerful at times. Shall we say students can be pushed fairly mercilessly, but all in the nature of helping them keep up to speed with a rapidly changing Universal Consciousness by ensuring that they continue to be on the crest of the Wave of Time, as it is only from this place of absolute synchronicity with the vibration of Universal Consciousness that you can be truly effective in uplifting and empowering others.

Drawing to a Close

Finally, The Guides are ready to draw this first book in *The Keys* series to a close and have chosen to speak to you directly, so without further ado, I shall stand aside.

35

The Last Chapter

Jesus said,
    'I stood boldly in the midst of the world
    and I manifested to them in the flesh
    I found them all drunk;
    I found none among them athirst,
    and my soul was afflicted for the sons of men
    because they are blind in their heart.'

The Gospel of Thomas

The Guides Speak:
The healers of today have been at the forefront of the transformation of consciousness, bringing in the healing rays for both themselves and others to experience. However, there is a sleeping sickness in the healing camp at this time, a malaise, a total misunderstanding and lack of comprehension of our present position regarding the Ascension of Man.

Yes, it is true that at one level the energies and light, which are entering the planet now will be working to uplift and transform human consciousness. But, at another level there is a misconception that all one has to do in order to evolve and ascend is to sit back and bathe in the new light and this will be all that is needed. This belief is way off the mark. If you think that you can just cruise into a New Age without the slightest effort, then you will be in for a shock. What is needed is vision, determination, courage, tenacity and drive, plus a great understanding of what it means to shift from the vibration of one age to the next.

The problem lies in that there is little reference for this journey. As humans, you are stepping into new territory. Seeded amongst you are those who have made this journey before and are here to guide you now, but even in these souls, who have journeyed previously, the deeply embedded knowledge of transformations in other worlds will bring up the Fear of Transformation from the heart as the ancient memories are illuminated by this incoming light. As the fear rises, so even your experienced warriors of light will become stuck until they find the necessary assistance to move through the tremendous energies, which will hold you in stasis.

The first major wave of transformation has been and gone and humanity is still standing on the shore, looking out to sea and marvelling at what it has seen and experienced. Those who are awakening marvel at what they are a part of, but don't realise that the wave, which raised them up has now receded into history. They are experiencing a mirage. The wave arrived, it uplifted those who were ready to move with it as it opened up the healing rays for humanity and it has now passed. That was a time, which came and went, a time, which has now been submerged by the next incoming wave. This new wave, the wave of evolution, is travelling faster and at a much higher vibration than the previous wave, which gave birth to the Age of Healing. Time and consciousness have moved on, but so subtly and at such speed that hardly anyone has noticed.

Who are we speaking about here? All those who were awakened by the first wave. All those who stepped up and learned how to ride the wave of healing light as it began to crash upon the shores of our future through the late 1980s, and into the 90s. All those who became illuminated and stepped into the learning zone of healing. All those who had the courage to open their hearts and lives to a new direction and called forth change within themselves. All those whose inner voice spoke loudly to them, saying, 'this is my time.' All those with the courage to take action. You, who now read these words are the ones who have awakened. If you had not awakened as you rode that first wave, then you would not be reading these words now. You are reading them because their light has called to you, just as the light of the first wave called you and you responded. It is the vibration of the words, which calls and only those with a vibration, which is ready to receive the light of the next level will perceive that call.

The second wave began to roll inwards in 1999, and has been surging forward since then. The vast majority have not seen or appreciated its value, for this wave is very different. It is not so profound. It is more subtle. It is a wave of consciousness as opposed to an energy wave and the subtle action of the consciousness demands that you pay attention. This wave demands that you take even greater responsibility than did the first. This wave demands that you actively seek to go beyond the place where the first wave carried you. This wave is truly the wave of triumph, but you must learn how to ride it, whereas the first one uplifted you almost without effort.

Celebration

What has happened to many of you is this. The first wave has raised your vision and perspective of the world. You have stepped into power and for the most part that power has opened you into certain truths about yourself. These truths are humanity's truths and so you are not alone in what you experience. The power exposes the inner being, with all its imperfections, challenges and failures as a vehicle of light. But this is no criticism of you. No, this is a celebration, for as the light of truth illuminates and exposes these imperfections, so we can all begin to sit up and take notice of how frail and weak we are. In reality, the imperfections or issues represent the challenges to which each individual must rise and then overcome. The imperfections are built into us in order that we might transcend them a little at a time and thus truly step into the real power that awaits us as the second wave continues to surge through the Earth Plane.

For the most part, that first wave has only shown you the very tip of the iceberg of power. You have no idea what awaits you when you begin to truly seek the second wave and climb aboard it. There is nothing to compare it with, but unlike the first wave, in order to begin to surf at this level, there is some work to do.

Seek and You Shall Find

Truly, you will not find the second wave until you are ready to challenge yourself to go beyond your present limitations. As we sit within the ethers and gaze upon you, we see the reflection of so much wonder at what you have stepped into and achieved these past few years. We see transformation of so many lives, which have moved beyond the drudgery and imprisonment of the patterns of many centuries. Truly, humanity is awakening and beginning to take its place in the higher conscious realms. But, what we say to you now is to uplift you even further.

We say to you that there is a world you have not yet experienced, which at this very moment is passing you by. You can't see it, for you have become intoxicated with the rise in consciousness and vibration from the first wave. You are standing in a microcosm within a macrocosm. The vista is so large that you cannot see it. You have a saying, 'You can't see the wood for the trees'. You know what it means, but we will tell you, nevertheless. It means that when you stand in a forest you cannot see it for your vision is obscured by the trees. If we were to lift you up above the forest, say in a helicopter, then you would see the magnificent organism, which is the forest, spreading out for miles in all directions. From a higher perspective one can see and appreciate more. From our perspective, we are looking down upon you in your wonder, but we also see how lost you all are within the wood or forest of your illumination. You have become blinded by the light. You think you know where you are going, but in reality, most of you are not going anywhere new. You have stepped onto the path of healing and travelled a certain distance, but you have now reached a point where you are either going round in circles or treading water, but you don't realise it. The second wave has passed you by because you don't know how to recognise it. As we write this to you, we are already ten years on from when the Evolutionary Wave began to surge through you. It has been travelling and accelerating daily for ten years and there are very few upon it.

This second wave is opening new portals around the world. As they open, new teachers will come forth, new schools will open. Some of these teachers will develop from among those who were awakened by the first wave and some will spontaneously awaken in a dramatic way, remembering the ancient knowledge and producing new teachings and pathways to help uplift the seekers amongst you. Many new schools of thought will emerge. All will be valid, because they will all be speaking to and for the person who is uplifted by their individual message. You must raise your awareness so that you can perceive that call when it comes. You must be aware that the path, which calls you may be very different from anything experienced previously and it may well be very challenging to those who know you, to see you going in a new direction. There will be no right or wrong way, there will just be, 'The Way' for each individual amongst you. Because consciousness is moving so quickly, you will drink from these fountains of vision and perception of the new ways of living and working and as you sup your fill, you will, perhaps, move on to a new teacher or school until you find what you are truly looking for. Until you find your true soul group.

It took around ten years for the first wave to gather momentum and bring so many into the healing light. That momentum continues apace and is helpful for those who are only just beginning their awakening journey. But those of you who awoke in the 80s, and 90s, should now be at the cutting edge of evolutionary work, not healing work. Do you not think this is bizarre that so many have not moved forward? Do you not think this is interesting? We think it is alarming that so many have failed to see the second wave and its potential.

This failure or inability to see and perceive the truth of what is happening is not so much due to complacency as to the intoxication we mentioned earlier. When a person is intoxicated their perception becomes impaired. In reality what has happened to the surfers of the first wave is that you have become comfortable and the comfort has taken the fire out of your seeking, because you think that you have moved far enough in terms of life change and illumination. It is true that many of you have indeed moved what we might term light-years ahead of the crowd. You have stepped up. You have learned to heal. You have learned to teach. You have learned how to uplift others, but who amongst you is teaching from the experience and knowledge of having walked the path of evolutionary light? We say to you that there are not many, in fact almost none at this time. How do you judge it, we hear you ask? The answer is simple. If you are still healing, then you have not learned how to transcend that position. If you are working with evolutionary light, you have gone beyond a place where you do the work. You have learned how to conduct the Universe.

What is happening now is that the evolution of human consciousness is stalling, like an old car that can't get up a hill. The hill of illumination has been placed before your feet, but it is a struggle to climb, even for those who can perceive it. But, perceive it you must, otherwise you will be left drifting in a time period akin to the Victorian age when space rockets were not even in the realm of fantasy, let alone a possibility.

The first train of the evolution of human consciousness has already left the station and we can see from our vantage point that there are very few upon it. The sad thing is that the second and third trains have also left the station and these too are almost empty.

We say to you in all sincerity and urgency, that there is no tomorrow. There is only, 'now' and if you do not begin to awaken to what you are doing with your lives; begin to drive them forward into the new light, then you will be sadly missed at the reunion later.

David has written most of this book, based upon his experience and we have interjected from time to time in our enthusiasm to teach. However, we wanted to communicate these words, which we have entitled, *The Last Chapter*. We would tell you now that the first wave of healing light, which awakened you could very well be your own last chapter in change. We would say that this could be your last chapter in this life. We do not mean that you are preparing to leave the planet soon, but if you do not spur yourselves into action, you will, for certain, be reliving the last chapter of time over and over again, until you eventually do pass from this life. Is that what you really want, when there is so much more to have?

See the first wave as the first chapter of an instruction book, the light of which is teaching you new ways of being. You have risen to its call and challenge, but is that where it ends for you? Will you continue to reinvent yourself at this same vibrational level, learning to cling on to the life raft of what you have already created for yourself? Or, will you respond to the invitation of evolution, which the second wave has been offering these past years and allow your rising vibration to bring you new and challenging opportunities? We say to you that you have only just tasted the beginning of your journey. Don't allow this first chapter to be your last. Take action and learn how to see what is going on. Continually seek ways of allowing your vibration to rise.

Dissolving Attachment in Order to Become

There is so much we could teach you, but first there must be a desire; a thirst to drink from the well. To help you understand this, here is a paraphrase of the saying of Jesus from the head of this chapter:

> Jesus stood boldly in the midst of the world,
> and found none of them arthirst
> and His soul was afflicted for the sons of men
> because they are blind in their heart.

Here we give you one key point to observe as guidance. When power is given forth, it allows you to become more than you are. It raises you up. It allows you to be more than you could previously imagine. What the healers tend to do with their power is become attached to it. They use the power to create themselves as healers, then they become attached to their own creation. In order to step into the new age, you must constantly dissolve your attachment to who you have become, otherwise you will cease to become the next thing.

Bless yourself with the God within you and allow that light to emerge and shine forth into the lives of others. Remember, it is by uplifting others that we are uplifted ourselves.

Blessings be upon you. Peace be with you.

The Guides
2:13 – 3:30 a.m. 14th July 2007

36

Afterword

Jesus said,
> 'Indeed the harvest is great,
> but the labourers are few.
> Entreat therefore, the Lord,
> to send labourers to the harvest.'

The Gospel of Thomas

Through the gifts, which have been bestowed on me, it is my task in this life to offer as much as I know to those who seek that knowledge, in order that you might transform your consciousness to maximum effect, even if that effect should allow you to overtake me so that I become the student.

Apart from student and teacher, we are equal in every other way, but especially so as student and teacher, for it is from each other that we learn. We are all students. We are all teachers. Should you overtake me with the gifts, which may be bestowed upon you through your journey and you then become the Master, I would welcome the rest and the opportunity to learn at your feet. It would be a blessing as being the teacher can be a lonely, difficult and frustrating place at times.

On this journey, you might find that whatever it is that I know, is of no use to you. All I know are directions to another place. I am but a guide and a messenger. You might find that you have no desire to travel to that place, or should you glimpse it, that the place is too challenging for you to enter and you turn away from the journey. In which case, whatever it is that I think I know becomes of no use to you.

That is how it should be, for we are all on our own journey. We touch with others from time to time as the Universal Consciousness cares to bring us together to learn what we need to learn, to touch a vibration that will accelerate us, to receive a single word that brings the answer we seek. Then we continue by ourselves on our own path, sometimes illuminated and in wonder, sometimes in difficulty and pain through the challenges that come forth for our continued learning.

It is only when we are challenged that we need the teacher or the guide, whoever that may be at the time and the teacher or guide is often the most unlikely person you could imagine: the old lady who lives across the street, the bank clerk who smiles at you, a stranger who gives you a passing word. The Consciousness of the Universe is the teacher and it chooses humble, simple people to deliver its message at the time you need to receive it. So go in peace and without worry, knowing that if you need a teacher or a guide, then the Universe *will* provide.

At this point we will take our leave, but The Guides and I wish to present you with one thought that will help you more than any other to understand what is happening at the very moment that you read these words, as we continue to enter this new age, the age which is spilling forth the Light of Christ into simple souls, so that ordinary folk can uplift ordinary folk into truth and glory.

> If you are doing today, what you were doing yesterday,
> then you have already been left behind.
>
> If you rise tomorrow and choose to be the same as today,
> then you have already been left behind.
>
> Universal Consciousness is changing by the second,
> you must learn to do the same.
>
> And soon, it will accelerate again.

Peace be with you.
Blessings be upon you.

> Dave Ashworth
> Red Bank, 16th July 2008

Contact Us:

For practical help and guidance for spiritual issues, please use these contact details.

Tel: · +44 (0)161 772 0207

E-mail: dave@davidashworth.com

Web: www.davidashworth.com

See also:

Essence of Evolution   www.essenceofevolution.co.uk

The Vision Journey   www.thevisionjourney.com

Direct Connections   www.direct-connections.co.uk

Address: David Ashworth
P.O. Box 312
Whitefield
Manchester
M45 8PW
United Kingdom

The Emerald Heart School

Working with The Emerald Heart takes you beyond the limitations of healing and opens your ability to unlock spiritual evolution in all those who seek this path.

David personally teaches all the advanced spiritual concepts which have been revealed to him through the guidance and Light of The Emerald Heart including the Universal Laws which govern Evolution of Consciousness and accessing the Universal Flow.

For more information about training, see: www.emerald-heart.co.uk